John Timbs

Ancestral Stories and Traditions of Great Families

Illustrative of English History

John Timbs

Ancestral Stories and Traditions of Great Families
Illustrative of English History

ISBN/EAN: 9783337208745

Printed in Europe, USA, Canada, Australia, Japan

Cover: Foto ©ninafisch / pixelio.de

More available books at **www.hansebooks.com**

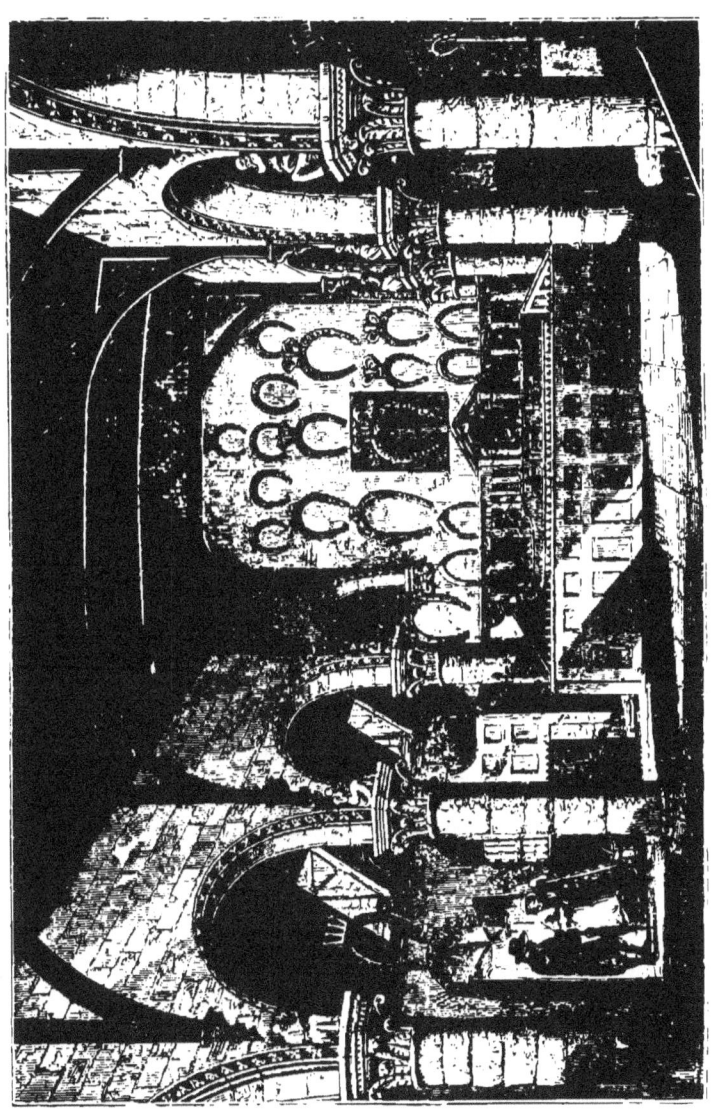

HALL AND HORSE SHOES, OAKHAM CASTLE.

ANCESTRAL STORIES

AND

TRADITIONS OF GREAT FAMILIES

Illustrative of English History.

BY

JOHN TIMBS, F.S.A.,

AUTHOR OF 'NOOKS AND CORNERS OF ENGLISH LIFE,' ETC.

LONDON:
GRIFFITH AND FARRAN,
SUCCESSORS TO NEWBERY AND HARRIS,
CORNER OF ST. PAUL'S CHURCHYARD.
MDCCCLXIX.

PREFACE.

THE Ancestral Histories of the Great Families of England are rich beyond compare in Episodes of Thought and Action, such as are the mastersprings by which the world is moved. It has been said:

> 'The evil that men do lives after them;
> The good is oft interred with their bones.'

Such is the dictum of the Dramatist; but in actual life the proportion of good is more equitably adjusted.

The gravity of History has been estimated as 'Philosophy teaching by example.' In this long lesson, how intricate is the chequer-work of success and defeat, of light and shade; yet how interesting to those who delight to seek out the motives of human action in the lives of masterminds, their rise and fall!

In the Histories of Great Families, which are the nooks and byeways of History proper, are to be found garnered many records of vicissitudes, which sometimes make men giddy by looking too long upon their wheels. In the present volume an attempt is made to *focus* some of these Scenes and Stories from English History, and the parts which the leaders of Great Families have played in the great drama of our country's fame: in its Monastic and Castle Life; its Traditions and Legends; its Domestic Tragedies; its Battles and Sieges; as well as its 'trivial fond records' of Private Life, and its abodes of quiet contentment; for we do not share the opinion of those historians who seem to think the whole world consists of some 150 persons, dignified as emperors, kings, popes, generals, and ministers. On the other hand, the *inner life* of the people, as well as of their rulers, has been here glanced at, with their habits and modes of living, as well as the great changes by which they have been influenced.

In the preparation of this volume we have not been content with merely breaking up and re-arranging the stereotype blocks of History, but have sought rather by the evidence of contemporaneous neglected documents to correct the verdict or modify the opinion of past centuries. The general aim has been to present such a book as, by seizing salient points in our History, should supplement narratives of striking events of domestic interest, which are already popular, and thus add to their attractiveness as well as completeness. Localities and love of country have not been overlooked, but studied for the charming character with which they invest scenes and circumstances, and people the historic page with actual life.

CONTENTS.

LACOCK ABBEY, AND ELA COUNTESS OF SALISBURY.

Village of Lacock, 1; Nunnery of Lacock, 2; William Longspé, Earl of Sarum, 2; Childhood of Ela, 2; Annals of Lacock, 3; Pilgrimage of William Talbot, 3, 4; Marriage of Ela, 4; Salisbury Cathedral founded, 5; Death of the Earl of Salisbury, 6; Ela Sheriff of Wiltshire, 7; Lacock Abbey founded, 7; Ela's Abbacy, 8; Death of Ela, 9; Lacock preserved, 11; A Love Adventure, 12; Mr. Fox Talbot and Photography, 13; Lacock Abbey described, 14, 15; Mrs. Crawford's account of Lacock, 15; Lady Shrewsbury and Miss Dormer, 16; Legend of Spye Park and the Bayntons, 17, 18.

THE LUMLEY PORTRAITS.

Lumley Castle, Durham, 19; Liulph the Saxon, 19; Series of Family Portraits, 20; Surtees' and Planché's accounts of the Pictures, 20–22.

FOTHERINGHAY AND ITS MEMORIES.

Village of Fotheringhay, 23; Fotheringhay Castle built, 23; Mary of Valence, her good works, 24; Fetterlock plan of the Castle, 25; College and Church of Fotheringhay, 25–27; Cicely Duchess of York, 26; History of the Castle, 28; Henry V. buried, 29; Richard III. born, 29; State Funeral, 30; The Duchess Cicely, death of, 32; Catharine of Aragon at Fotheringhay, 33; Ampthill Park, 33; Fotheringhay a Prison of State, 34; Mary Queen of Scots imprisoned here, 34; Mary's Trial, 35; Sentence, 36; Elizabeth and Mary, 37; Souvenirs of Mary, 37, 38; Execution of Mary, 42;

Conduct of Elizabeth, 42; Portraits of Mary, 43; Ruins of Fotheringhay Castle, 44, 45; Case of Mary Queen of Scots and Mr. Froude's Views, 46, 47.

TRADITIONS OF WALLINGTON AND THE CALVERLEYS.

Wallington Border Tower, 48; Sir John Fenwick's Hospitality, 48; his Execution, 49; Walter Calverley's Adventures, 50; the Vavasours of Weston, 51; Yorkshire Tragedy, 51; Headless Horse Superstition, 52; Calverley Wood, 52.

FORTUNES OF THREE EARLS OF KILDARE.

The Irish Geraldines, 54; The Earl of Kildare saved from fire in Woodstock Castle, 54; The Vescis and the Geraldines, 55; The Baron of Offaly, 56; Gerald the Great Earl of Kildare, 57; Lambert Simnel and Perkin Warbeck, 57, 58; The Lord of Clanricarde, 58, 59; Death of Kildare, 59; Gerald Oge, ninth Earl, 60, 61; Strange Story, 61; 'Silken Thomas,' 62; His Rebellion, 63; Lord Edward Fitzgerald, 64.

SIR ANTHONY BROWNE AND HIS DESCENDANTS.

Sir Anthony Browne's family connection with Royalty, 66, 67; Hunsdon House and the Earl of Surrey, 66; The Fair Geraldine's Story, 67; Mabel Browne, 67; Gerald eleventh Earl on his Travels, 68, 69; Cardinals Pole and Farnese, 69; Battle Abbey and Sir Anthony Browne, 71; Schaffhausen catastrophe, 71, 72; Cowdray Castle and Viscount Montague, 72; The Family of Browne, 72, 73.

THE OSBORNE AND LEEDS FAMILIES.

Edward Osborne, the Gallant Apprentice of London Bridge, and Sir William Hewet, Cloth-worker, 76; Hewet's Daughter saved, 76; Family of Osborne, 77; Prints and Pictures of Osborne, 78, 79.

CONTENTS.   ix

FATALITIES IN FAMILIES.

House of Neville, 80; Calamities of Cicely Duchess of York, 80–83; House of Percy and its Misfortunes, 83; Reverses of the Paulets, Marquises of Winchester, 84; Sacking of Basing House, 86; John Earl of Oxford imprisoned Twelve Years, 86; a Duke of Exeter Begging his Bread, 86; Brancepeth Castle, its vicissitudes, 87; Tresham Family and Rushton Hall, 88; Sir Edward Dering the anti-royalist, 88; Staffords of Penshurst, 89; Fallen Fortunes of the Buckinghams, 91; Bosworth Field strategies, 92, 93; Thornbury Castle and Edward Stafford, Duke of Buckingham, 93; His Trial and Execution, 93, 94; Duke of Buckingham assassinated by Felton, 95; Buckingham and Shrewsbury Duel, 95; Pope's Lines on the Death of Buckingham, 96; John Villiers, 97; Dukes of Buckingham and Chandos, 97–101; Princely Stowe, 97–99; Lineage of the Duke of Buckingham, 101; Reresbys of Thrybergh Park, Fall of, 102; Two Unfortunate Baronets, 102; Plantagenets fallen, 102; Conyers' Family reverses, 103.

THE HUNGERFORD FAMILY.

The Hungerfords of Somerset and Wilts, 104; Sir Richard Colt Hoare's *Hungerfordiana*, 104; Farleigh Castle, History of, 104, 105; An Episode of Bosworth Field, 106; Lady Hungerford Executed at Tybourn, 106; Hungerfords, 107; Lord Hungerford of Heytesbury, 108; Inventory of Lady Hungerford's Goods, 108; The Hungerford Badge and Crest, 113, 114; Heytesbury Manor-house, 116; Bottreaux Shield in the Hungerford Arms, 117; Hungerford House, Strand, 117; A Five Hundred Guinea Wig, 118; Aubrey and Britton's Accounts of the Hungerford Family, 119, 120.

THE HOUSE OF FERRERS.

The Family of Shirley, 121; Lordship of Etington, 121; Sir Thomas Shirley, 122; Chartley Estate, 123; Staunton Harold Church, 123; Sir Robert Shirley, 123, 124; Laurence Earl Ferrers murders his Steward, 124; Trial of Lord Ferrers, 127; Execution of Lord Ferrers, 129–132; Chartley Tradition, 133.

THE HOUSE OF TALBOT.

The Earl of Shrewsbury, 135; Gooderich Castle, 136; John Talbot, 136; Wars of Henry V., 137; Monument at Whitchurch, 138; Sir Gilbert Talbot at Bosworth, 138; George Earl of Shrewsbury and Mary Queen of Scots, 139; The Duke of Shrewsbury and Addison, 140; The Great Shrewsbury Will Case, 140, 141; Inscription in Bromsgrove Church, 142.

GEORGE VILLIERS, DUKE OF BUCKINGHAM, ASSASSINATED BY JOHN FELTON.

Buckingham the Favourite of James I. and Charles I., 143; 'Sweet Steenie,' 144; Death of Dr. Lambe, 'the Duke's Devil,' 145; Attempts upon Buckingham's Life, 146; Assassination by Felton at Portsmouth, 146, 147; Paper found in Felton's Hat, 148; Charles I. at Southwick, 149; Account of Felton, 149; Purchase of the Knife, 150; Execution of Felton, 151; Funeral of Buckingham, 151; D'Israeli on the Assassination, 152; Poems and Songs printed by the Percy Society, 153; Mutiny at Portsmouth, 154; Forster's *Life of Sir John Eliot*, 154.

DRAGON LEGENDS.

Wolves exterminated, 156; Serpent, Dragon, and Crocodile Stories, 157; Lindwurm or Dragon in Moravia, 158; The Dragon of Wantley, 159-161; St. Leonard's Forest Serpent or Dragon, 161-163; Geological Lights, 163, 164; Sir John Conyers, the Dragon-slayer, 165; Worm of Lambton Hall, 166, 167; The Lambton Family, 168; Gigantic Snail and Laidly Worm, 169; 'Serpent in the Sea,' 170.

LEGENDS OF 'THE RED HAND.'

Heraldry, its uses, 171; 'The Red Hand of Ulster,' 171; Hatchment at Hagley, 172; Holt Tradition and Aston Church, 172, 173; Red Hand at Wateringbury and Gray's Inn, 175, 176; Legend of Sir Richard Baker, 176-178; Stoke D'Abernon Church, 178; Legend of the Bodach Glass, 179-182; Oxenham Family and white-breasted Bird, 182.

DONINGTON CASTLE AND CHAUCER.

Castles near Newbury, and Leicestershire, 183; Castle Doningtons, the two, 185; Chaucer's Residence question, 185; 'Chaucer's Oak,' 186; Death of Chaucer, 188; The Stauntons and the Shirleys, 190.

THE HOUSE OF HOWARD.

Sir John Howard, the eminent Yorkist, 191; Creation of Earl Marshal, 192; Catherine Howard, 193; The Earl of Surrey, statesman, poet, and warrior, 193; Thomas Duke of Norfolk, 194; Lines by Queen Elizabeth, 195; Philip Earl of Arundel, 'the Renowned Confessor,' 196-199; The Earls of Arundel and Charles I., 199; The Howards and the Deepdene, 200.

THE TRAGEDY OF SIR JOHN ELAND.

Eland Hall and the Family of Eland, 201; Fray and Feud in Yorkshire, 202; Eland, Beaumont, Lockwood, and Quarmby, 202; Attack on Crossland Hall, 202; Sir John Eland slain, 204-207; Search for his Murderers, 207; Revenge at Eland Mill and Hall, 208-211; Quarmby's Fate, 211; The Lockwoods extirpated, 212; Old Ballad quoted, 213.

PONTEFRACT CASTLE AND ITS ECHOES.

Pontefract Town and its Castle, 214; Three Sieges, 215; Towers of the Castle, 216; Magnificence of Thomas Earl of Lancaster, 216; The Earl tried in Pontefract Castle, and beheaded, 218, 219; Remorse of Edward II., 220; Deposing of Richard II., 221; Richard in Flint Castle, 221, 222; Richard II. in the Tower, 222, 223; Tradition of the King's Death, 223; Murdered by Sir Piers of Exton, 224; Execution of Rivers, Grey, and Vaughan, 225; Tragedies at Pontefract, 226; Three Sieges of the Castle, 226-228; Views from the Heights, 228, 229; Pontefract and Pomfrete, 229; Pontefract Cakes, 230.

THE RADCLIFFES OF DERWENTWATER.

The Derwentwater Family, 231; Charles Radcliffe and his Support of the Chevalier, 232, 233; Rebellion of 1745, Walpole's account, 233, 234; Dilston or Devilstone Hall, 235; Lord Derwentwater's 'Corpse Lights,' 236; Derwentwater Estates and Greenwich Hospital, 237; Relics of the Derwentwaters, 237, 238; Genealogical details, 238.

THE BRAVE EARL OF LEVEN.

The House of Lesley or Leslie, 239; General Lesley's Brave Services, 239, 240; Imprisoned in the Tower, and liberated by the mediation of the Queen of Sweden, 241.

FYNDERN AND THE FYNDERNES.

Village of Fyndern, County Derby, 242; Family of the Fyndernes, 242, 243; Mary Queen of Scots in Tutbury Castle, 244; 'The Fynderne Flowers,' 244; Sir Bernard Burke's *Vicissitudes of Families*, 245, 246.

THE GOLDSMITH OF LEEDS: A TRAGIC TALE.

Mace of the Corporation, its Maker hanged for High Treason, 247; Clipping Case, 248; The Mystery cleared up, 249, 250.

A COUNTRY GENTLEMAN OF THE SEVENTEENTH CENTURY.

Mr. Henry Hastings, Son, Brother, and Uncle to the Earl of Huntingdon, his Park and Mansion, and love of Hunting; A foundling Knight, 251-254.

CONTENTS. · xiii

THREE EARLS OF STANHOPE.

The First Earl, Soldier and independent Statesman, 255; Earl Philip, Patron of learned Men, and honest Statesman, 256; Earl Charles, universal Genius (Improver of the Printing-press), 257.

HORSE-SHOES AT OAKHAM CASTLE.

Drayton's Lines on Rutland, 258; Oakham Hall, 259; Walkeline de Ferrers, 259; Horse-shoes nailed upon the Castle Gate, origin of the custom, 260; Possession of the Castle and Manor, 262; Castle in the last century, 263; List of Shoes on the Castle Walls, 265–267; The 'Golden Shoe,' 267.

CHRISTMAS MUMMERS IN THE OLDEN TIME.

Origin of Mumming, 268, 269; Christmas in Guildford Castle in 1348, 269; Mummers in 1377, 270; Cornish Miracle-plays, 271; Mumming in Worcestershire and Northamptonshire, 272; Haddon Hall and its Festivities, 273; Possessors of Haddon, 274; Stanzas, 275.

LOVE PASSAGE FROM THE DIARY OF LADY COWPER.

Lady Cowper's *Diary*, 276; Lady Harriet Vere and Lord Cowper, 277–280; History of the *Diary*, 280, 281.

THE SIEGE OF LATHOM HOUSE.

Lathom House and its Possessors, 282; The Earls of Derby and their Magnificence, 284; Siege of Lathom in 1644, and its Defence by the heroic Countess of Derby, 284, 285; Sir Thomas Fairfax at Lathom, 286; Capture of Bolton, 287; Fall of Lathom, 288; The Earl of Derby defeated in 1651, 288; Lathom and Knowsley Proverbs, 290, 291; Legend of the *Eagle and Child*, 291–293; 'The Great Stanley,' his career, 293, 294; His Execution at Bolton, 295; The Rev. Mr. Cumming's Narrative, 295, 296.

THE MANOR OF WAKEFIELD AND SANDAL CASTLE.

Wakefield Manor, 297; William first Earl of Warren, 297; Discovery of the Remains of Gundreda at Lewes, 298, 299; Sandal Castle and the Battle of Wakefield, 300, 301; The Battle-field, 301; The Battle of Towton, 302; Towton and Waterloo compared, 302; Wakefield in olden times, 303; Pindar's Fields and Robin Hood, 303, 304; Sandal Castle, its history, 304, 305; The Civil Wars, 306; Wakefield Park, 306.

MIDDLEHAM CASTLE AND RICHARD III.

Middleham Castle, History of, 308; Character of Richard III., 309-312; His love of Music, 313; Richard and Richmond at Bosworth, 315; Richard's personal appearance, 315.

THE VALE OF WHITE HORSE.

Uffington Castle and White Horse Hill, 316; Battle of Ashdown, 316; The White Horse and Scouring, 317; Saxon Standard of the White Horse, 319; Dragon Hill and Wayland Smith, 320; Wayland Smith Cave described, 321; Blowing-stone described, 322; Vale of White Horse, a retrospect, 323, 324.

THE DUKE OF MONMOUTH'S LAST DAYS.

Monmouth's Progress in Somerset and Dorset, 325, 326; White Lackington House and Norton St. Philip's, 326; Capture of Monmouth, 327-329; The Ash-tree, 329; Monmouth-close, 330; Monmouth's Attainder, 331; Execution of Monmouth, 333, 334; Burial of Monmouth, 334-336; Monmouth House, Soho, 336; Memorials of the Duke, 337; Pocket-book, 337; Verses and Prayers, 340; *Diary*, 341; Charles II., 341; Interesting Documents, 342.

THE LADY ALICE LISLE.

Miles Court, 343; 'The Merciful Assize,' 344; Trial of Lady Alice Lisle, 344-347; 'Kirke's Lambs,' 346; Chief Justice Jeffreys, 347; The Sentence and Execution, 347; The Last of Jeffreys, 348, 349.

WEST HORSLEY PLACE AND THE WESTONS.

West Horsley Place and its Possessors, 350, 351; The Berners Family, 351; Lord Berners and the *Chronicles of Froissart*, 352–354; West Horsley Manor, Sir Anthony Browne, and the Fair Geraldine, 355; The Career of Beddington and Carew Raleigh, 355; Sir Walter Raleigh and Sherborne Castle, 355, 356; The Head of Sir Walter Raleigh, 358, 359; Owners of West Horsley, 359; Great Storm of 1703, 360; The Weston Family, 360, 361; Historical Portraits, 361; The Westons of Sutton, 362; Sutton Place described, 363; Armorial Cognizances, 364; Curious Devices, 365; Old Portraits, 366; Chapel, 367.

THE CLIFFORDS OF CRAVEN.

Scenery of Craven, 368; The Cliffords, and Skipton Castle, 369; The Shepherd Lord Craven, 369, 370; The Profligate Earl of Cumberland, 371; Ballad of 'The Nut-Brown Mayde,' 372; Earls of Cumberland, second and third, 373; The Countess of Pembroke and Montgomery, 373; Town Mansion of the Cliffords in Clerkenwell, 374.

SCRIVELSBY AND THE QUEEN'S CHAMPIONSHIP.

Office of the Champion, the Dymokes and Scrivelsby, 375; The Marmyons, 376; The Champions at the Coronations, Henry IV. to George IV., 377, 378; Scrivelsby Court, 379; Anglo-Norman Ballad on the Lands of Scrivelsby, 379–381.

BRADGATE AND LADY JANE GREY.

Memoir of the Greys of Groby, 382; Bradgate described, 383; Families of Ferrers and Grey, 384, 385; Birthplace of Lady Jane Grey, 386; Ruins of Bradgate, 386, 387; Aylmer, Lady Jane's Master, 388; Education and Character of Lady Jane, 388; Ascham's Visit to Bradgate, 389; Scholarship of Lady Jane, 390, 391; The Greys of Groby, 391; The Countess of Stamford, 392, 393; Marriage of Lord Dudley and Lady Jane, 394; Committed to the Tower, 395; Wyat's Insurrection, 395; Execution of Lord Dudley.

and Lady Jane, 396-401 ; Lines by Lady Jane, 401, 402 ; Burial of Lady Jane, 401, *note;* Prison in the Tower, 404 ; Lines on Bradgate, 405.

ASSASSINATION OF THE HARTGILLS BY LORD STOURTON.

Stourton, in Wiltshire, 407 ; The Hartgills of Kilmington, 407 ; Lady Elizabeth Stourton, 407 ; Affray in Kilmington Church, 408, 409 ; Lord Stourton committed to the Fleet, 409 ; The Hartgills attacked by Lord Stourton's Men, 410 ; Star Chamber business, 411 ; Affray in the Church, 412 ; The Murder, 413, 414 ; Trial of Lord Stourton and four of his Servants, 415 ; Execution at Salisbury, 416 ; The Stourton Family, 416.

THE RED AND WHITE ROSES.

Dispute in the Temple Garden, 418 ; Badges of York, 418 ; Rose Tenure, 419 ; Clifford Castle, 419, 420.

APPENDIX.

Peerages *per saltum*, 421 ; 'Bell the Cat,' 423.

ANCESTRAL STORIES.

LACOCK ABBEY, AND ELA COUNTESS OF SALISBURY.

ABOUT thirteen miles east of Bath, and nearly half-way between the towns of Chippenham and Melksham, in a spacious and level meadow, surrounded by elms, and watered by the Avon, rise the walls and tall spiral chimneys, and arches hung with ivy, of the ancient Nunnery of Lacock. The site, it may be supposed, was originally a solitary glade, adjoining the village or town of Lacock. The name is derived from *Lea* and *Lay*, a meadow, and *Oche*, water; and here, in the Avon, Aubrey found large round pebbles, 'the like of which he had not seen elsewhere.' Lacock was, in the Saxon times, of greater importance than at present; for in an ancient record, quoted by Leland, we read that Dunvallo founded three cities, with three castles, Malmesbury, Tetronberg (? Troubridge), and Lacock. We need scarcely remark, that what might have been then called cities or castles, would not be much in accordance with our ideas of such places in the present age.

The Nunnery of Lacock is far more interesting than the Castle of Dunvallo. In the year 1232, Ela, only child of William Earl of Salisbury, and sole heiress of all her father's vast landed possessions in Wiltshire, laid the foundation of this religious house in her widowhood, in pious and affectionate remembrance of her husband William Longspé (in her right Earl of Sarum), who had then been dead six years. This brave man was the eldest natural son of Henry II., by the lady whose transcendent beauty has become proverbial under the name of Fair Rosamond. He assisted in founding the magnificent Cathedral of New Sarum in the year 1220: six years afterwards he died of poison at the Castle of Old Sarum, and was the first person buried within the walls of New Sarum Cathedral, where his tomb now remains. The earliest ancestor of Ela, whose existence rests on credible record, was Edward of Salisbury, Sheriff of Wilts, whose name occurs in Domesday book, and attesting several charters of the Conqueror.

The childhood and early life of the pious Ela are fraught with romantic interest. She was born at Amesbury in 1188. Until her father's death in 1196, Ela was reared in princely state. Earl William, her father, was one of the distinguished subjects of the chivalric lion king, Richard, and took a prominent part at both his coronations. He also kept the king's charter for licensing tournaments throughout the country. One of the five steads or fields then appointed for tournaments in England was situated between Salisbury and Wilton; and on that spot, when a child, the future Abbess of Lacock may have first witnessed the perilous gaiety of knightly enterprise, and its proud exhibitions of personal courage and external splendour and gallantry. The situation is well known on the downs in front of the site of Sarum Castle.

Such was the scene on which Ela in her childhood might have gazed when animated with the glitter of arms and banners; but from which, on the death of her father, this richly-portioned heiress was suddenly snatched and subjected to seclusion in a foreign country. All that is said in the transcript of the annals of the Abbey of Lacock—the original perished in the fire at the Cotton Library—is that Ela was secretly taken into Normandy by her relations, and there brought up in close and secret custody. These relations, it is conjectured, were her mother and her mother's family, whose estates were either in Normandy or Champagne. Immediately upon the inquisition held after her father's death, Ela's land would, in due course, be taken into the possession of the king, as she had become a royal ward: but such was not the case. The event which arose from these circumstances is highly characteristic of the court of the minstrel monarch. An English knight, named William Talbot, undertook to discover the place of the youthful heiress' concealment; the idea having been suggested, if the fact be admitted, by King Richard's own discovery, a few years before, by aid of the minstrel Blondel.

Assuming the garb of a pilgrim, the gallant Talbot passed over into Normandy, and there continued his search, wandering to and fro for the space of two years. When at length he had found the Lady Ela of Salisbury, he exchanged his pilgrim's dress for that of a harper or travelling troubadour, and in that guise entered the court in which the maid was detained. As he sustained to perfection his character of a gleeman, and was excellently versed in the jests or historical lays recounting the deeds of former times, the stranger was kindly entertained, and soon received as one of the household. At last his chivalric undertaking was fully accomplished; when, having found a convenient opportunity for returning, he carried with him the heiress, and presented her to King Richard. Immediately after, the hand of Ela was given in marriage to William Longspé by his brother King Richard,—Ela being then only ten years old, and William twenty-three.

After the marriage of Ela, we have little to recount of her for several years, unless it were to enumerate the names of her flourishing family of four sons and as many daughters. The Earl was in frequent attendance upon King John; but the Countess Ela appears to have passed most of her life in provincial sovereignty at Salisbury, or in the quiet retirement of some country manor,—most frequently, perhaps, in the peaceful shades of her native Amesbury.[1]

---

[1] Aubrey tells us that 'the last Lady Abbess of Amesbury was a Kirton, who, after the Dissolution, married to ——— Appleton of Hampshire. She had during her life a pension from King Henry VIII.

We pass over the career of the Earl; his assumption of Ela's hereditary office of the Shrievalty of Wiltshire; his attendance at the coronation of John, and upon the king in Normandy; his progresses with John in England, and his appointment to military command and as Warder of the Marches; his ruinous campaign in Flanders; and his presence at the signing of Magna Charta. After the death of John, the Earl returned to his Castle of Salisbury, and to that most interesting scene in which the pious Ela was an active partaker with him. This was no less than the ceremony of founding the present beautiful Cathedral of Salisbury, the fourth stone of which was laid by the Earl, and the fifth by the Countess Ela. We next pass the Earl's visit to Gascony in the spring of 1224, and his disastrous return, when, according to Matthew Paris, he was 'for almost three months at sea' before he landed in England. During the interval all his friends had despaired of his life, except his faithful wife, who, though now a matron, became an object of pursuit to the fortune-hunters of the Court. The Justice Hubert de Burgh, with most indecent haste, now put forward a nephew of his own as a suitor to the Lady of Salisbury. It is related by Matthew Paris, that whilst King Henry was deeply grieved at the supposed loss of the Earl of Salisbury, Hubert came and required him to bestow Earl William's wife (to whom the dignity of that

She was 140 years old (?) when she dyed. She was great-great-aunt to Mr. Child, rector of Yatton Keynell, from whom I had this information. Mr. Child, the eminent banker in Fleet Street, is Parson Child's cousin-german.'—*Natural History of Wiltshire*, 4to, p. 70.

earldom belonged by hereditary right) on his own nephew Reimund, that he might marry her. The king having yielded to his petition, provided the Countess would consent, the Justice sent Reimund to her, in a noble, knightly array, to endeavour to incline the lady's heart to his suit. But Ela rejected him with majestic scorn, and replied that she had lately received letters and messengers which assured her that the Earl, her husband, was in health and safety; adding, that if her lord the Earl had indeed been dead, she would in no case have received *him* for a husband, because their unequal rank forbade such a union. 'Wherefore,' said she, 'you must seek a marriage elsewhere, because you find you have come hither in vain.' Upon the Earl's return, he claimed reparation from the Justiciary, who confessed his fault, made his peace with the Earl by some valuable horses and other large presents, and invited him to his table. Here, it is said, the Earl was poisoned (probably with repletion). He returned to his castle at Salisbury, took to his bed, and died March 7, 1226; and, as already mentioned, was buried in Salisbury Cathedral.

Ela, now a widow, continued firm in her resolution to remain faithful to the memory of her first lord, and to maintain her independence in what was then termed, in legal phrase, 'a free widowhood.' Her choice, however, was singular; for ladies of large estate, at that period, were seldom permitted to remain either as virgins or widows without a lord and protector, unless they had arrived at an advanced age. Her case is deemed extraordinary in the chronicles. Her son, when he became of age, claimed the inheritance of the earldom; but the king refused it, by the advice of his judges, and according to the principles of feudal law. The objection probably was, that the earldom was then vested in his mother. Thus Ela's entrance into the profession of a recluse may possibly have partaken of a worldly motive, as being likely to facilitate her son's admission to his hereditary dignity; but if so, it was still unsuccessful. In consequence of her protracted life, the earldom of Salisbury continued dormant; and as she survived both her son and grandson, it was never revived in the house of Longspé.

Ela was permitted to exercise in person the office of Sheriff of Wiltshire, and Castellane of Old Sarum. Her great seal, an elegant work of art, is extant, and represents her noble and dignified deportment, and her gracefully simple costume: 'her right hand is on her breast; on her left stands a hawk, the usual symbol of nobility; on her head is a singularly small cap, probably the precursor of the coronet; her long hair flows negligently upon her neck on each side; and the royal lions of Salisbury appear to gaze upon her like the lion in Spenser on the desolate Una!'

We at length reach the time of the foundation of Lacock Abbey. 'When,' says the Book of Lacock, 'Ela had survived her husband for seven (six?) years in widowhood, and had frequently promised to found monasteries pleasing to God, for the salvation of her soul and that of her husband, and those of all their ancestors, she was directed in visions (*per revelationes*) that she should build a monastery in honour of St. Mary and St. Bernard in the meadow called Snail's Mead, near Lacock.' This she did on April 16, 1232, although the requisite charters bear prior dates.

Among the earliest coadjutors with the pious Ela was Constance de Legh, who assisted by giving 'her whole manor.' Ela had likewise founded a monastery of Carthusian monks at Hinton, in Gloucestershire, in which, as also at Lacock, she is supposed to have fulfilled the intentions of her husband; indeed, the profits of his wardship of the heiress of Richard de Camville were assigned to the foundation at Hinton by the Earl's last will.

The first canoness veiled at Lacock was Alicia Garinges, from a small nunnery in Oxfordshire, which was governed under the Augustine rule, the discipline to be adopted at Lacock. In the transcripts from the Book of Lacock another person is mentioned, either as abbess or canoness, during the eight years which elapsed after the foundation, and before Ela herself took the veil as abbess of her own establishment, in the year 1238, in the fifty-first year of her age; she 'having, in all her actions and doings, been constantly dependent on the counsel and aid of St. Edmund, the Archbishop of Canterbury, and other discreet men.'

The records of Ela's abbacy are neither copious nor numerous. Among them is a charter, dated 1237, in which the king grants to the Prioress of Lacock, and 'the nuns there serving God,' *a fair to last for three days*,—namely, on the eve, feast, and morrow of St. Thomas the Martyr. In the year 1241 Ela obtained two other charters from the king; one to hold a weekly market. A beautiful cross stood in the market-place at Lacock until about the year 1825, when its light and elegant shaft was destroyed to furnish stone for building the village school-room. By the second charter the king gave the abbess the privilege of having, every week, one cart to traverse the forest of Melksham, and collect 'dead wood' for fuel, without injury to the forest, during the royal pleasure.

Five years before her death, Ela retired from the peaceful rule of her monastic society, and appointed in her place an abbess named Beatrice, of Kent. Yet Ela obtained several more benefits for the abbey from the king. At length, in the seventy-fourth year of her age, August 24, 1261, yielding up her soul in peace, Ela rested in the Lord, and was most honourably buried in the choir of the monastery. Aubrey has this strange entry in his *Natural History of Wiltshire*: 'Ela Countess of Salisbury, daughter to Longspé, was foundress of Lacock Abbey, where she ended her days, being above a hundred years old: she outlived her understanding. This I found in an old MS. called *Chronicon de Lacock in Bibliotheca Cottoniana*.' Now, the chronicle referred to was burnt in 1731, and the extracts preserved from it do not confirm Aubrey's statement, but place Ela's death in her seventy-fourth year.

Ela had been deprived by death of her son and grandson, and her daughter Isabella, Lady Vesey; and in the last year of her life she was preceded to the tomb by her son Stephen; so that, of all her family, she left only two sons and three daughters surviving, one of whom died in the following year. Ela's son William Longspé the second, having joined the expedition of St. Louis to the Holy Land, perished at the assault of Mensoura. His mother, according to the monkish legend, seated in her abbatial stall in the church at Lacock, saw, at the same moment, the mailed form of her child admitted into heaven, surrounded by a radius of glory. His son William Longspé III. was killed in a tournament near Salisbury.

The annals of the abbey after the death of Ela are by no means complete. In 1291 we first collect a view of its yearly revenue, £191, 12s. 4d. Among the possessions here included is a manor in the Isle of Wight, which had been given to the abbey by Amicia Countess of Devon, and 'Lady of the Isle,' *together with her heart.* The *obit* of the Countess was yearly celebrated in the church of Lacock Abbey, on the feast of St. Andrew (November 30), when four bushels of corn were distributed to the poor; and on the eve and day of that feast, three poor persons were fed with bread, drink, and meat, to the value of 2d. each. Another instance of pious affection in 1297, is the bequest of the heart of the aged Nicholas Longspé, Bishop of Salisbury, the last surviving son of the foundress.

The last abbess was Joanna Temys. Lacock was one of the thirty monasteries which the king spared in 1536; but it was surrendered in 1539, and the fatal document is still preserved in the Augmentation Office. It is ratified by the abbey common seal, which is of the same age as the foundation, and represents the Virgin and Child, with the lady abbess in a niche below, kneeling in prayer. To the last abbess was assigned a pension of £40; and the prioress and 15 other nuns had proportionate provisions. The yearly value of the abbey and its estates, at the surrender, was £171, 19s. 3½d. Among the payments are those for observances in memory of the foundress and others, in candles about their tombs, and doles to the poor: there were maintained three priests for the daily celebration of divine services, and 'the general confessor to the convent.' Some of the principal gentry in the neighbourhood, as well as the abbess' own kinsmen, are also named as holding honourable offices in the service of the abbey.

Lacock has preserved, from the Dissolution to this day, its most perfect form: the cloisters and cells of the nuns—its ancient walls and ivied chimneys almost entire. But the church was wholly destroyed, and not a vestige can be traced of its ancient altars. The bones of the honoured foundress and her family were alike disregarded. One single mark of respectful remembrance has been paid to the Countess Ela: her epitaph is still preserved on a stone within those cloisters which echoed once to her footsteps, and resounded the Ave Marias of the nuns.

After the Dissolution we find that Lacock was sold to Sir William Sherington in 1544 for £783, 12s. 1½d. Thirty years subsequently Lacock was visited by Queen Elizabeth, who was also this year at Longleat and Wilton; and, most probably, the queen then knighted her host, Sir Henry Sherington. In the Civil War, 1645, the house was garrisoned for the king, and taken by the opposite party shortly after Cromwell had won Devizes, the Lord of Lacock having previously been sent prisoner to London.

Aubrey relates this romantic story, which has the appearance of authenticity: 'Dame Olave, a daughter and co-heir of Sir [Henry] Sherington of Lacock, being in love with [John] Talbot, a younger brother of the Earl of Shrewsbury, and her father not consenting that she should marry him, discoursing with him one night from the battlements of the abbey church, said she, "I will leap down to you." Her sweetheart replied he would catch her then, but he did not believe she would have done it. She leapt downe; and the wind, which was then high, came under her coates, and did something break the fall. Mr. Talbot caught her in his arms, but she struck him dead. She cried out for help, and he was with great difficulty brought to life again. Her father told her that, since she had made such a leap, she should e'en marrie him. She was my honoured friend Colonel Sharington Talbot's grandmother, and died at her house at Lacock about 1651, being about an hundred years old. Quære, Sir Jo. Talbot?'

The above anecdote was missed by the venerable historian of Lacock, the Rev. Canon Bowles, to which work we are largely indebted for the materials of this sketch. John Carter, the antiquary, when he visited Lacock in 1801, was told a tradition, that 'one of the nuns jumped from a gallery on the top of a turret there into the arms of her lover.' He observes, as impugning the truth of the story, that 'the gallery appears to have been the work of James or Charles the First's time.' This may have been founded upon Aubrey's story: though the abbey church had then been destroyed, there is a galleried tower of later date.

From the Sheringtons the property descended to Sir Anthony Mildmay of Apthorp, Northamptonshire, by his marriage with Grace, daughter of Sir Henry Sherington, but had no issue; so that the whole inheritance of Lacock came to her sister Olive, the wife of John Talbot, Esq. of Salwarp, county Worcester, fourth in descent from John the second Earl of Shrewsbury, from whom it has descended to Henry Fox Talbot, Esq., who in this delightful retreat, in chemical researches for his own recreation, here worked out the secret of Photography. He took up the ground to which Davy and Wedgwood had made their way. Paper was the medium, which he made sensitive to light by nitrate of silver, and then fixed the image by common salt. He first called his process Photogenic Drawing, then Calotype, which his friends changed to Talbotype, in imitation of Daguerre's example. Mr. Fox Talbot is stated, in the *Quarterly Review*, No. ccii., to have sent his method to the Royal Society in the same month that Daguerre's discovery was made known, January 1839; but Sir David Brewster dates Mr. Talbot's communication six months earlier.[1]

[1] As a new art, which gave employment to thousands, Mr. Fox Talbot brought photography to a high degree of perfection. 'He

Lacock Abbey, as it now exists, consists of the octangular turret, with a gallery, already referred to ; and the cloisters, of the time of Henry IV. There are several sepulchral relics, as grave-stones, coffin-lids, etc. The site of the church is now a terrace-walk. The residential portion of the building has handsome bayed windows, pierced parapet, and twisted chimney-shafts. The middle chamber of the tower is reserved as a depository for writings; here is the Magna Charta of King Henry III., of inestimable value, being the only one perfect in the kingdom. It is $12\frac{3}{4}$ inches broad ; and in length, including the fold, $20\frac{1}{2}$ inches : the seal is of green wax, pendent by a skein of green silk. This charter seems to have been designed for the use of the knights and military tenants in Wiltshire, and to have been deposited here by the Countess Ela, who succeeded her husband in the office of Sheriff of Wiltshire.

expended large sums of money in obtaining for the public the full benefit of his invention ; and towards the termination of his patent he liberally surrendered to photographic amateurs and others all the rights which he possessed. As Mr. Talbot had derived no pecuniary benefit from his patent, he had intended to apply to the Privy Council for an extension of it ; but in this he was thwarted by interested parties.'
'Although,' says Sir David Brewster, 'we are confident that a jury of philosophers would have given a verdict in favour of Mr. Talbot's patent, taken as a whole, and so long unchallenged, yet we regret to say that an English judge and jury were found to deprive him of his right, and transfer it to the public. The patrons of science and art stood aloof in the contest ; and none of our scientific institutions, and no intelligent member of the Government, came forward to claim from the State a national reward to Mr. Talbot. How different in France was the treatment of Niepce and Daguerre !'

A singular domestic relic is shown here—the *Nuns' Boiler*, which formerly stood in the abbey kitchen. It is very massive, is supported on three legs, and bears this inscription :

'A PETRO WAGHUENS IN MECHLINIA EFFUSUS FACTUS VE FUERAM, ANNO MILLESIMO QUINGENTESSIMO. DEO LAUS ET GLORIA CHRISTO.'

'I was moulten or made by Peter Waghuens, of Mechlin, in the year 1500. Praise be to God and glory to Christ.'

Mrs. Crawford, in a sketch of the old place, remarks : 'There is something highly picturesque and moving to the feelings in the appearance of this fine abbey, standing in a fertile vale, with its old avenue, broad terrace-walks, and extensive cloisters, breathing, as it were, the heavenly music of those holy spirits that once animated the vestal forms of beauty now mouldered into dust, and of which the profane foot that treads over it takes no account.

'The entrance-hall is a magnificent apartment, with a double row of niches round its sides, filled with statues : one of a bishop, with a book in hand, is instinct with life. Over the high mantel are the effigies of the Countess of Shrewsbury and her two beautiful nieces, habited as nuns. From a door on one side of the hall you enter the inner cloisters, which still bear the name of " the nuns' burying-ground." The great dining-room has full-length portraits painted on panel. There is a gallery hung with pictures, among which is the legendary leap of the nun, who "escaped with her lover, having leaped from the high tower, in which the abbess had confined her, and sustained no injury from her fall but the fracture of her little finger."' Mrs. Crawford relates some interesting recollections of an inmate of the abbey, Lady Shrewsbury, a strict Catholic, eighty years of age, who had been in her youth a great beauty. She had frequently friends staying here; the Blounts, Cliffords, and Hydes being her most frequent guests. The family priest, a sort of 'Will Wimble,' had three rooms for his special use: a bed-chamber hung with tapestry, and filled with all sorts of curious things; and two chambers—a printing-office and turning-shop.

Lady Shrewsbury was pious without parade, and one of the old aristocracy, without any of those unbecoming airs of pride too often attending high rank. She was sent by her father, Lord Dormer, to a French convent to be educated. Her own account of her first interview with the Earl of Shrewsbury is amusing: 'Being told that an English gentleman had brought letters from my father, I hurried into the Lady Abbess' parlour, where the Earl, then a beautiful young man, was waiting to see me. I had been so long within those dismal walls, and never seen a man but our own confessor, and a hideous-looking creature who came to draw my tooth, that the Earl looked like an angel to me.' They were soon married, and spent some time at the French court. On her arrival in England, Lady Shrewsbury went, in all her bridal state, to visit her sister, Miss Dormer, at the convent where she was passing her novitiate, previously to her taking the veil. Lady Shrewsbury used all her sisterly arts to entice back the young recluse to the gay world she had forsaken,—but in vain.

LEGEND OF SPYE PARK.

Mrs. Crawford appends: Half-way up to Bowden Hill, and between Bowood and Lacock Abbey, stands Spye Park, the seat of the Bayntons, a family of great antiquity. In 1652, at the defeat of Sir William Waller by the Lord Wilmot, Bromham House, the former seat of the Bayntons, was burnt down, after which they removed to Spye Park. There is now in the Royal Museum a curious old pedigree, showing that the Bayntons, in the reign of Henry II., were Knights of St. John of Jerusalem. Sir Henry Baynton held the office of knight-marshal to the king, a place of great authority at that time; and his son, who was slain at Bretagne in the year 1201, was a noble Knight of Jerusalem. Sidney, in his *Treatise on Government*, mentions this family of 'great antiquity, and that in name and ancient possessions it equals most, if it is not far superior to many, of the nobility.' As all old mansions in the country must be associated with some portion of the superstitious and the wonderful, Spye Park was not without its share. There was a story told (and credited by the peasantry) of a knight, clad in armour, haunting one of the chambers—supposed to be the spirit of the gallant Sir Henry Baynton, who was beheaded at Berwick, in the time of Henry IV., for taking part with the rebel Earl of Northumberland. More modern spirits also were said to trouble the indwellers of Spye Park; for old Lady Shrewsbury used to tell that old Sir Edward Baynton, the father of Sir Andrew, was continually seen at nightfall in the park and grounds, and that the latter had often (when in company with his mistress) been startled by the apparition of his father. Sir Andrew, in early life, was remarkable for the possession of engaging and high moral qualities; but the misconduct of his first wife, to whom he was fondly attached, altered, it was said, his very nature; and to banish thought, he plunged into reckless libertinism. The circumstances were these: A gentleman of great personal attractions, and related to Lady Maria Baynton, arrived on a visit at the house. The wretched wife and mother forgot her twofold duty; and after many stolen meetings among the shades of Spye Park, she fled with her paramour. Sir Andrew was at first inconsolable, and, despite her shameless desertion of him, long lamented the mother of his child. Alas! that sinful mother and guilty wife was speedily visited by an awful retribution. Her infamous companion in guilt treated her with cruelty and brutality. Death at last put an end to her sufferings; and the young, the elegant, and accomplished Lady Maria, nurtured upon the bosom of indulgence, died in a low house, without a single friend or attendant to minister to her last wants, or a charitable hand to close her dying eyes.

THE LUMLEY PORTRAITS.

IN Lumley Castle, in the village of Lumley, Durham, built in the reign of Edward I., the entrance-hall contains full-length portraits of the Lumley family, commencing with Liulph, the Saxon progenitor of the family, and ending with his descendants, who lived in the reigns of Elizabeth and James I. Mr. Planché, Rouge Croix, describes these pictures as evidently ancient, the greater number displaying the well-known and accurately-represented costumes of particular periods, ranging from the fourteenth to the seventeenth centuries. 'Until,' says Mr. Planché, ' I learned from the Rev. John Dodd that they had all been painted by order of Lord John Lumley, in the reign of Elizabeth or James I., I was perfectly ready to believe that each portrait was contemporary with the costume in which the figure was attired; for though, of course, Liulph the Saxon and the early Norman Lumleys could never have worn the dresses they were painted in, the pictures themselves might have been executed at the various periods when such dresses were worn, according to the invariable practice of mediæval artists. Had this been the case with these pictures, the hall of Lumley Castle would have presented us with the most curious and valuable series of family portraits that could perhaps be found in the world. But such is not the case.' Still they are a remarkable collection of imaginary portraits. Surtees, who wrote nearly fifty years ago, says of them: 'The collection of paintings at Lumley is dispersed; those only remain which are strictly family portraits. . . . In the great hall, besides a portrait of Liulph armed *cap-à-pie*, like a gallant knight' (in plate armour, with a helmet of the sixteenth century!), and bestriding his war-horse, are fifteen pictures of my lord's ancestors, with a pillar of his pedigree; all which are noted in the inventory of 1609, and then valued at £8. These, whether in robes or armour, are evidently fictitious or restored, and need no further notice. The most genuine and ancient piece Mr. Surtees considers to be: 'King Richard II., in the bloom of youth, and with bright auburn hair, sits on a chair of state in his royal robes—scarlet lined with ermine, his inner dress deep blue or purple, powdered over with golden R's, and crowned. He holds the sceptre in his left hand, and with his right gives a patent of nobility to Sir Ralph Lumley, who kneels before him in his baron's robes.' The frame bears the date 1384. This picture Mr. Planché considers a close imitation of the celebrated original portrait of Richard, preserved in the Jerusalem Chamber at Westminster. The figure of Sir Ralph Lumley is not authentic, since he was slain at Cirencester, in arms against Henry IV., in 1400, when he had not attained the age of thirty-eight, and could scarcely even then have presented the portly and venerable appearance displayed in the picture.

Mr. Planché describes the portraits as representing the descendants of Liulph for fourteen generations, in various military or civil costumes, some exceedingly picturesque, and all bearing strong evidence to the fact that the robes and armour were painted from authorities of some description, and not from the fancy of the artists. They were executed about 1600, when various histories and chronicles were printed and published in Germany, Holland, and Flanders especially, illustrated by very spirited engravings representing the sovereigns and princes whose reigns or biographies were included in them. A great similarity exists in the styles of drawing and the character and costume of all these figures,—the dress and armour of the earlier personages being invariably of the fifteenth century. Mr. Planché was therefore struck by the strong general resemblance the paintings at Lumley Castle bear to the aforesaid engravings.

We have not space for further details; but to add, that among the discrepancies should be noted the portrait of Theoderick the first Count of Holland, who lived in the ninth century, in armour and dress of the fifteenth century; his shield has on it an heraldic lion rampant, some 300 years before the earliest appearance of heraldic devices. Mr. Planché, in conclusion, considers the pictures to have been painted by Richard Stevens, a Dutchman, mentioned by Walpole as 'an able statuary, painter, and medallist.'

Surtees considers 'the connection of Liulph, a southern noble' (grandfather of William de Lumley, Baron of the Bishopric), 'as asserted in the pedigree, with the blood of Syward and Waltheof (Earls of Northumberland), is confirmed by evidence not very usual in claims of such high and splendid antiquity.'

Pennant relates that when James I., on his way to the south, visited Lord Lumley in his castle, 'William James, Bishop of Durham, expatiated to the king on the pedigree of their noble host, and wearied him with a long detail of the family ancestry to a period even beyond belief. "Oh, mon!" said the king, "gang na farther; let me digest the knowledge I ha' gained; for, by my saul, I did na ken Adam's name was Lumley."'[1]

[1] See the able paper by Mr. Planché in the *Journal of the British Archæological Association*, March 1866, p. 31.

FOTHERINGHAY AND ITS MEMORIES.

FEW of the historical villages of England possess such interest as Fotheringhay, celebrated as the peculiar seat of the House of York, the birthplace of Richard III., and memorable as the place where Mary Queen of Scots was condemned to close on the scaffold a life of captivity and sorrow. Fotheringhay lies in the eastern division of Northamptonshire, on the north bank of the river Nen; and though now reduced to a small village, it formerly held the rank of a market-town; had its royal castle and market cross, its college, nunnery, hermitage, and other votive buildings, in addition to its collegiate church of highly enriched architecture.

The Castle of Fotheringhay, not one stone of which remains upon another, was originally built by Simon de St. Liz, or by the second Earl of Northampton, at the close of the eleventh or early in the twelfth century; the manor having been granted by the Conqueror to his niece Judith, from whom it descended by marriage to the above Earl. It was in the possession of the Crown in the reign of Edward I., who granted it to his nephew, John de Britain Earl of Richmond, who in the second year of Edward II. obtained a grant of the castle to himself and his heirs, and seven years later was certified to be Lord of Fotheringhay. He dying without issue, the castle and manor reverted to the Crown, and were granted to Mary de St. Paul, daughter of Guido de Chatillon, Comte de St. Paul in France, by Mary, daughter of the Earl of Richmond aforesaid. She was Baroness de Voissu and Montanzi, and married to Andemare de Valence, Earl of Pembroke, who fell in a tournament on the day of their nuptials; whence she is characterized by Gray as the

> 'Sad Chatillon on her bridal morn,
> That wept her bleeding love.'

She passed the greatest part of her life in the exercises of religion, and employed her estate in founding Denny Abbey, near Ely; and Pembroke Hall, in the University of Cambridge. Her residence at Fotheringhay is thus described: 'The castle, with a certain tower, is built of stone, walled in, embattled, and encompassed with a great moat. Within are one large hall, two chambers, a kitchen and bakehouse, built all of stone, with a porter's lodge and chambers over it, and a drawbridge beneath. Within the castle walls is another place called the manor. The site of the whole contains ten acres.'

Upon the death of Mary of Valence, the castle and manor again reverted to the Crown, and were granted by Edward III. to his fifth son, Edmund of Langley, then a minor. The castle had fallen into decay, and on his taking actual possession, was so much dilapidated as to induce him to rebuild the greater part of it, the ground plan being in the form of a *fetterlock ;*[1] and the fetterlock, enclosing a falcon, was afterwards the favourite device of the family of Edmund of Langley. He also, having projected the building of a college at Fotheringhay, began to fulfil his intention by erecting 'a large and magnificent choir' at the east end of the old parish church. After his death, the building was carried on by his son, and completed by his grandson Richard, whose body was in 1466 buried there, under a handsome shrine on the north side of the high altar. The agreement for the buildings was with 'William Howard, a freemason of Fotheringhay;' but they were not completed till the time of Edward IV., who erected 'the fair cloister,' and the shrine already mentioned, which Leland describes as 'a pratie chapelle,' and Camden as 'a magnificent monument.' The college

---

[1] Mr. Planché (Rouge Croix), setting aside the old origin of this badge, traces it, by aid of the *Promptorium Parvulorum* (a Latin and English dictionary of the fourteenth century), to *langelyn*, 'to bind together;' and, according to Mr. Halliwell, *langele* is still used in the north to signify hopling or fettering a horse. Without asserting that a fetterlock was actually called a *langel*, there is quite enough similarity of sound between *langelyn* or *langele*, 'to bind or fetter,' and Langley, the name by which he was known to suggest its adoption for his badge, the object being to typify the name or title of the bearer. The falcon may have been added as a token of descent by his grandson Richard, the said falcon being described by itself as 'falco imagine *Ricardi Ducis Ebors.*' See a paper 'On the Badges of the House of York,' *Journ. Brit. Archæol. Association*, 1864.

being suppressed under Edward VI., and its site granted to Dudley Duke of Northumberland, the church was dismantled. Some of the richly carved stalls have been preserved in the neighbouring churches of Hemington and Tansor: they are decorated with the Yorkist badges and crests. The royal tombs fell to decay. At length Queen Elizabeth, visiting the spot, ordered the bodies to be removed to the parish church, where monuments, 'by no means worthy,' says Camden, 'of such princes, sons of kings, and progenitors of kings of England,' still exist to their memory. On opening the graves, the bodies were found enclosed in lead; and round the neck of Cicely Duchess of York was a silver ribbon, with a pardon from Rome, written in a fine Roman hand, 'as fair and fresh,' says Fuller, 'as if it had been written yesterday.'

When Dugdale visited the spot in 1641, the glass was in the windows of the cloister and college halls, and the shields of arms remained. The windows of the nave and side aisles were also painted, and contained figures of saints, cardinals, and prelates. Above these were angels playing on musical instruments. Here, too, were the Bohemian plume, and the falcon, enclosed by a fetterlock, already mentioned as the device of the House of York. Whilst that powerful family was contending for the crown, the falcon was represented as endeavouring to expand its wings and force open the lock. When the family had actually ascended the throne, the falcon was represented as free, and the lock open. The western windows were ornamented with the rose, the white hart, the fetterlock, and the lion. 'The whole,' says Stukeley, 'were saved during the Civil War by the minister of the parish, who bribed the soldiers to preserve them.' Many of these figures were perfect in the year 1787, but at present not a window retains its former beauty. In 1817, when the canopy of the pulpit was under repair, some of the ancient gilding was discovered. At the back is a shield of arms, bearing France and England quarterly, supported on the dexter side by a lion rampant guardant, for the earldom of March, and a bull for Clare; on the sinister by a hart, showing descent from Richard II., who took that device; and by a boar for the honour of Windsor, possessed by Richard III. Gray, alluding to the murder of the princes, characterizes Richard by this badge :

> 'The bristled bore, in infant gore,
> Wallows beneath the thorny shade.'

It should be mentioned that the device of the fetterlock remained in most of the windows of the church till the year 1807; and it is retained to this day upon the point of the flag-pole on the lantern-tower.

'The Church of Fotheringhay,' says Mr. Richard Brooke, who visited the site in 1857 and 1858, 'must once have been a magnificent edifice; but at present, all that remains of it is the nave with its side aisles, and the tower, which are very beautiful. The nave is now used for divine service. The church contains a very handsome and large stone font, apparently of the early part of the fifteenth century, which is not only an object of interest from its beauty, but, as King Richard III. was born at Fotheringhay on October 2, 1452 (see *William of Wyrcester*), it is only a reasonable inference that he was baptized at that font' (*Notes and Queries*, 2d S. vi.).

Resuming our history of the castle at the death of Edmund, who had been successively created Earl of Cambridge and Duke of York, the fortress descended to his son Edward Earl of Rutland, who succeeded also to his father's honours. But on his falling in the battle of Agincourt, and dying without issue, the castle and lordship descended to his nephew Richard, the son of his brother Richard Earl of Cambridge, who was beheaded in the third year of Henry V., for conspiring against that king. Fotheringhay thus became the residence of the House of York, and the birthplace of Richard III. :

> ' Lo ! on that mound, in days of feudal pride,
> Thy tow'ring castle frown'd above the tide;
> Flung wide her gates, where troops of vassals met
> With awe the brow of high Plantaganet.
> But, ah ! what chiefs in sable vest appear !
> What bright achievements mark yon warrior's bier!
> 'Tis York's, from Agincourt's victorious plain,
> They bear the fallen hero o'er the main ;
> Through all the land his blooming laurels spread,
> And to thy bosom give the mighty dead.
> When from thy lap the ruthless Richard sprung,
> A boding sound through all the borders rung :
> It spoke a tale of blood—fair Neville's woe,
> York's murd'rous hand, and Edward's future foe.'
> *Antonia's Banks*, MS., 1797.

The hero of Agincourt left minute directions for his funeral, ordering his body to be buried in the church of Fotheringhay, in the midst of the choir, near the steps, under a flat marble. His remains were accordingly brought over to England and carried to Westminster, and thence to Fotheringhay, where, on December 1, 1415, they were interred. The tomb is described by Leland, who saw it, 'as a flat marble stone, and upon it was his image flat in brass.'

Richard III. was the eleventh child of Richard Plantagenet, Duke of York, and nearest of kin to Edward III., the common ancestor of all the royal houses which have, since his death, reigned in Great Britain. His mother was also of royal blood, being the daughter of Ralph Neville, who had married Joan Beaufort, daughter of John of Gaunt. From his earliest childhood at Fotheringhay he was bred up amidst the violence and confusion of civil war, and was only seven years old when, with his mother, he was imprisoned by Henry VI.; and one of his earliest recollections must have been his father's death in the battle of Wakefield. Although Shakspeare assigns him a prominent part in this battle, where his father the Duke of York was taken and put to death after exclaiming,

'Three times did Richard make a line to me,
And thrice cried, Courage, father, fight it out,'

Richard was then only in his ninth year. His father's body was first interred at Pontefract, but afterwards removed, with that of his son Edmund Earl of Rutland, in great pomp, to Fotheringhay. On July 22, 1466, their remains were put into a chariot covered with black velvet, richly wrapped in cloth of gold and royal habit. At the feet of the Duke stood the figure of an angel clothed in white, and bearing a crown of gold, to signify that of right he was a king. The chariot was drawn by seven horses, trapped to the ground, and covered with black, charged with escutcheons of that prince's arms. Every horse carried a man, and upon the foremost rode Sir John Skipwith, who bore the Duke's banner displayed. The bishops and abbots in their robes went two or three miles before, to prepare the reception of the remains. Richard Duke of Gloucester followed next after the chariot, accompanied by several of the nobility and officers of arms. In this order they left Pontefract, and that night rested at Doncaster, where they were received by the convent of Cordeliers in grey habit. Thence, by easy stages, they proceeded to Blithe, Tuxford-in-the-Clay, Newark, Grantham, and Stamford; and on Monday, July 29, the procession reached Fotheringhay, where the bodies were received by several bishops and abbots in their robes, and supported by twelve servants of the deceased.

At the entrance of the churchyard, King Edward IV., accompanied by several dukes, earls, and barons, in mourning, were in attendance, and proceeded to the choir of the church, near the high altar, where was a hearse covered with black, furnished with banners and other insignia. Upon this hearse were placed the remains of the Duke and his son Edmund. The queen[1] and her two daughters were also present in mourning, attended by ladies and others. Over the image was a cloth of majesty and black sarcenet, with the figure of our Lord, sitting on a rainbow, of beaten gold; it had in every corner an escutcheon of the arms of France and England quarterly, with a valence round the hearse, fringed half a yard deep, and ornamented with three angels of beaten gold, holding the Duke's arms within a garter, in every part above the hearse.

Upon the morrow, the 30th, several masses were said; and at the offertory of the mass of requiem, the king offered for the prince his father; and the queen, her two daughters, and the Duchess (Countess) of Richmond, offered afterwards. Then Norroy King-of-arms offered the prince's coat-of-arms; March King-of-arms the target; Ireland King-of-arms the sword; Windsor herald of England, and Ravendor herald of Scotland, offered the helmet; and M. de Ferreys, the harness and courser:

> 'So sumptuous, yet so perishing withal!
>
> . . . . . .
>
> A thousand mourners deck the pomp of death:
> To-day, the breathing marble glows above
> To decorate its memory, and tongues
> Are busy of its life; to-morrow, worms
> In silence and in darkness seize their prey.'

Edward Earl of March, afterwards Edward IV., succeeded his father both in the honours of his house and the

[1] Elizabeth, daughter of Sir Richard Woodville, and widow of Sir John Gray, Kent, who was killed in the battle of St. Albans.

possession of Fotheringhay Castle and lordship; Cicely, his mother, still retaining her right in it until the ninth year of his reign, when Guy Woolston, Esq., was appointed constable of the castle and keeper of the great park, Erleswood, and Newhaugh, lying within the bailiwick of Clyve in Rockingham Forest; here the lord of the castle had *housebote* (timber out of the lord's wood for repairs) and *heybote* (thorns and other wood for hedges, gates, fences, etc.), and two leets, held yearly at Easter and Michaelmas. From Leland's account, Fotheringhay appears to have been the favourite residence of this powerful and royal house; for the Duchess Cicely, who survived her husband thirty-six years, during the greatest part of her widowhood inhabited the castle. She died in the tenth of Henry VII., 1495, in her castle at Berkhampstead, where the kings of Mercia had a palace and castle, afterwards enlarged and strengthened in the Norman times, and where Henry II. kept his court. The Duchess Cicely was buried in the choir at Fotheringhay beside her husband. She was the youngest of twenty-one children; she survived the whole of her family the Nevilles, and by their conquering swords became the mother of kings; she saw three of her descendants kings of England, and her grand-daughter Elizabeth queen of Henry VII. By her death she was saved the additional affliction of the loss of her grandson Edward Earl of Warwick, the last male of the princely house of Plantagenet, who was cruelly put to death by a tyrannical monarch in 1499.

After the death of Edward IV., the castle continued in

the Crown, and by Act of Parliament 1 Henry VII. was declared to be part of the royal possessions. Henry settled it upon his queen Elizabeth, the only representative of the House of York. Reverting to the king on her death, it continued in the Crown till Henry VIII. gave it in dower to Catharine of Aragon, who seems to have been much attached to the castle. Leland records that 'she did great cost of refreshing it.' He describes it as being at that time 'a castle fair and neatly strong, with very good lodgings in it, defended by double ditches, with a very ancient and strong keep.' Queen Catharine removed from Fotheringhay to Ampthill Castle[1] whilst the process of her divorce from Henry VIII. was going on at the neighbouring Priory of Dunstable; after her divorce she resided some time in Kimbolton Castle. 'I pity Catharine of Aragon,' says Walpole, 'for living at Kimbolton; I never saw an uglier spot.' The queen died there in 1536.

[1] Ampthill Park, on the site of the old castle, has a grove of firs, in the centre of which, in 1773, Lord Ossory erected an octagonal shaft, raised on four steps, surmounted by a cross, bearing a shield, with Queen Catharine's arms of Castile and Aragon. On a tablet in the base of the cross is the following inscription, by Horace Walpole:

> 'In days of yore, here Ampthill's towers were seen,
> The mournful refuge of an injured queen;
> Here flowed her pure but unavailing tears,
> Here blinded zeal sustained her sinking years.
> Yet Freedom hence her radiant banner wav'd,
> And Love avenged a realm by priests enslav'd :
> From Catharine's wrongs a nation's bliss was spread,
> And Luther's light from lawless Henry's bed.'

Close to Ampthill is Houghton Park, with a pear-tree under which Sir Philip Sidney is said to have written part of his *Arcadia*.

Such is an outline of the history of the Castle of Fotheringhay, until it was converted to a prison of state. This seems to have taken place in the reign of Mary, when, 25th May 1554, according to Stow, Edward, the last of the Courtneys, Earls of Devonshire, was removed from the Tower of London, to which he had been committed on suspicion of his having consented to Sir Thomas Wyat's conspiracy, by Master Chamberlayne of Suffolk, and Sir Thomas Tresham, Knt., and conveyed to Fotheringhay, to remain under their custody at the queen's pleasure. The Earl's confinement here was of short duration; for in the Easter of the year following, 1555, he again appeared at court.

The next and last person who entered the castle as a prisoner, and from whose fate it is noted in English history, was the unfortunate Queen of Scots, who was closely confined here, in the custody of Sir William Fitzwilliam of Milton, during the last six years of her life. When Fuller the historian visited the castle, he read in one of the windows the following distich, written on the glass with a diamond by the royal captive:

> 'From the top of all my trust
> Mishap hath laid me in the dust,'

which is taken from an old ballad preserved in Ellis's *Specimens*.

It will be recollected that the indictment against Babyngton and his companions charged them not only with intending to kill Elizabeth, but also to rise in arms to favour an invasion from Spain, and to release the Queen of Scots. This last was probably the chief object with most of them, but the project terminated as fatally for her as for themselves. Babyngton had been recently in France, and had brought letters for Mary; and, in return, she is stated in his indictment to have written letters to him, 'in which she not only signified that she allowed and approved of such intended treasons, but therein also urged Babyngton and his confederates, by promises of great reward, to fulfil the same.' The truth of this assertion, at least as regards any design on the life of Elizabeth, is very doubtful; but it answered the purpose of the framers of the Association, and it was forthwith resolved to proceed to the judicial murder of the unhappy prisoner. Her secretaries (Nau and Curle) and her papers were seized, and both subjected to rigid examination; and Mary was removed to Fotheringhay Castle preparatory to her so-called trial.

On October 11, 1586, the commissioners assembled at Fotheringhay; Sir Thomas Bromley, Lord Chancellor, and the Earls of Kent and Shrewsbury, being the leading members. Three days after, the presence-chamber of the castle was fitted up for the trial. The court sat two days. Mary at first refused to plead; then acknowledged negotiating with foreign powers to obtain her freedom; but earnestly disdained any intention against the life of Elizabeth. She also charged Walsingham with forging letters (which he denied), and desired to be confronted with her secretaries, one of whom (Nau) she accused of treachery. Her demand was refused. The commissioners adjourned, and, October 25, re-assembled in the Star Chamber at Westminster, and pronounced a sentence, 'that Babyngton's conspiracy was with the privy (*cum scientiâ*) of Mary;' as also, 'that she had herself compassed and imagined within this realm of England divers matters tending to the hurt, death, and destruction of the royal person of our sovereign lady the queen.' On October 28 the Parliament met, their principal business being the attainder of Babyngton and his associates, and applications to the queen to consent to the execution of Mary. Elizabeth desired them to reconsider their request; they again urged it, and then she dismissed them with an ambiguous speech, which she herself termed ' an answer without an answer.'

The sentence against Mary was confirmed by the queen and her council at Richmond. The proclamation was made in seven different places, 'to the great and wonderful rejoicing of the people of all sorts,' says Stow, 'as manifestly appeared by ringing of bells, making of bonfires, and singing of psalms in every one of the streets and lanes of the city.' Stow adds, that the proclamation was made with serjeants-at-arms and by sound of trumpets: it was witnessed by several of the nobility, the Lord Mayor and aldermen in their scarlet dresses, the city officers, the principal part of the gentry of London, and the most eminent citizens habited in velvet, with gold chains, all mounted on horseback. The sentence was next communicated to the prisoner, who wrote to Elizabeth, praying that she might not be put privately to death; that she might be buried in France, as the Scottish sepulchres had been profaned; and that her servants might be allowed to go free, and enjoy her legacies.

Next, James of Scotland and Henry III. of France interceded for Mary's life; but the Scottish ambassador is said to have abused his trust, and urged Mary's execution; the French ambassador's representations were not attended to, as his master's sincerity was doubted. The queen gave ambiguous answers. At length, February 1, 1587, she signed the warrant for execution, and gave it into the care of William Davison, the secretary, who, by direction of the council, despatched it to Fotheringhay.

Elizabeth either felt or affected extreme reluctance to take the life of Mary; but her courtiers (according to Camden) argued that 'the life of one Scottish and titular queen ought not to weigh down the safety of all England;' and 'some preachers more tartly than was fit, and some of the vulgar sort more saucily than became them, either out of hope or fear,' held the same language; and there can be no doubt that her council conceived they were carrying her wishes into effect by acting on the warrant. Yet they had the meanness and cruelty to sacrifice their tool, Davison, who was tried in the Star Chamber, sentenced to a fine of £10,000, and imprisoned for years.[1]

Sir William Fitzwilliam, the constable of Fotheringhay Castle at this time, conducted himself towards the Queen

[1] *Annals of England*, vol. ii. p. 303.

of Scots with such regard and humanity, that, a short time before her execution, she told him she was unable to make him a proper return; but if he would accept the picture of her son, then King James VI. of Scotland, and which was hanging at her bed's-head, he should have it. The present was accepted, and is still in the collection of the Fitzwilliam family. The queen also presented to the governor her watch, which passed into the possession of so many different persons, that ultimately, the one who had it was scarcely known; until towards the end of the last century, Lady Godolphin was the owner of it, and she restored it to the family that originally possessed it, for she stood sponsor to the son and heir of a Lord Fitzwilliam, and made the infant a gift of the watch. Another of the Queen of Scots' watches, of French workmanship, with an elegant little jewel called a solitaire, were given or bequeathed to a French lady by Mary the night before her execution.

On February 7, the Earls of Kent and Shrewsbury waited on Mary, and warned her for death. The hall of the castle had been fitted up with a scaffold, two feet high and twelve feet broad, with rails about, hanged and covered with black, with a low stool, a fair long cushion, and a block covered also with black. Mary having received the said sentence that she was to die 'about eight o'clock on the morning of the morrow,' devoted her few last hours to consoling her servants, and making her will: it was near two o'clock in the morning when she had finished writing.[1] Feeling somewhat fatigued, she went to bed. Her women continued praying; and during this last repose of her body, though her eyes were closed, it was evident, from the slight motion of her lips, and a sort of rapture spread over her countenance, that she was addressing herself to Him on whom alone her hopes now rested. At daybreak she arose, saying that she had only two hours to live. She picked out one of her handkerchiefs, with a fringe of gold, as a bandage for her eyes on the scaffold, and dressed herself magnificently. She next read to her servants her will, which she then signed; and afterwards gave them letters, papers, and presents, of which they were to be the bearers, to the princes of her family, and her friends on the Continent. She had already distributed to them, on the previous evening, her rings, jewels, furniture, and dresses; and she now gave them the purses which she had prepared for them, and in which were, in small sums, five thousand crowns. With finished grace, and with affecting kindness, she mingled her consolations with her gifts, and strengthened her servants for the affliction into which her death would soon throw them. She now retired to her oratory, and was for some time engaged in reading prayers for the dead. A loud knocking at the door interrupted these last orisons. She bade the intruders wait a few minutes. Shortly afterwards, eight o'clock having struck,

---

[1] Pasquier says: 'The night before her execution, Mary, knowing her body must be stripped for her shroud, would have her feet washed, because she used ointment to one of them which was sore.'

there was a renewed knocking at the door, which this time was opened. The sheriff entered, bearing a white wand, advanced close to Mary, who had not yet moved her head, and said, 'Madam, the lords await me, and have sent me to you.' 'Yes,' replied Mary, rising from her knees, 'let us go.' Just as she was moving away, Bourgoin, her physician, handed to her the ivory crucifix which stood on the altar; she kissed it, and ordered it to be carried before her. Not being able to support herself alone, on account of the weakness of her limbs, she walked, leaning on two of her own servants, to the extremity of her apartments. There they, with peculiar delicacy, which she felt and approved, desired not to lead her themselves to execution, but entrusted her to the support of two of Paulet's servants, and followed her in tears.

On reaching the staircase, where the Earls of Shrewsbury and Kent awaited her, and by which she had to descend into the lower hall, where the scaffold was raised, the attendants were refused the consolation of accompanying her farther. They threw themselves at her feet, kissed her hands, and clung to her dress: when they were removed, Mary resumed her course—the crucifix in one hand, and a prayer-book in the other—evincing the dignity of a queen with the calm composure of a devout Christian. At the foot of the staircase she was allowed to stop and take farewell of the master of her household, Sir Andrew Melville, whom her keepers had not suffered to come into her presence for some weeks before. Melville kissed her hand,

and in tears declared this was the heaviest hour of his life. 'No so to me,' said Mary. 'I now feel, my good Melville, that all this world is vanity.' 'When you speak of me hereafter, say that I died firm in my faith, willing to forgive my enemies, conscious that I never disgraced my native country, and rejoicing in the thought that I had always been true to France, the land of my happiest years. Tell my son'—and here she burst into a flood of tears—'Tell my son I thought of him in my last moments, and that I said I never yielded, by word or deed, to aught that might tend to his prejudice : tell him to remember his unfortunate parent; and may he be a thousand times more happy and prosperous than she ever was.' The sentence was then read to her ; and, says Camden, 'she heard it attentively, yet as if her thoughts were taken up with something else.' She then made a short speech, in which she repeated the words so frequently in her mouth, 'I am queen born, not subject to the laws;' and declared that she had never sought the life of her cousin Elizabeth. She then began to pray. Fletcher, Dean of Peterborough, offered his services, but she declined them, and prayed in Latin with her servants (from the offices of the blessed Virgin); she also prayed in English for the church, for her son, and for Queen Elizabeth, and forgave the executioner; then, having kissed her women, and signed the men with the sign of the cross, she prepared for death, and had sufficient command of herself to comfort her weeping attendants. Having covered her face with a linen handkerchief, and laying herself down on the block, she recited that psalm, 'In Thee, O Lord, do I trust; let me never be confounded.' Then stretching forth her body, and repeating many times, 'Into Thy hands, O Lord, I commend my spirit,' her head was stricken off at two strokes, the dean crying out, 'So let Queen Elizabeth's enemies perish!' the Earl of Kent answering 'Amen,' and the multitude sighing and sorrowing.

Nichols tells us that the executioner at two strokes separated her head from her body, saving a sinew, which a third stroke parted also. When the fatal blow was struck, 'her face was in a moment so much altered that few could remember her by her dead face; her lips stirred up and down a quarter of an hour after her head was cut off' (*Ellis*). The executioner that went about to pluck off her stockings found her little dog had crept under her coat, which, being put from thence, went and laid himself down betwixt her head and the body, and being besmeared with her blood, was caused to be washed.

In her last moments, the Scottish queen exhibited a religious dignity, resignation, and apparent serenity of conscience, that tend greatly to counteract the popular impression regarding her guilt. We are at a loss to believe that one who had not lived well could die so well.

Heretofore the strange conduct of Elizabeth towards her unfortunate cousin had not tended to exculpate her from authorizing the Fotheringhay tragedy. But it now appears that she really did not give the final order for the act, but that the whole was managed, without her consent, by

Burleigh, Walsingham, and Davison; the signature to the warrant being forged, at Walsingham's command, by his secretary Thomas Harrison (Strickland's *Lives of the Queens of England*, vii. 465); so that the queen's conduct to these men afterwards was not hypocritical, as hitherto believed. A fortnight and a day elapsed before King James, while hunting at Calder, was certified of the event. It put him into 'a very great displeasure and grief,' and well might; and he 'much lamented and mourned her many days.'

Walpole says of her portrait: 'At the Duke of Devonshire's, at Hardwicke, there is a valuable though poorly painted picture of James v. and Mary of Guise, his second queen: it is remarkable from the great resemblance of Mary Queen of Scots to her father—I mean in Lord Morton's picture of her, and in the image on her tomb at Westminster, which agree together, and which I take to be genuine likenesses.' In a very old trial of her, which Walpole bought from Lord Oxford's collection, it is said 'she was a large, lame woman.' (See note at page 39, *ante.*)

The beauty, accomplishments, and hard fortune of this extraordinary princess, who was a captive eighteen years, have given such an interest to the place in which she suffered, that the stranger is apt to imagine he shall find some relic on the spot to gratify his curiosity. He will regret that the ground on which it stood, with the surrounding moats, and small fragments of the walls near the river and on the east of the mound, are the only marks of this once strong and memorable castle.[1] When Walpole visited the spot in 1763, he wrote: 'The castle is totally ruined. The mount on which the keep stood, two doorcases, and a piece of the moat, are all the remains. Near it are a front and two projections of an ancient house, which, by the arms about it, I suppose was part of the palace of Richard and Cicely, Duke and Duchess of York. . . . You may imagine we were civil enough to the Queen of Scots, to feel a pity for her while we stood on the very spot where she was put to death.'

During the rest of the reign of Elizabeth the castle is passed over unnoticed, and was probably uninhabited; but in the first year of James I. it was granted to Charles Lord Mountjoy, created afterwards Earl of Devonshire; Sir Edward Blount, Knt.; and Joseph Garth, Esq. Upon the death of the Earl, four years after, the two other proprietors conveyed the castle and lordship to his natural son, Mountjoy, who was afterwards created Earl of Newport. In 1625, the last year of the reign of James I., the castle was surveyed, and is described as 'very strong, built of stone, and moated about with a double moat.' The great barn and part adjoining were in 1821 tenanted by a farmer. On the east side of what was then the dwelling-house was a Gothic doorway, the only fragment of original architecture on the premises.

---

[1] *Historic Notices*, by the Rev. H. K. Bonney; a book wrought with the most trustworthy materials, including an unpublished record of Dugdale.

Soon after this survey, we gather from Mr. Bonney's *Notices*, the castle seems to have been consigned to ruin; for Sir Robert Cotton, who lived at that time, purchased the hall in which the Queen of Scots was beheaded, and removed it to Connington, in Huntingdonshire. The stone of other parts was purchased by Robert Kirkham, Esq., to build a chapel in his house at Fineshade, in the neighbourhood; and the last remains of the castle were destroyed in the middle of the eighteenth century, for the purpose of improving the navigation of the Nen. There is a tale of Fotheringhay having been destroyed by order of James I., on account of its having been the scene of his mother's sufferings; but this has been disproved, although it was long believed that the Talbot Inn at Oundle, which is evidently of the age of James I., was built with the stone from the castle.

In June 1820, the earth on the eastern side of the mount on which the keep stood was removed, when the workmen laid open one of the servants' apartments on the western side of the castle court, and part of the pavement of Norman bricks could be traced. About the same time, in the earth outside the fortification, were found a groat of Edward II. and a shilling of Edward IV.

Mr. Brooke's visit to Fotheringhay in 1858 gives us this brief but minute account of the aspect of this very interesting historic site: 'Sufficient remains of the earthworks and ramparts of the castle are yet there to show that it was built in the form of a fetterlock, with a flat face or portion on the side (westward) nearest to the village, and circular on the eastward portion. A very small mass of masonry, a few feet long, lies near the river, and seems to have slipped or been thrown down from the outer wall.'

The events of Mary's life have been minutely discussed by a host of writers. The site we have here described was the closing scene of this most unfortunate of sovereigns. The opposite views of the several authors have led to a protracted controversy as to the guilt of Mary in her ambitious schemes. Of late years evidences from forgotten archives have thrown a flood of light upon her dark career; and the Simancas papers and the collection at Hatfield have been adduced for the first time, and proved of great importance and interest. These novel materials Mr. Froude has ably digested in his valuable *History of England.* Of Mary Stuart's history he takes a most unfavourable view. Entirely unprincipled, save in her fidelity to the Church of Rome, which led her into conspiracy against her cousin Elizabeth, Mary was not habitually vicious or depraved. But her passions were strong; and when they were once aroused, no obstacle either of virtue or of fear could turn her from her purpose. Her energy, her fiery strength of will, were perhaps unequalled in the history of woman. 'There are only two views which can be entertained of Mary Stuart's character,' says an impartial reviewer. 'Either she was the most curiously and extraordinarily unfortunate woman who ever lived, or she was a foul adulteress and murderess, who lured her husband to his death with circumstances of peculiar treachery and baseness. Mr. Froude has convinced the large majority of his readers that the latter view is the true one. The broad facts of the case point unquestionably to the worst conclusion. Nor can it be well denied, that if Mary had been old and ugly, and had died in her bed, probably not a single voice would have been raised in her defence. Her beauty, her misfortunes, the injuries which she received at the hands of her rival, and her early and tragical death (at the age of forty-five), have thrown a halo of romance round her name which has raised up defenders of her innocence; but they have been persons led by the heart and not by the head.' Their number must be greatly reduced by evidence recently produced; and if Mary Stuart was innocent, no conclusion can be considered worthy of reliance.

The few fragments which remain of this palace and prison can only be duly appreciated by the archæologist. It is not a little curious, that of so celebrated an edifice in its entirety, not a view exists, or is of extreme rarity. Even a large folio history of the county represents but a few stones.

TRADITIONS OF WALLINGTON AND THE CALVERLEYS.

IN the time of Henry VI., there was erected by William de Strother, in Northumberland, a border tower named Wallington, which is described in a survey of 1542 as consisting of 'a strong toure and a stone house of the inherytance of Sir John Fenwyeke, in good reparacion.' So profuse was the hospitality kept up here, as to become the subject both of song and legend, narrating the frays and frolics that followed a hard day's chase. 'Show us the way to Wallington' is an old and favourite air in the neighbourhood:

> 'Harnham was headless, Bradford breadless,
>   Shafto picked at the craw;
> Capheaton was a wee bonny place,
>   But Wallington banged them a'.'

But this hospitality could not be supported after a frequent residence in London, and the profligate habits of Charles II.'s court encroached too deeply upon the rentals. This led to the sale of the property, and not improbably was the cause of Sir John Fenwicke, its last owner, being implicated in the plot for the assassination of King William III., for which he was beheaded on Tower-hill, Jan. 28, 1696. All his hopes of court favour being extinguished, disappointment and revenge were likely enough to make him adopt any measures to retrieve his broken fortunes. Be this as it may, the estate passed by sale to Sir William Blackett, who rebuilt the mansion at the end of the seventeenth century. From this family Wallington passed to the Trevelyans, in whose hands the place has lost none of its former interest. There is a museum in the mansion, where is preserved a portrait of Joyce, the widow of Henry Calverley, the only survivor of the Yorkshire tragedy: 'My brat at nurse, my beggar boy.' In this portrait the spiteful old dame is represented with a scroll in her right hand, whereon these lines are inscribed:

> 'Silence, Walter Calverley;
> This is all that I will leave W. C.:
> Time was I might have given thee me.'

This Walter was her son; and, whatever may have been his faults, he showed a gentle spirit in not committing this legacy to the flames.

To the family of Calverley a very tragical story attaches. Walter Calverley having married Philippa Brooke, the daughter of Lord Cobham, became, soon after this marriage, jealous of the then Vavasour of Weston. In a moment of ungovernable fury, arising from suspicion of his wife's infidelity, he killed his two eldest sons, and then with his dagger attempted to stab the lady herself. Luckily, however, she wore a steel stomacher, according to the fashion of the day, and the weapon glancing aside, only inflicted a slight wound. Meanwhile the terrified nurse had caught up the youngest son, and fled with him to a square building about half a mile from the village, said to have been a banqueting-hall of the family. It was situated in a large oak wood, that forms a striking feature in the property.

After the murder Calverley mounted his horse and endeavoured to escape; but about ten miles from his dwelling the animal stumbled upon a smooth turf, throwing the rider. This accident enabled the pursuers to overtake the fugitive, when they immediately seized and brought him before Sir John Bland of Kippax, who committed him to York Castle.

It was now that by some means—we are not told how—he became convinced of his wife's innocence and the legitimacy of his children. This change of feeling determined him to atone for the past by saving his estate for his family by an obstinate refusal to plead: otherwise, in the case of conviction, of which there could be little doubt, all his property would escheat to the Crown. He was then condemned to be *pressed* until he yielded or died, according to the old law. While he was under this horrible torture, a faithful servant—and it is saying much for the culprit that he had a servant so attached—requested permission to see his master. His prayer was granted, when Calverley, in the agonies of his torture, begged the poor fellow to sit upon his breast, and thus at once put an end to his suffering.

The man complied, and was tried at York, and condemned to death for murder,—a sentence which was actually carried into effect. The victims in this tragedy, the two children, are simply entered in the parish register as having died, without any particulars as to the cause of their death.

The younger son of Calverley, who, as we have seen, had the good fortune to escape, obtained a baronetage, and continued the family; but the last baronet of that name, having inherited large property in Northumberland from the Blacketts, sold both his old possessions of Calverley and his acquired property of Edshall, where he had always lived till he finally left the country. The family in the direct male line is now extinct. The Vavasours of Weston are also extinct, the last of them having died thirty-six years ago, when Weston passed to a son of his sister. In utter opposition to the pride of most landed proprietors so situated, he forbade his elected heir to take the name of Vavasour, declaring that he would be the last Vavasour of Weston, which estate, he maintained, had been in his family since the time of Henry II.

The tradition above related is the basis of the drama called *The Yorkshire Tragedy*. In our day it has been adopted by Ainsworth in his romance of *Rookwood*, who has marred its interest by transferring the date of action from its proper era to the prosaic times of George II., for no other reason, as it would seem, than to introduce the highwayman Turpin. 'I remember,' says the venerable informant who communicated this tradition to Sir Bernard Burke, 'detailing it, with its appended superstitions, to the late Mr. Surtees, our Durham antiquary, expecting him to deliver it to Sir Walter Scott, who, I felt sure, would manufacture it into a clever romance, by keeping it to the true time—the beginning of the reign of James I. He promised to do so, but ere long both he and Sir Walter Scott were called away.' The 'appended superstitions' are as follow: 'It was currently reported that Mr. Calverley and his men galloped about through the extensive woods at dead of night on *headless horses*, their cry being, "A pund of more weight—lig on, lig on!" So ran my native vernacular. As you are perhaps a Southron, I give you the English: "A pound of more weight—lay on, lay on!" Their favourite haunt was said to be the *Cave*, a romantic natural cavern in the midst of the wood. Sometimes the ghosts of the two murdered children were thought to appear,—a remarkable instance of which occurred to my father's old clerk in his younger days, though he admitted that he had sat up drinking and carding to "the Sabbath-day morning." It was said that at one time master and men were wont to ride their infernal horses into the very village, to the great terror of all quiet people. However, a skilful exorcist prohibited them from passing the church so long as hollies grew green in Calverley wood; and there was in my time no lack of hollies in the wood.'

A good deal of the superstition was in existence some twenty years ago, of which here is an instance: 'In going his rounds, a Methodist preacher was hospitably received by a clothier who lived in the old hall. Whether to account for the fact by the goodness of the cheer, we pretend not to say; but, as the detail ran, the old haunted hall was close to the church, and the window of the room where the gentleman slept looked very awfully into the churchyard. In the dead of the night he felt his bed repeatedly raised from the floor, and then let down again. Whereupon he called up his host; but the bed-mover was provokingly invisible, and nothing could the two worthies find.

'Now, to a native, the amusing part of the story is its topography. The old hall is about a quarter of a mile from the church, with the whole village intervening; so that if the good man saw into the churchyard from his window, he must have rivalled Lynceus by looking through a dozen good stone walls; for all the houses are built of stone.'

FORTUNES OF THREE EARLS OF KILDARE.

OF the Irish Geraldines—whose great ancestor was a favourite of Edward the Confessor, whose English possessions were numerous, and whose successor was treated after the Conquest as a fellow-countryman of the Normans, and who, moreover, put the copestone to his prosperity by marrying a daughter of a prince of North Wales, as did his son by wedding the daughter of a prince of South Wales—here are three noteworthy histories.

First is John Thomas Fitzgerald, who nearly lost his life in an accidental conflagration. In his infancy he was in the Castle of Woodstock when there was an alarm of fire. In the confusion that ensued the child was forgotten; and on the servants returning to search for him, the room in which he lay was found in ruins. Soon after a strange voice was heard in one of the castle towers; and upon looking up, they saw an ape, which was usually kept chained, carefully holding the child in its arms. The Earl, afterwards, in gratitude for his preservation, adopted a monkey for his crest; and some of his descendants, in memory of it, took the additional motto, 'Non immemor beneficii.'

The life of the child thus miraculously preserved abounds in romantic adventures. He was at variance with William de Vesci, lord of Kildare, a baron much esteemed by the reigning monarch, Edward I.; their disputes arising from the contiguity of their estates. De Vesci, who was Lord Justice of Ireland, openly declared that John Fitzthomas was the cause of the existing disturbances, and that he was 'in private quarrels as fierce as a lyon, but in publicke injuries as meeke as a lambe.' This having been reported to Fitzgerald, he, in the presence of the Lords of the Council, replied: 'You would gladly charge me with treason, that by shedding my blood, and by catching my land into your clouches, that but so neere upon your lands of Kyldare, you might make your sonne a proper gentleman.' 'A gentleman!' quoth the Lord Justice; 'thou bold baron, I tell thee the Vescis were gentlemen before the Geraldines were barons of Offaly; yea, and before that Welsh bankrupt, thyne ancestaur, fethered his nest in Leinster;' and then accused him of being 'a supporter of thieves and upholder of traytours.' 'As for my ancestor,' replied the baron, 'whom you term a bankrupt, how riche or how poore he was upon his repayre to Ireland, I purpose not at this time to debate; yet this much I may boldly say, that he came hither as a byer, not a beggar. He bought his enemies' land by spending his blood; but you, lurking like a spider in his cobweb to entrappe flies, endeavour to beg subjects' livings wrongfully by despoiling them of their lives. I, John Fitzthomas, Baron of Offaly, doe tell thee, William Vesci, that I am noe traytour, noe felon; but that thou art the only battress by which the king's enemies are supported.' Both parties being summoned to the royal presence, Fitzgerald maintained the same bold language, accusing the justiciary of corruption, and saying that, while the nobility were excluded from his presence, 'an Irish cow could at all times have access to him. But,' continued Offaly, 'so much as our mutual complaints stand upon, the one his yea and the other his nay, and that you would be taken for a champion, and I am known to be no coward, let us, in God's name, leave lieing for varlets, bearding for ruffians, facing for crakers, chatting for twatlers, scolding for callets, booking for scriveners, pleading for lawyers; and let us try, with the dint of swords, as it becomes martial men to do, our mutual quarrels. Therefore, to justify that I am a true subject, and that thou, Vesci, art an arch-traitor to God and to my king, here, in the presence of his highness, and in the hearing of this honourable assembly, I challenge the combat.' De Vesci accepted the challenge amidst the applauses of the assembly; but either he doubted the goodness of his cause, or feared to contend with so formidable an adversary. Before the appointed day he fled to France, whereupon the king declared Offaly innocent; adding, 'Albeit De Vesci conveyed his person into France, yet he left his lands behind him in Ireland;' and he granted them to the Baron of Offaly, who subsequently, in many a hard-fought day, showed himself no less true than valiant. For his good services the English monarch, Edward II., created him Earl of Kildare, and assigned to him the town and castle of that name.

We now pass over many illustrious chiefs of this house to come to Gerald eighth Earl of Kildare, called the Great, who was constituted, on his accession to the peerage, lord-deputy to Richard Duke of York. In 1480 he was reappointed lord-deputy; and again, upon the accession of Henry VII., deputy to Jasper Duke of Bedford, the Lord-lieutenant. Upon the arrival, however, of Lambert Simnel, and his tutor Richard Simon, an Oxford priest, in Ireland, the lord-deputy, the chancellor (Thomas Fitzgerald, the deputy's brother), treasurer, and other nobles in the York interest, immediately acknowledged the impostor, and had him proclaimed in Dublin by the style of Edward VI.; and the lord-deputy assisted with the others at his coronation in Christ's Church, May 2, 1487, where the ceremony was performed with great solemnity; the chancellor, the Archbishop of Dublin, the Earl of Lincoln, Lord Lovel, Jenico Mark, Mayor of Dublin, and several other persons of rank attending. The crown was borrowed from the image of the Virgin Mary. John Pain, Bishop of Meath, preached the coronation sermon; and the pretender was subsequently conveyed upon the shoulders of Darcy of Platen, a person of extraordinary height, to the Castle of Dublin, amidst the shouts of the populace. In the engagement which afterwards decided the fate of Simnel, near Stoke, the chancellor

Fitzgerald fell; but the lord-deputy had the good fortune to make his peace with the king. And well, both by his fidelity and his talents as a statesman and a soldier, did this great man repay the king's confidence.

Perkin Warbeck, on his landing at Cork in 1497, was successfully opposed by the Earls of Kildare and Desmond, and narrowly escaped being taken prisoner. For this good service King Henry conferred on Kildare several manors in the counties of Warwick and Gloucester. With a strong hand, too, the Earl controlled the unruly native chieftains; and if he could not entirely extinguish the spirit of revolt, rebellion was instantly put down.

This unquiet spirit, however, showed itself in formidable array against the king's authority amongst many of the most powerful native chiefs under the Lord of Clanricarde, who had married Kildare's daughter, but had so neglected her as to excite much ill blood between the lady's husband and her father. Never had the Earl's son Gerald's pre-eminent skill and courage been more severely tested. When he came in sight of the rebels, they were drawn up in full force under *Knock Taugh*, or the *hill of axes*, now called *Knockdoe*, about seven miles from Galway. Many of the lords of the Pale began to be alarmed for the result, the enemy having collected the largest army ever seen in the country since the invasion of 1169. They would have persuaded the Earl to offer terms of peace, but the stout old soldier refused to listen for a moment to such timid counsels. Having drawn up his men in battle array, he bluntly told them that their own safety, as well as the king's honour, rested on their unflinching valour in that day's service. The onset was made by the rebels in gallant style; but they were received with such a volley of arrows from the Leinster men, that they fell back in confusion. The Earl then commanded his vanguard to advance, when his son Gerald, in the impatience of youthful courage, charged without orders at the head of his men most bravely and resolutely. 'Far away from the troops,' says the Irish chronicler, 'were heard the violent onset of the martial chiefs, the vehement efforts of the champions, the charge of the royal heroes, the noise of the swords, the clamour of the troops when endangered, the shouts and exultations of the youths, the sound made by the falling of brave men, and the triumph of nobles over plebeians.' It was a fierce battle, such as had not been known in latter times. Of Clanricarde's nine divisions which were in solid array, there survived only one broken battalion. The rebels were completely routed, their slain being computed at nearly 9000 men, though this may be exaggeration. For this good service Kildare was created by Henry a Knight of the Garter.

The days of this great man were now drawing fast to a conclusion. In 1513 he marched against Lemyvannon, or 'O'Carroll's Castle,' now called Leap Castle, in the King's County; but as he was watering his horse in the River Greese, at Kilkea, he was shot by one of the O'Mores of Leix, and after lingering for a few days he died of his wound, and was buried in his own chapel at Christ's Church before the high altar. Holinshed describes him as a 'mightie man of stature, full of honours and courage, who had been Lord-deputie and Lord Justice of Ireland three and thirtie yeares. Kildare was in government milde, to his enemies sterne. He was open and playne, hardly able to move himself when he was moved; in anger not so sharp as short, being easily displeased and sooner appeased.'

Gerald Oge, that is, Gerald the younger, the ninth Earl of Kildare, entered upon his office of lord-deputy under less favourable auspices than his predecessor had done. As governor of Ireland, Gerald seemed to consider himself as representing the king's interests only in the Pale, which at that time included the counties of Dublin, Louth, Meath, and Kildare, ruling the rest of his possessions as independently as any native chief; and these were tolerably extensive, for he and his kinsmen occupied the counties of Kildare and Carlow as far as the bridge of Leighlin, exacting coin and livery within these bounds. In fact, while he was English to the Irish, he was, to a certain degree, Irish to the English who were placed in this unfortunate dilemma: they must of necessity support the lord-deputy, from his influence over the Pale, which was their instrument for curbing the rest of Ireland, then divided amongst thirty great Anglo-Irish lords and sixty Irish chieftains. On the other hand, there was always a danger of the lord-deputy's growing over-powerful, and turning round upon his master.

It happened to Gerald Oge, as it had happened to his predecessors, to more than once incur the jealousy of the English Government, and to be deprived of his office of lord-deputy. What was yet worse, he unluckily drew upon himself the hatred of the stern and lynx-eyed Wolsey, and nearly lost his head in consequence. The stout Earl weathered the storm which had well-nigh foundered him, and even again attained his former dignity; but it was only to relapse into suspicion and disgrace. He was once more called over to England, and recommitted to the Tower. Before his departure from Ireland, he constituted his son Thomas Lord Offaly vice-deputy, and strictly enjoined him to be 'wise and prudent,' and submissive to the council. Nevertheless, the 'hot and active temper' of the young lord could not be restrained. The murder of Archbishop Alen, perpetrated by his followers, led to the severe sentence of excommunication pronounced against him; which being shown to the old Earl in the Tower, had such an effect on him that he died shortly after of a broken heart. His remains received sepulture within the Tower walls, in St. Peter's Chapel,—a sorry recompense for all his services.

Some time before the ninth Earl died, a report reached Ireland that he was to be beheaded. A strange story is told by Holinshed, how this report was confirmed in secret letters written by certain servants of Sir William Skeffington. 'One of these letters fell into the hands of a priest, who threw it among other papers, meaning to read it at leisure.

'That nighte, a gentleman, a retainer of Lord Thomas', lodged with the priest, and sought in the morning when he rose for some paper to darne on his strayte stockings; and as the divell would, he hit upon the letter, and bore it away in the heele of his stocke.' At night he found the paper; and seeing that it announced the Earl's death, he carried it to his son Lord Thomas, who immediately resolved to throw off his allegiance to the English Crown.

From this moment the adventures of Thomas tenth Earl of Kildare, known (from the fringes on the helmets of his retainers) as *Silken Thomas*, form a chapter of romance; and, after all, his determination was not so hopeless of success as many at the time imagined it to be, so extensive was the influence of the Geraldines. In disclaiming the English rule, the young Earl proceeded with all the chivalric honour of a knight of old. He called a meeting of the council at St. Mary's Abbey; and when he had seated himself at the head of the table, a party of his followers rushed in, to the sore amazement of those who had not been previously warned of his intentions. The words in which he then addressed them were worthy of his great ancestors, and show of what metal the Geraldines were made. He then tendered his sword of state to the chancellor (Cromer). The gentle prelate, who was a well-wisher of the Geraldines, besought him with tears to abandon his purpose. He might perhaps have succeeded, but that Nolan, an Irish bard then present, burst out into a heroic strain in his native tongue, in praise of 'Silken Thomas,' and concluded by warning him that he had lingered there over long. This aroused the Earl, who, addressing the chancellor somewhat abruptly, renounced all allegiance to the English monarch, saying that he chose rather 'to die with valiantness and liberty.'

The subsequent career of 'Silken Thomas' fully corresponded with the above commencement. For a length of time he resisted successfully the famous lord-deputy Skeffington, with all the support that England could afford him, or that could be derived from Irish septs. When, finally deserted by the last of his allies, Kildare was obliged to surrender, it was upon a promise sealed upon the holy sacrament, that he should receive a full pardon upon his arrival in England. But this pledge was shamefully violated by Henry VIII. For sixteen months the Earl was imprisoned in the Tower of London; and then, together with his five uncles, two of whom had always been staunch adherents of the king, was hanged, drawn, and quartered at Tyburn, on the 8th of February 1537, the Earl being then but twenty-four years of age.

The rebellion of 'Silken Thomas' is a most romantic and touching episode in Irish history. It is melancholy to contrast the early condition of the gay, glittering noble, 'the Silken Lord,' vice-deputy of Ireland, and head of one of the most illustrious families in the world, with that bitter suffering which he described in a letter to an adherent while a prisoner in the Tower. He writes: 'I never had any money syns I cam unto prison but a nobull, nor I have had nethyr hosyn, dublet, nor shoys, nor shyrt buton. . . . I have gone barefote dyverse tymes (when y^{tt} hath not been very warme), and so I should have done styll, and now, but that pore prysoners, of their gentylnes, hath sometyme geyven me old hosyn, and shoys, and old shyrtes. This I wryte unto you, not as complaynyng on my fryndes, but for to show you the trewth of my gret ned.' The generous, self-sacrificing spirit of the youth still shines throughout his sufferings; and the reader will scarcely fail to be struck with the marked resemblance between 'Silken Thomas' and another equally ill-fated Geraldine of a much later period, the amiable and high-minded Lord Edward Fitzgerald. Both were led away by the enthusiasm of their nature; both were chivalrously honourable; both displayed throughout the contest an unflinching spirit; and each in the bloom of manhood paid the penalty of his error in a violent death.

Though attainder followed, the House of Kildare was not destined to perish. Thomas's half-brother Gerald, the eleventh Earl of Kildare, then only twelve years old, became the male representative of the Geraldines. His fortunes will be found narrated in connection with the history of Sir Anthony Browne and his descendants.

SIR ANTHONY BROWNE AND HIS DESCENDANTS.

THE famous Sir Anthony Browne, standard-bearer to King Henry VIII., stands out from the canvas of history by his devotion to a worthy cause and course of upright action. He was twice married: his second wife was a more celebrated lady than his first. She was the second daughter of the ninth Earl of Kildare, the Lady Elizabeth Fitzgerald; and was the issue of that unfortunate nobleman's second wife, the Lady Elizabeth Grey, fourth daughter of Thomas Marquis of Dorset by Cicely his wife, daughter and heir of William Bonville, Lord Bonville and Harrington. The Lady Elizabeth was a great beauty, and had been brought up with the Princesses Mary and Elizabeth, afterwards Queens Mary and Elizabeth of England, at Hunsdon House; she being by descent and relationship their second cousin, and her mother being a granddaughter of the Lady Elizabeth, daughter of Sir Richard Woodville, Earl Rivers, and relict of Sir Thomas Grey of Groby, whose beauty and high character had caused Edward IV. to make her his queen. Thus, again, was Sir

Anthony's family connected with royalty: for his second wife's mother, the Countess of Kildare, was niece in half-blood to King Edward V. and his brother Richard Duke of York, who were both so cruelly murdered in the Tower; and to the Princess Elizabeth, in her own right Queen of England, and wife of King Henry VII.: consequently she was cousin to the husband's royal patron and friend, Henry VIII.

At Hunsdon House Lady Elizabeth Fitzgerald was seen by Henry Howard the poet, Earl of Surrey; and by the sonnet he has left behind him in commemoration of her attractions, it is not only natural to conceive that he admired her, but that he would have married her if he could. The sonnet is as follows:

> 'From Tuscane came my ladie's worthie race,
>   Fair Florence was sometime her ancient seat;
> The Western Ile, whose pleasant shore doth face
>   Wild Camber's cliffes, did give her livelie heat.
> Fostered she was with milke of Irish breste;
>   Her sire an earle, her dame of prince's blood.
> From tender years in Britaine she doth rest
>   With king's child, where she tastes costlie food.
> Hunsdon did first present her to mine eine:
>   Bright is her hew, and Geraldine she hight.
> Hampton me taught to wish her first for mine;
>   And Windsor, alas! doth chase me from her sight.
> Her beautie of mind, her vertues from above;
>   Happie is he that can obtain her love.'

'Windsor' refers to Surrey's imprisonment in Windsor Castle, where many of his sonnets were composed; and the 'dame of prince's bloude' applies to her grandmother, the

Marchioness of Dorset, who was daughter and heiress of Henry Duke of Exeter by the Lady Anne, sister of Edward IV. This lady has ever since been known as the 'Fair Geraldine,' although by that confusion which is frequently caused by careless writing, the first wife of Anthony Browne, Alice, is in some works called by the second one's just *sobriquet*.[1] This 'Fair Geraldine' had no children by Sir Anthony Browne; but marrying soon after her husband's demise, she had a large family by her second husband, Sir Edward Clinton, first Earl of Lincoln of that name, and ancestor of the Duke of Newcastle.

A very remarkable and interesting event occurred in this family,—namely, the marriage of Mabel Browne, second daughter of Sir Anthony by his first wife, with Geraldine Fitzgerald eleventh Earl of Kildare, and brother to the Lady Elizabeth, Sir Anthony Browne's second wife.

Mabel's husband's career had been a most romantic one; for he was, as a child, hunted down by the rancour of Henry VIII., who had not only executed his half-brother, Thomas tenth Earl of Kildare, with his five uncles—Sir James, Oliver, Richard, Sir John, and Walter Fitzgerald— but by keeping his father Gerald, ninth earl, in the Tower, and for many years cruelly treating him, caused him to die, after the execution of his son and brothers, of grief and

---

[1] At p. 529 of the *History and Antiquities of Sussex*, by Thomas Walker Horsefield (2 vols. 4to, 1835), occurs the following note in a reference to the tomb of Sir Anthony Browne: 'It is said that Alice was a great beauty, and celebrated by the Earl of Surrey, at the tournaments, under the name of the "Fair Geraldine."'

pain. Gerald had been Lord-Deputy of Ireland, and was a man of high estate and character, who at times had been in much favour with his sovereign, although he was always hated and envied by Wolsey. His death took place on December 12, 1534, and he was buried in the chapel of the Tower, as attested by an inscription on a chest found there in 1580.

After many stirring adventures in Ireland and in Scotland, the young Gerald was sent, in the custody of his tutor, Thomas Leverons, who was foster-brother to his father, and was afterwards created Bishop of Kildare as a meet reward for his fidelity, to France. Thence his tutor, having reason to suspect the sincerity of the French (Sir John Wallop, the English ambassador, demanding him in his master's name), removed him secretly to Flanders, whither he had no sooner conveyed him, than an Irishman, one James Sherlock, a spy, arrived in pursuit of him. Leverons waited on the governor, and desired his protection from Sherlock's wicked intention to betray the innocent child to his enemies, whereupon the governor sent for Sherlock and examined him; and finding him guilty, and without reasonable defence, he imprisoned him, until the generous youth interceded for his liberation.

From Flanders they went to Brussels, where Charles v. held his court. Here, too, the hatred of Henry pursued him, and he was again demanded by the English ambassador; but Charles answered that he had nothing to do with him, and, for aught he knew, he intended to make but a short stay in the country, and so sent him to the Bishop of Liege, allowing him for his support one hundred crowns a month. The bishop gave him an honourable reception, and placed him in an abbey of monks for greater safety of his person; whence Cardinal Pole, his kinsman by his mother's side, sent for him to Rome, receiving him very kindly, and had him educated under the care of the Bishop of Verona and the Cardinal of Mantua.

After some year and a half the Cardinal Pole sent for him to Rome; and the Duke of Mantua gave him an allowance annually of 300 crowns. He continued in Rome some three years an inmate of the cardinal's house. He travelled, with his relative's permission, to Naples, and accompanied the Knights of Rhodes to Malta; thence he went to Tripoli, on the coast of Barbary, then belonging to those knights, where he remained a short time, serving valiantly against the Turks, or rather Moors; he returned with a rich booty, first to Malta and then to Rome.

Some three years after, he one day, in the heat of the chase, when accompanying Cardinal Farnese to hunt the stag, narrowly escaped death. In the violent pursuit, his horse leaped into a deep pit which had been concealed from view. Finding himself falling, the young man clung to some roots of trees, by which he hung, leaving his unfortunate horse to precede him to the bottom of this deep pit; but at last tired out, he relinquished his hold, and fell on his dead horse. In the pit he remained ankle-deep in water some three hours, no one coming to relieve him, notwithstanding his cries for help. When the chase was over, his hound missing his master, tracked him to the edge of the precipice, where he stood howling over him. The cardinal, perceiving something was wrong by the manner of the dog, hastened with his attendants to the spot, and had his kinsman relieved by causing one of the company to be let down by ropes in a basket; and the nearly exhausted Gerald was thus brought out of the pit to the surface. He remained abroad till the death of King Henry, when he returned to London.

It was at a masque or ball in the time of Edward VI. that Gerald met with Mabel Browne; and as he was one of the handsomest men of the age, and she a very beautiful young woman, it is not surprising that they fell at once in love with each other. His marriage with Mabel, the daughter of his king's honoured servant and former guardian, Sir Anthony Browne, brought him into especial favour with the young monarch, who not only made him a Knight of the Garter, but honoured him with the knighthood in 1552, restoring to him all his forfeited estates in Ireland. In the time of Queen Mary, Cardinal Pole returing to England, our knight was fully restored to his titles of Earl of Kildare and Baron Offaly; and with an almost uninterrupted good fortune, the Earl of Kildare and his Countess Mabel lived for many years, to prove the rule true by being an exception to it, that 'the course of true love never did run smooth.' He died November 16, 1555; and his widow, 'a lady of great worth and virtue, at her fair home of Maynooth,' died

August 10, 1610, being the mother of three sons and two daughters.

From this chequered story we pass to a circumstance related of the same family which bears out the curious reasoning upon which Sir Henry Spelman wrote in his *History of Sacrilege* in the year 1632,—namely, that 'all those families who took or had church property presented to them, came, either in their own persons or those of their ancestors, to sorrow and misfortune.'

One of the many curious occurrences relating to Sir Anthony Browne was sent some years since to *Notes and Queries*, being communicated in a letter to the Editor of that periodical by a clergyman of Easebourne, near to the famous Cowdray Castle, the principal seat of the Montagues. It stated, that at the great festival given in the magnificent hall of the monks at Battle Abbey, on Sir Anthony Browne taking possession of his sovereign's munificent gift of that estate, a venerable monk stalked up the hall to the dais, where the worthy knight sat, and in prophetic language denounced him and his posterity for the crime of usurping the possessions of the church, predicting their destruction by fire and water, which fate was eventually fulfilled. The last viscount but one, just before the termination of the eighteenth century (1793), was drowned in an unsuccessful attempt to pass the Falls of Schaffhausen on the Rhine, accompanied by Mr. Sedley Burdett, the elder brother of the late distinguished Sir Francis. They had engaged an open boat to take them through the rapids, and had appointed six o'clock on the following morning to make their voyage; but the fact coming to the knowledge of the authorities, they took measures to prevent so very dangerous an enterprise. They resolved, however, to carry out their project, regardless of all its perils; and in this spirit they decided on starting two hours earlier than the time previously fixed, namely at four o'clock in the morning instead of at six, the season of the year being early summer. They commenced their descent accordingly, and successfully passed the first or upper fall; but unhappily the same good fortune did not continue to attend them, as the boat was swamped and sunk in passing the lower fall, and was supposed to have been jammed in a cleft of the submerged rock, as neither boat nor adventurers ever again appeared. In the same week as that in which this calamity occurred, the ancient seat of the family, Cowdray Castle, was destroyed by fire, and its venerable ruins still stand at Easebourne—the significant monument, at once of the fulfilment of the old monk's prophecy, and of the extinction of the race of the great and powerful noble.

The last inheritor of the title—the immediate successor and cousin of the ill-fated young nobleman of Schaffhausen, Anthony Browne, the last Viscount Montague, who died at the opening of this century—left no male issue; but his estates, so far as he could alienate them from the title, devolved on his only daughter, who intermarried with Mr. Stephen Poyntz, a great Buckinghamshire landholder and a member of the Legislature, who, from his local importance,

was desirous of obtaining a grant of the dormant title
'Viscount Montague' in favour of the elder of his two
sons, issue of this marriage; he was a very large contributor to the then 'Loyalty Loan,' and through his family
connections, he was sanguine of success. His hopes, however, were suddenly and painfully destroyed by the deaths
of the two boys, his only male issue, who were drowned
together while bathing at Bognor, in the seventeenth and
nineteenth years of their respective ages; the fatal 'water'
thus becoming again the means in fulfilment, as it were, of
the monk's terrible denunciation on the family in his fearful
curse! As if, too, Time had identified himself with the
fate involving their doom, the most indefatigable efforts of
those who have considered themselves collaterals have been
frustrated in their attempts to draw evidence from the
'shadowy past;' for although they have been most energetic 'tomb-searchers,' yet they have now nearly abandoned
their efforts to lift successfully the 'shroud that Time has
cast' over the scattered records of their ill-fated race.

The obscurity of the present gradually darkens as years roll
on; and the proofs which now 'demonstrate thinly,' decline
to their extinction, and appear to be verifying the doom which
the monk of old foreshadowed; for this once proud family
of other days is rapidly becoming altogether lost in the
mists of obscurity. It once occupied the highest position
in the land; whereas its honours are now only remembered in the ruins of its ancestral houses, leaving it for the
wandering antiquary to bring them once more to light,

by the tower and the tomb to read a few records of their former greatness, and in the melancholy yet truthful strains of the poet to exclaim :

> 'Out upon Time! who for ever will leave
> But enough of the past for the future to grieve.
> Out upon Time ! who will leave no more
> Of the things to come than the things before.
> Two or three columns and many a stone,
> Ivy and moss with grass o'ergrown ;
> Remnants of things that have passed away,
> Fragments of stone raised by creatures of clay !'

It may be interesting to add, that 'the name of Browne is not derived, as believed, from the colour brown, but boasts of a much higher origin : it is now well understood to be taken from the name of an office or position of dignity allied to chieftainship, which in a Scandinavian form is known as "*brân,*" or "*bren,*" and which was, with the numerous tribes of the north-west of Europe, the title of the chieftain or head of the clan. From this may possibly have come the French *Brun,* from which we get easily enough Brown and Browne.

'The family of Browne was no doubt derived from the Normans ; for on the Roll of Battle Abbey, amongst others, occurs the name of Browne. On Stow's "auncient Role," which he received from "Master Thomas Scriven," as containing the surnames of the "chefe noblemen and gentlemen which came into England with William the Conqueror," the name does not appear, although that of Montague occurs on both lists or rolls. The original Roll is said to have perished in the great fire at Cowdray, whither Sir Anthony or his successors had carried it from Battle Abbey. Of all the copies of this famous deed, that of Leland, made in Henry VIII.'s reign, is generally thought to be the most reliable, as the monks, no doubt to gratify the pride of some of the great families, falsified and Frenchified names on the so-called copies they made of the Roll; but Leland copied his from the Roll itself, and states in notes to his copy that some particular marks are the same in the original.'

The above narrative has been selected and abridged from an interesting paper contributed by Mr. George R. Wright, F.S.A., to the *Journal of the British Archæological Association*, 1867.

THE OSBORNE AND LEEDS FAMILIES.

TOWARDS the middle of the sixteenth century (1536), when London Bridge was covered with picturesque towers and gateways, and houses of business, there occurred, in one of the latter, an incident which is probably better known and more often related than most other portions of its history. We allude to the anecdote of Edward Osborne leaping into the Thames from the window of one of the bridge houses, to rescue the daughter of Sir William Hewet, a cloth-worker, the son of Edmund Hewet of Wales, in Yorkshire. He possessed an estate of £6000 per annum, and is said to have had three sons and one daughter, Anne, to which daughter this mischance happened, the father then living upon London Bridge. It happened that the maid-servant, as she was playing with the infant on the edge of the open window over the river Thames, by chance dropped her in, almost beyond expectation of her being saved; but a young gentleman named Osborne, then apprenticed to Sir William, the father, seeing the accident, leaped into the river after her boldly, and brought the child out safe, to the great joy of its parents and the admiration of the spectators. In memory of this deliverance, and in gratitude, when the child was grown to woman's estate, and asked in marriage by several persons of quality, particularly by the Earl of Shrewsbury, Sir William betrothed his daughter with a very great dowry to her deliverer, and with this emphatic declaration : 'Osborne saved her, and Osborne shall enjoy her.' Part of the property given her in marriage was the estate of Sir Thomas Fanshaw of Barking, in Essex ; together with several other lands in the parishes of Harthil and Wales, in Yorkshire, now in the possession of the noble family of the Duke of Leeds. Sir William Hewet was one of the eminent members of the Cloth-workers' Company, and served the office of Lord Mayor in 1539. He was buried, under a magnificent tomb, between those of Dean Colet and Sir William Cockain, in the south aisle of the old Cathedral of St. Paul.

Now the family of Osborne, whence sprung 'the gallant apprentice of London Bridge,' is one of considerable antiquity in Kent, and was early seated at Ashford in that county. So far back as the twelfth of Henry VI., John Osborne of Canterbury occurs on the list of Kentish gentry. Sir Edward Osborne, who married Sir William Hewet's daughter, served as Sheriff of London in 1575, and Lord Mayor in 1583-84, the twenty-fifth of Queen Elizabeth, when he received the honour of knighthood at Westminster. He dwelt, according to a MS. in the Herald's College, in Philpot Lane, in Sir W. Hewet's house, and was buried in 1591 in the old church of St. Dionis Backchurch in Fenchurch Street. On the 15th of August 1675, Sir Thomas Osborne, the great-grandson of Sir Edward, was raised to the peerage by the titles of Viscount Latimer and Baron Kiveton, in the county of York, by patent from King Charles the Second. On the 27th of June in the year following he was created Earl of Danby; on the 20th of April 1680 he was advanced to the dignity of Marquess of Caermarthen; and he became first Duke of Leeds on May the 4th, 1694. 'Ancient as is the paternal family of the noble family of Osborne,' says Sir Bernard Burke, 'the illustrious houses of Conyers, D'Arcy, and Godolphin, which the present Duke of Leeds represents, and his descent through various lines of the royal House of Plantagenet, add a lustre to his Grace's coronet of which few other families can boast' (*Peerage*, 1865). We may here add that Sir Edward Osborne, when Lord Mayor, introduced the custom of *drinking* to the new Sheriff, although there is a ludicrous instance of such a ceremony in 1487.

The courageous action of Osborne at London Bridge has been commemorated in various pictures and prints. We even remember its illustration in a little book of our childhood. The Leeds family preserve the picture of Sir William Hewet, in his habit as Lord Mayor, at Kiveton House in Yorkshire to this day, valuing it at £300. Pennant describes this portrait as half-length, on board; dress, a black gown, furred, red vest and sleeves, a gold chain, and a bonnet. There is also an engraved portrait of Osborne himself, said to be unique, in a series of woodcuts, consisting of the portraits of forty-three Lord Mayors in the time of Queen Elizabeth. There is also a small but uncommon engraving of Osborne leaping from the window, executed for some ephemeral publication, from a drawing by Samuel Wale. As this artist died in 1786, it is of course but of little authority as being a representation of the fact: it is nevertheless interesting for its portraiture of the dwellings on London Bridge in the artist's time. With this print may be mentioned one designed by the same hand, and engraved by Charles Grignion, of the first Duke of Leeds pointing to a portrait of Hewet's daughter, and relating to King Charles II. the foregoing anecdote of his ancestors.

So much, then, for an historical and genealogical illustration of the anecdote of the gallant apprentice of London Bridge.

FATALITIES IN FAMILIES.

THE fates of the House of Neville are read in the history of Cicely Duchess of York, who died on the 31st of May 1495, after having witnessed in her own family more appalling calamities than probably are to be found in the history of any other individual. She was a Lancasterian by birth, her mother being Joan Beaufort, a daughter of John of Gaunt. Her father was that rich and powerful nobleman, Ralph Neville Earl of Westmoreland. She was the youngest of twenty-one children, and, on her becoming the wife of Richard Plantagenet Duke of York, her numerous wealthy and powerful family exerted all their influence to place her on the throne of England. But after a series of splendid achievements, almost unparalleled in history, the whole of the Nevilles were swept away long before their sister Cicely, who by their conquering swords became the mother of kings, had descended in sorrow to the grave.

Here is the sad record of her calamities in chronological sequence. Her nephew, Humphrey Earl of Stafford, was killed at the first battle of St. Albans in 1455. Her

THE HOUSE OF NEVILLE. 81

brother-in-law, Stafford Duke of Buckingham, was killed at the battle of Northampton in 1460. Her husband, Richard Duke of York, was slain in 1460 at the battle of Wakefield, just as the crown of England was almost within his ambitious grasp. Her nephew, Sir Thomas Neville, and her husband's nephew, Sir Thomas Bourchier, were killed at the same time and place. Her brother, the Earl of Salisbury, was taken prisoner, and put to death after the battle; and her son, Edmund Earl of Rutland, a boy about twelve years of age, was captured when flying with his tutor from the fatal field, and cruelly murdered in cold blood by Lord Clifford, ever after surnamed the Butcher. Her nephew Sir John Neville was killed at the battle of Towton in 1461, and her nephew Sir Henry Neville was made prisoner and put to death at Banbury in 1469. Two other nephews, Richard Neville, Earl of Warwick, 'the king-maker,' and John Neville, Marquis of Montague, were killed at the battle of Barnet in 1471. Edward Prince of Wales, who married her great-niece, was barbarously murdered after the battle of Tewkesbury in the same year. Her son, George Duke of Clarence, was put to death—drowned in a malmsey-butt, it is said—in the Tower of London in 1478, his wife Cicely having previously been poisoned. Her son-in-law, Charles the Bold, Duke of Burgundy, was killed at the battle of Nancy in 1477. Her eldest son, Edward IV. King of England, fell a victim to his passions in the prime of manhood in 1483. Lord Harrington, the first husband of her niece, Catherine

Neville, was killed at Wakefield; and Catherine's second husband, William Lord Hastings, was beheaded, without even the form of a trial, in 1483. Her great-nephew, Vere, son of the Earl of Oxford, died a prisoner in the Tower, his father being in exile and his mother in poverty. Her son-in-law, Holland Duke of Exeter, who married her daughter Anne, lived long in exile, and in such poverty as to be compelled to beg his bread; and in 1473 his corpse was found stripped naked on the sea-shore near Dover. Her two grandsons, King Edward v. and Richard Duke of York, were murdered in the Tower in 1483. Her son-in-law, Sir Thomas St. Ledger, the second husband of her daughter Anne, was executed at Exeter in 1483, and her great-nephew, Henry Stafford, Duke of Buckingham, was beheaded at or about the same time. Her grandson, Edward Prince of Wales, son of Richard III., through whom she might naturally expect the honour of being the ancestress of a line of English kings, died in 1484, and his mother soon followed him to the tomb. Her youngest son, Richard III., was killed at Bosworth Field in 1485; and her grandson, John de la Pole, Earl of Lincoln, was slain at the battle of Stoke in 1487.

Surviving all these troubles and all her children, with the exception of Margaret Duchess of Burgundy, the Duchess Cicely died at a good old age, after seeing three of her descendants kings of England, and her granddaughter Elizabeth queen of Henry VII. By her death she was saved the additional affliction of the loss of her grandson,

Edward Earl of Warwick, the last male of the princely house of Plantagenet, who was treacherously put to death by a cruel and jealous monarch in 1499.

When her husband was killed at the battle of Wakefield, the conqueror cut off his head, and putting a paper crown on it, in derision of his royal claims, placed it over the principal gate of the city of York. But when her son Edward came to the throne, he caused the mangled remains of his father to be collected, and buried with regal ceremonies in the chapel of the collegiate church at Fotheringhay. Here also Cicely, according to directions contained in her will, was laid beside her husband, whose loss she had mourned for thirty-five long years. It was fated that she should be denied the last long rest usually allotted to mortals. At the Reformation the church at Fotheringhay was almost razed to the ground, and the bodies of Edward and Cicely were exposed to public view; and the discovery having been made known to Queen Elizabeth, she ordered the remains to be reinterred with all decent solemnities. We quote this very interesting *précis* from Chambers's *Book of Days*, vol. i. pp. 711, 712.

The great house of Percy was singularly unfortunate. Henry first Earl of Northumberland was slain at Bramham Moor. His son, the gallant Hotspur, had already fallen at Shrewsbury; and his grandson Henry, second Earl of Northumberland, fell at the battle of St. Albans in 1455. The next and third possessor of the title was slain at

Towton; and his son, the fourth Earl, was murdered by a mob at Thirsk in 1480. Henry, the fifth Earl, died a natural death; but his second son, Sir Thomas Percy, was executed in 1537 for his concern in Ask's rebellion. Henry, the sixth Earl, the first lover of Anne Boleyn, died issueless in 1537, and the family were deprived of the honours of the peerage by Sir Thomas Percy's attainder. During this period the rightful heirs had the mortification to see the dukedom of Northumberland conferred on John Dudley, Earl of Warwick. This nobleman, however, being attainted, the earldom was restored to Thomas Percy, who became seventh Earl, and eventually ended his life on the scaffold, August 1572. His brother Henry, eighth Earl of Northumberland, still blind to the hereditary sufferings of his race, intrigued in favour of Mary Queen of Scots, and being imprisoned in the Tower, there committed suicide. His son Henry, ninth Earl, was convicted on a groundless suspicion of being connected with the Gunpowder Plot, stripped of all his offices, adjudged by the Star Chamber to pay a fine of £30,000, and sentenced to imprisonment for life in the Tower. His grandson Jouline, eleventh Earl of Northumberland, left an only daughter; and thus ended the male line of the greatest perhaps of all our English families (Burke's *Family Romance*, vol. ii.).

The reverses of the Paulets have been very striking. The first Marquis of Winchester was one of those members of the peerage who stand out as prominent persons in the national history, giving direction to public affairs, exercising vast influence, acquiring great accumulations of honours and wealth, and leaving families to dwindle behind him in splendid insignificance. Born about 1475, the son of a small Somersetshire gentleman, William Pawlet, or Powlett, devoted himself to court life, and prospered so well that he became successively comptroller and treasurer of the household to King Henry VIII. Under the boy-king, who succeeded, he rose to be Lord Treasurer, the highest office in the State, being then over seventy years of age. In the same reign he was ennobled, and finally made Marquis of Winchester. It has never been said that he possessed masterly abilities: he is only presented to us as a man of great policy and sagacity. When the death of the young king raised a dynastic difficulty, old Powlett foresaw that the popular sentiment would not ratify the pretensions of Lady Jane Grey; and throwing himself in the opposite scale, he was the chief instrument in preserving the crown for Mary. Through that bloody reign he continued to be Lord Treasurer. When Elizabeth and Protestantism succeeded, he still contrived to keep his place. In fact, this astute old man maintained uninterrupted prosperity down to his death in 1571-2, when he was ninety-seven, enormously wealthy, and had upwards of 100 descendants. It might well excite surprise that a statesman should have kept high place from Edward's reign, *through Mary's*, into Elizabeth's; and the question was one day put to him how it was he did so. He answered that he was 'born of the willow, not of the oak.'

The old Marquis built in his later years a palatial house at Basing, in Hants. But we hear no more of the cautious wisdom which founded the greatness of the family. We hear of the third Marquis writing poetry, and giving away large estates among four illegitimate sons; of the fourth impoverishing himself by a magnificent entertainment to Queen Elizabeth; and of the fifth taking the losing side in the civil war, when Lord Winchester fortified Basing House for the king. He defied a powerful besieging force, and made upon it many deadly sallies, and wrote on every window of the house *Aimez Loyauté*, since continued the motto of the family crest. He swore to maintain his position so long as a single stone of his mansion remained; and it was not till after a two years' siege (October 1645) that the investing army succeeded. The house, in which the captors found valuables worth £300,000, was burnt to the ground. The Marquis survived to 1674, and his loyal faith and courage were commemorated in an epitaph by Dryden.

Among the nobles who surrendered to Edward VI. after the battle of Barnet, was John Earl of Oxford, who had his life pardoned, but was sent over sea to the Castle of Hammes: here for the space of twelve years he was shut up in a strong prison and narrowly looked to; his lady all that time was not suffered to come unto him, nor had anything to live upon but what people of their charity gave her, or what she could get by needle or other work.

About this time, Henry Holland, Duke of Exeter and

Earl of Huntingdon, disinherited by Act of Parliament in the fourth year of the reign of Edward IV. (though he had married this king's sister), grew to so great misery, that, passing over into Flanders, Comines there saw him running barelegged after the Duke of Burgundy's train begging his bread for God's sake. The Duke at that time not knowing (though they had married two sisters), but hearing afterwards who it was, gave him a small pension to maintain him, till not long after he was found dead, as stated at p. 82; but how he came to his death, could never by any inquiry be brought to light.

Among the vicissitudes of historic seats, the famous Castle of Brancepeth, in Durham, stands prominently. 'Of all the feudal fortresses of England,' says Sir Bernard Burke, 'whether we regard their venerable antiquity, the rank and authority of their early possessors, or the wealth and taste which have been, in modern times, expended upon them, there are few which can claim precedence over this home of the Nevilles. Built, in all probability, *temp*. Stephen, by the Bulmers, lords of Sheriff Hutton, in Yorkshire, it was conveyed, after a few generations, by an heiress, Emma de Bulmer, to her husband, Geoffrey de Neville. Thus originated the illustrious House of Neville of Brancepeth, in which this grand old castle continued down to the time of Elizabeth, when the last Neville of Brancepeth, Charles Earl of Westmoreland, by his participation in 'the Rising of the North,' forfeited both Raby and Brancepeth, and was driven into exile, where he died penniless in 1601. Brancepeth, thus lapsed to the Crown, was granted by James I. to his favourite, Robert Carr, who was created Baron Brancepeth and Earl of Somerset; but his attainder again forfeited the property, and it was sold in 1636.

The Tresham family appear to have been very unstable in their possession of Rushton Hall, in the county of Northampton. The property belonged to the Treshams in the reign of King Henry VI., and was forfeited not long afterwards to the Crown, in consequence of the attainder of the first Sir Thomas Tresham. He was beheaded at the commencement of the reign of Edward IV.; but the estate was subsequently restored to the family, which attained the meridian of its greatness under Queen Elizabeth. In the succeeding reign its star once again declined: the possessions of the family were confiscated once more, and the head of it being attainted, was confined, and died in the Tower. He had been implicated in the Gunpowder Plot, and proved, though with no such intention upon his part, the cause of its timely discovery. From his hand proceeded the well-known letter addressed as an anonymous warning to Lord Monteagle. It was in a summer-house at Newton, belonging to another branch of the Tresham family, that the framers of the Gunpowder Plot used to concoct their plans.

Sir Edward Dering, who rebuilt Surrenden Dering in Kent in 1626, appears to have been a very singular character, full of levity and of learning, and which he was at all times anxious to display, in season and out of season. To such a pitch did he carry this passion, that, although in principle a royalist, he one day brought before the House of Commons a bill for extirpating bishops, deans, and chapters, solely, as it was said at the time, with a view to show his learning by appending to it two lines from Ovid's *Metamorphoses*:

> ' Cuncta prius tentanda, sed immedicabile vulgus
> Ense recidendum est ne pars sincera trahetur.'

In a short time he repented of this anti-royal demonstration, and publicly apologized for it, in doing which he gave so much offence to the Parliamentary party that they committed him to the Tower. From this prison he contrived to escape and join the king; but he was declared a delinquent, his estate was sequestrated, and his house repeatedly plundered, so that he died in much distress and poverty.

The history of the Staffords of Penshurst presents us with remarkable instances of rise and fall. At the decease of Humphrey the Good, Duke of Gloucester, without children, Penshurst vested in the king his cousin, and was shortly after granted to Humphrey Earl of Stafford, a nobleman of great influence and power, nearly related to the royal family through his mother Lady Anne Plantagenet. Serving with great gallantry in the French wars, his lordship received in requital, and in regard of his near propinquity to the throne, a grant of the dukedom of Buckingham, with precedence of all dukes whatsoever. But the fate of the illustrious house was chequered by dire misfortune. Edmund Earl of Stafford, his son Humphrey Duke of Buckingham, and his grandson Humphrey Earl of Stafford, all fell in the desolating Wars of the Roses; and Henry, second Duke of Buckingham, and his son Edward, third and last Duke, were both beheaded and sacrificed to the feuds of party and private malignity. With the third duke sank for ever the splendour, princely honour, and great wealth of the ancient and renowned family of Stafford.

Its last male representative, Roger Stafford, grandson of Henry Lord Stafford by Ursula Pole his wife, grand-niece of King Edward IV., went in his youth by the name of Fludd —for what reason has not been explained—perhaps with the indignant pride that the very name of Stafford should not be associated with the obscurity of his lot. At the age of sixty-five he became, by the early death of his cousin Henry Lord Stafford, heir-male of his noble house, and petitioned Parliament accordingly; but he eventually submitted his claim to King Charles, who decided, that having no part of the inheritance of the Stafford lands, he should surrender the title to His Majesty; which order being obeyed by the petitioner, the honour was conferred upon Sir William Howard and Mary Stafford his wife. Roger Stafford died unmarried in 1640. His only sister, Jane Stafford, married a joiner, and had a son a shoemaker living at Newport, in Shropshire, in 1637. Thus the great-grandson of Margaret Plantagenet, the daughter and heiress of George Duke of Clarence, sank to the grade of a cobbler!

The fallen fortunes and vicissitudes of the Buckinghams have been favourite topics with many writers, who have traced the extraordinary fatalities which happened to this noble family through the long lapse of eight centuries.

The fate of Buckingham at Bosworth Field will be remembered. He had changed sides, to try whether he could not pull down what he had so largely contributed to set up. His motives were, however, probably mixed. He may (as Shakspeare takes for granted) have been refused the promised earldom and domains of Hereford, although a formal grant of them had been discovered among some old records; or, being of the blood royal, he might have hoped to get the crown for himself. He told Morton that he could no longer abide the sight of Richard after the death of 'the two young innocents.' He accordingly transferred his allegiance to the Earl of Richmond, who, when the arrangements for a simultaneous rising in several parts of England were complete, set sail from St. Malo with a force computed at 5000 soldiers. His friends keeping faith, the insurrection assumed formidable proportions in Devonshire, Wiltshire, Berkshire, and Kent. Buckingham had collected a large force in Wales. But it was impossible to elude Richard's watchfulness; and fortune had not yet deserted him. Richmond's fleet was driven back by a tempest; and Buckingham was stopped by an inundation of the Severn and the neighbouring rivers, so terrible that, for a century afterwards, it was spoken of as Buckingham's Great Water. The result is succinctly told by Shakspeare :

> '*Mess.* My lord, the army of great Buckingham—
> *K. Rich.* Out on ye, owls! nothing but songs of death!
> (*He strikes him.*)
> *Mess.* The news I have to tell your Majesty,
> Is, that by sudden floods and fall of waters,
> Buckingham's army is dispersed and scatter'd;
> And he himself wander'd away alone,
> No man knows whither.'

After another messenger has delivered an equally cheering report,

> '*Enter* CATESBY.
> My liege, the Duke of Buckingham is taken :
> That's the best news. That the Earl of Richmond
> Is with a mighty power landed at Milford,
> Is colder tidings, yet it must be told.
> *King.* Away towards Salisbury; while we reason here,
> A royal battle might be won and lost;
> Some one take order Buckingham be brought
> To Salisbury; the rest march on with me.'

Then we have the popular reading, interpolated by Cibber :

> '*Enter* CATESBY.
> My liege, the Duke of Buckingham is taken.
> *Rich.* Off with his head : so much for Buckingham.'

Thornbury, in Gloucestershire, exhibits a fine specimen of the last gradation of Gothic architecture in its application to castellated houses. The whole is a picturesque group, with many beauties of battlemented tower and turret and enriched chimney shafts.[1]

[1] Thornbury has been in part restored by its present possessor, Henry

Edward Stafford, Duke of Buckingham, who commenced building this interesting pile—the condition of which is emblematic of the fortunes of its founder—was the fifth in descent from Anne Plantagenet, daughter and heiress of Thomas of Woodstock, the youngest son of King Edward III. The line of his pedigree is marked in civil blood. His father was beheaded by Richard III.; his grandfather was killed at the battle of St. Albans; his great-grandfather at the battle of Northampton; and the father of this last at the battle of Shrewsbury. More than a century had elapsed since any chief of this great family had fallen by a natural death,—a pedigree which may be sufficient to characterize an age. Edward was doomed to no milder fate than his forefathers. Knivett, a discarded officer of Buckingham's household, furnished information to Wolsey which led to the apprehension of his late master. The most serious charges against Buckingham were, that he had consulted a monk about future events; that he had declared all the acts of Henry VII. to be wrongfully done; that he had told Knivett, that if he had been sent to the Tower when he was in danger of being committed, he would have played the part which his father intended to perform at Salisbury, where, if he could have obtained an audience, he would have stabbed Richard III. with a knife; and that he had told Lord Abergavenny if the king died he would have the rule of the land. All

Howard, Esq. of Greystoke Castle, Cumberland. The noble banqueting rooms are among the restorations.

these supposed offences, if they could be blended together, did not amount to an overt act of high treason, even if we suppose the consultation of the soothsayer to relate to the time of the king's death. The only serious imputation on his prudence rests on the testimony of the spy. Buckingham confessed the real amount of his absurd inquiries from the friar. He defended himself with eloquence. He was tried in the court of the Lord High Steward by a jury of peers, consisting of one duke, one marquess, seven earls, and twelve barons, who convicted him; although the facts, if true, amounted to no more than proof of indiscretion and symptoms of discontent. The Duke of Norfolk, Lord Steward for the occasion, shed tears on pronouncing sentence. The prisoner said, 'May the Eternal God forgive you my death, as I do!' The only favour which he could obtain was that the ignominious part of a traitor's death should be remitted. He was accordingly beheaded on the 17th of May 1521, while the surrounding people vented their indignation against Wolsey by loud cries of 'The butcher's son!'[1]

Thornbury Castle was restored to the founder's son in the reign of Mary, but great dilapidation had taken place in the interval. Leland, who saw the place twenty years after the Duke's death, describes the castle, and adds: 'Edward Duke of Bukkyngham made a fayre parke hard by the castle, and tooke muche faire ground in it very frutefull of corne, now fayr launds for coursynge. The inhabitants cursed the Duke

Sir James Mackintosh's *History of England*.

for these lands so incloysed.' Rudder, in his *History of Gloucestershire*, describes the place from an old manuscript, which he conjectures to have been written about the time of King James I. It is a curious record, as preserving the memory of what must else have been speedily forgotten. On one of the scrolls over the entrance is inscribed, 'Doresenavant,' an old French word, signifying 'henceforward' or 'hereafter,' in allusion, it is supposed, to the Duke's expectation of one day possessing the crown of England.

The title of Buckingham, which slept for many years, was revived in the person of George Villiers, the son of Sir George Villiers, knight of Brokesby. Although the favourite of two monarchs, he was heartily detested by the nation. He was stabbed to the heart with a knife by one John Felton, a lieutenant in the army; his age was but thirty-six years. The son of this unfortunate Duke was no less remarkable for the perfection of his form than for the extent and variety of his talents. But his vices would seem to have been more than equal to his abilities. Having first seduced the wife of Francis Talbot Earl of Shrewsbury, he killed that nobleman in a duel. The no less profligate Countess was a looker-on at this horrible scene, and held the Duke's horse by the bridle while he killed her husband. Walpole says of him: 'When this extraordinary man, with the figure and genius of Alcibiades, could equally charm the Presbyterian Fairfax and the dissolute Charles; when he alike ridiculed the witty king and his solemn Chancellor; when he plotted the ruin of his country by a cabal of bad ministers, or, equally unprincipled, supported its cause with bad patriots, one laments that a man of such parts should be devoid of every virtue. But when Alcibiades turns chemist; when he is a real bubble and a visionary miser; when ambition is but a frolic; when the worst designs are fore the foolishest ends, contempt extinguishes all reflections on his character.'

The Duke forfeited his friends, wasted his estate, lost his reputation with the world, and died, it is said, as miserable and as destitute as the meanest beggar. Pope thus describes his death, which he affirms to have taken place at a remote inn somewhere in Yorkshire:

> 'Behold what blessings wealth to life can lend!
> And see what comfort it affords our end.
> In the worst inn's worst room, with mat half hung,
> The floor of plaster and the walls of dung;
> On once a flock-bed, but repaired with straw,
> With tape-tied curtains never meant to draw;
> The George and Garter dangling from that bed,
> Where tawdry yellow strove with dirty red—
> Great Villiers lies; alas! how changed from him,
> That life of pleasure and that soul of whim!
> Gallant and gay in Cliveden's proud alcove,
> The bow'r of wanton Shrewsbury and love;
> Or just as gay at council in a ring
> Of mimicked statesmen and their merry king.
> No wit to flatter left of all his store;
> No fool to laugh at, which he valued more.
> There, victor of his health, of fortune, friends,
> And fame, the lord of useless thousands ends.'

It was at Kirkby Moorside where the wretched Villiers expired, though not in 'the worst inn's worst room,' but in a respectable farm-house occupied by one of the Duke's tenants, and which had never been an inn.

Next, John Villiers, who assumed on questionable right the dignities of Viscount Purbeck and Earl of Buckingham, had his share of the evil destinies that seem for ever attached to the name of Buckingham. He became the associate of gamesters; and having lived a life of debauchery and squandered his fortune, he married Frances, the daughter of the Rev. Mr. Moyser, and widow of George Heneage, Esq., of Lincolnshire, by whom he had two daughters, who, like their mother, sank to the lowest degradation. The last survivor, 'Lady Elizabeth Villiers,' died in Tavistock Court, Covent Garden, July 4, 1786 (Burke's *Family Romance*, vol. ii.).

In our own time, two Dukes of Buckingham and Chandos have fallen from their high estate into comparative neglect and poverty. Richard, the first Duke, lived on his noble estate, Stowe, 'with princely magnificence. His expenditure in the luxuries of literature and art was enormous; and the munificent spirit with which he entertained the royal family of France and their numerous followers during their residence here, not only drained his exchequer, but burdened him with debt. Neither Louis XVIII. nor Charles X. took the slightest notice of the obligation they had incurred, apparently regarding such imprudent generosity as the natural acknowledgment of their exceeding merit.'[1]

[1] Mr. Rumsey Forster, in his piquant historical notice of Stowe prefixed to the *Priced and Annotated Catalogue*, relates that Louis-Philippe

The Duke was in 1827 compelled to shut up his house at Stowe, and go abroad till his large estates could be *nursed*, so as to meet the heaviest and most pressing demands.

When the Duke and Duchess took their farewell of Stowe, and had reached the flower-garden, the Duchess burst out into a violent fit of tears, in which the Duke participated without saying a word. 'In this manner,' he writes, 'she went through the two gardens, and left them in silent sorrow. I gave her a rose which I gathered out of the garden as we passed, and I know that she treasured up the *last gift*.' While abroad, the Duke had a dream, which he has thus recorded in his private *Diary*, published in 1862:

'I am ashamed to say that I am more low than I should dare confess to any one, by a dream which haunted me in my sleep, with a degree of precision which is really frightful. I was at Stowe, my dear and regretted home. All was desolate—not a soul appeared to receive me. My good dog met me, and licked my hand. Accompanied by him I traversed all the apartments—all desolate and solitary:

---

being present when the royal family of France were enjoying the hospitality of the Marquis of Buckingham at Stowe, as they were seated together in the library, the conversation turned on events then enacting on the other side of the Channel; upon which Louis-Philippe, recollecting his own position with the Revolutionists, threw himself upon his knees, and begged pardon of his royal uncle for having ever worn the tricolored cockade. The anecdote is curious, when the subsequent career of the ex-monarch is borne in mind.

every room as I had left it. On my return from the state bedroom, I met my wife! She told me all my family were gone, and that she was left desolate—that even her little favourite dog, which had been her sole remaining companion, had died a few days ago. We went out at the north hall door together, and all was solitude and desertion. I awoke with the distress of the moment, and I slept no more that night. I do not like to confess how much effect this has had upon me. I have not the slightest faith in dreams, but this has strongly accorded with the feelings and tone of my mind, and I cannot shake it off. Those who will ever see this journal will, I am sure, not laugh at my feelings.'

The Duke died Jan. 17, 1839, and was succeeded by his only son, Richard Plantagenet, who, though crippled in fortune by the paternal virtues, celebrated the coming of age of his son with profuse hospitality at Stowe in 1844. In the following year the Duke entertained Queen Victoria and the Prince Consort with great sumptuousness. The mansion at Stowe was partly refurnished for the occasion, when the cost of the new carpets was £5000. In 1848 the dream of the first Duke was strangely realized by the dismantling of Stowe, and the compulsory sale of the whole of the costly contents; the sale occupying forty days, and realizing £75,562, 4s. 6d. The second Duke subsequently resided in the neighbourhood. He often indulged his sadness at his fallen fortunes by walking to Stowe, and there, in one of the superb saloons in which kings and princes had held courts and been feasted with regal magnificence, seated in a chair before a small table—the only furniture in the room—would Richard Plantagenet pass many an hour of 'bitter fancy!' Heir to a great position, the Duke took no mean part in public business, and enjoyed no small influence in the Legislature. It is less for this, however, than for the greatness of his misfortune, that he will be longest remembered. He lost everything but his name. Through his mother he represented one of the most noble houses in the land; the long line of his ancestors being all famed for their magnificence, this one known as 'the King of Cotswold,' and that as 'the Princely Chandos.' Through his father he was the head of the family of the Temples, which, including the Grenvilles, has given more statesmen to the nation than any other in the land. The family had wealth corresponding to its renown, but all vanished. The broad acres went with the treasures which it would be more difficult to replace, and the Duke of Buckingham found himself stripped of his heritage, the owner of little more than the titles of his ancestors. It was a great fall, that might in its way be compared with the descent of another Duke of Buckingham, to whom on a small scale he bore some resemblance, and who,

> 'Stiff in opinions, always in the wrong,
> Was everything by starts, and nothing long;
> But in the course of one revolving moon
> Was chymist, fiddler, statesman, and buffoon:
> Then all for women, painting, rhyming, drinking,
> Besides ten thousand freaks that died in thinking.

> In squandering wealth was his peculiar art;
> Nothing went unrewarded but desert.
> Beggared by fools, whom still he found too late,
> He had his jest, and they had his estate.'

He gave his name to a provision of the Reform Bill known as the 'Chandos clause,' which extends the franchise in counties to tenancies of £50. It is the only part of this Reform Bill which is identified with any one man's name. After his troubles overtook him, the public heard little of him save as an author. He collected all the correspondence of his family, and the friends of his family, which threw light on the political intrigues of Courts and Cabinets ever since George III. began to reign, and published it with a connecting narrative.

The Duke died July 30, 1861, at the age of sixty-four. Sir Bernard Burke, Ulster, writes of his lineage: 'Of all native-born British subjects, his Grace was, after the present reigning family, the senior representative of the Royal Houses of Tudor and Plantagenet.' Paternally, his Grace was a Grenville, not a Temple. His right to the latter surname was derived simply from his being the representative of Hester Temple (eldest daughter of Sir Richard Temple, Bart., of Stowe), who at the decease of her brother Richard succeeded to the Viscounty of Cobham, and was afterwards made Countess Temple. Among the male descendants of this same family of Temple was Viscount Palmerston.

The history of the Reresbys of Thrybergh Park—a family

with many illustrious names—affords a melancholy example of the decadence to which the great and noble may be subjected. Sir William Reresby, Baronet, son and heir of the celebrated Sir John Reresby, the author of the well-known *Memoirs of His own Times*, inherited from his father an estate of £17,000 a year; but by dissipation became so reduced, that he was forced to part with Thrybergh, eventually was a tapster in the King's Bench Prison, and was imprisoned for cheating in 1711. Gaming, and particularly cock-fighting, was his predominant vice; and there is a tradition at Thrybergh, that the estate at Dennaby was staked and lost on a single main!

Not long after, a Sir Charles Burton was tried at the Old Bailey for stealing a seal, and pleaded poverty as an excuse. At the beginning of the present century, the heir of the eminent and ancient family of Castleton, and the twelfth baronet of that name in succession, was a breeches-maker at Lynn, in Norfolk. He died in 1810, when the family became extinct.

Sir Bernard Burke has, in one of his popular works, instances how one co-heir of our Plantagenet kings was, at the time he wrote, a shoemaker, working at his craft in a suburb of London; another a butcher at Halesowen, and a third a toll-bar keeper near Dudley. An Earl of Traquair, ruined in the great civil war, was reduced to beg alms in the streets of Edinburgh; and the last baronet of the O'Neills, sprung from the ancient kings of Ireland, ended his days as 'boots' at a little inn at Dunleek, in the county of Louth.

Of 'Tees-seated Sockburn, where by long descent Conyers was lord,' not one stone is left on another, and not an acre of land in the county of Durham is held by one of the name. Sir Roger Conyers was, in the Conqueror's days, made Constable of the Keep of Durham. The family, by noble alliances, rose to great position and grandeur, and early in the eighteenth century were thus dispersed. The heirs or assigns of Ann Conyers, Countess of Shrewsbury, held Sockburn; Conyers d'Arcy, Earl of Holdernesse and Baron Conyers, the next branch, kept princely state in the Conyers Castle of Hornby; and Sir John Conyers of Horden possessed the fine mansion of Charlton, in Kent. Within a century, in the very county where the lords of Sockburn held such potent sway, might be seen poor old Sir Thomas Conyers, the last Baronet of Horden, in his seventy-second year, solitary and friendless, a pauper in the parish workhouse of Chester-le-Street! He was removed by his friends to a situation of ease and comfort; he did not long enjoy it, but expired without pain or a sigh, the last male heir of a long line of ancestry. He left three daughters, married to working men in the little town of Chester-le-Street.

THE HUNGERFORD FAMILY.

BLOTS on the escutcheon is an old phrase used to denote the black spots of disgrace which appear in .the records of many opulent families; but in few so darkly as that of the Hungerfords of Farleigh Castle, in Somersetshire, about nine miles west from Bath. There are other branches of the Hungerfords in Wiltshire; and their history is so complicated as to baffle collectors, who are ever on the look-out for additions to their stores, notwithstanding that accomplished antiquary, Sir Richard Colt Hoare, printed in 1823 a small octavo volume of this remarkable family, entitled *Hungerfordiana*. From these accumulations of evidence we may glean a narrative which not only portrays individuals, but affords us pictures of periods which are interesting as well as suggestive. The name of the Hungerfords has been preserved in our metropolis for several centuries; and that upon a spot which was long noted as a site of unfortunate speculation.

The Farleigh Castle estate is of high antiquity. For a long period it was held by Saxon thanes; and in the eleventh century it fell into the possession of Roger de

Curcelle, a Norman baron, who stood in high favour with William the Conqueror. After his death, the property reverted to the Crown, when William Rufus granted it, with other lands, to Hugh de Montfort; whence in old records we often find it denominated Farley Montfort. A strange character was this same Hugh. In opposition to the almost universal custom of the time, he chose to wear a long beard, whence he acquired the cognomen of *the bearded Hugh cum barbâ*. He was a right valiant soldier, but got killed in a duel with Walkeline de Ferrers, of Oakham Castle. The estate, however, remained in his family till the year 1335, when Sir Henry de Montfort granted this and other lands to Bartholomew Lord Burghersh, who figures in the unfortunate wars carried on by Richard II. against the Scots. His son and successor held the property but a short time, being compelled by his imprudence to part with it to Thomas Lord Hungerford. With his descendants it then continued for many generations, except only for a brief interval, when, its possessor having been beheaded, it was confiscated to the Crown and given to the Duke of Gloucester. Upon the Duke's accession to the throne it was granted by him to John Howard, Duke of Norfolk—'Jockey of Norfolk'—one of the staunchest of his adherents on Bosworth Field, where he fell in a personal encounter with the Earl of Oxford. After shivering their spears on each other's shields or breastplates, they fell to with their swords. Oxford, wounded in the arm by a blow which glanced from his crest, returned it by one which hewed off the vizor of

Norfolk's helmet, leaving the face bare; and then, disdaining to follow up the advantage, drew back, when an arrow from an unknown hand pierced the Duke's brain. We must spare room for the close of this striking episode of Bosworth. Surrey, hurrying up to assist or avenge his father, was surrounded and overpowered by Sir Gilbert Talbot and Sir John Savage, who commanded on the right and left for Richmond.

> 'Young Howard single with an army fights;
> When, moved with pity, two renowned knights,
> Strong Clarendon and valiant Conyers, try
> To rescue him, in which attempt they die.
> Now Surrey, fainting, scarce his sword can hold,-
> Which made a common soldier grow so bold,
> To lay rude hands upon that noble flower;
> Which he disdaining—anger gives him power—
> Erects his weapon with a nimble round,
> And sends the peasant's arm to kiss the ground.'[1]

If we may credit tradition or the chroniclers, all this was literally true. When completely exhausted, Surrey presented the hilt of his sword to Talbot, whom he requested to take his life, and save him from dying by an ignoble hand. He lived to be the Surrey of Flodden Field, and the worthy transmitter of 'all the blood of all the Howards.'

To return to the Hungerfords. The fact of a lady of this name having suffered execution at Tyburn on the 20th of February 1523, has been handed down by the Chronicle of Stow; and it is stated by that historian that

---

[1] *Bosworth Field*, by Sir John Beaumont, Bart., in Weaver's *Funeral Monuments*, p. 554.

she died for murdering her husband. Stow cites in his margin the Register of the Grey Friars, meaning a volume now preserved in the British Museum, and including a London Chronicle which was printed for the Camden Society in the year 1852. We find that the body of the convicted lady was buried in the Church of the Grey Friars, in the middle of the nave; and that circumstance evidently occasioned the notice taken of the execution in the chronicle. In a side-note, written by a later but old hand, is, 'Suspendit apud Tyborne.' The passage is as follows: 'And this yere in feverette the xx^{ti} day was the lady Alys Hungerford lede from the Tower unto Holborne, and there put into a carte at the churchyard with one of her servanttes, and so caryed unto Tiborne, and there both hongyd, and she burryed at the Grayfreeres in the nether end of the myddes of the church on the North syde.'

Sir Richard Colt Hoare, in his *Hungerfordiana*, already mentioned, connects this tragic event with that branch of the Hungerfords which resided at Cadenham, in Wiltshire; but the Rev. Mr. Jackson, F.S.A., who has formed large collections relative to the Hungerfords, corrects the statement of Sir Richard Colt Hoare, and adds: 'There were no knights in the Cadenham branch of the Hungerfords before a Sir George, who died in the year 1712; and the only knights of the family living at the date of the execution in 1523 were Sir Walter Hungerford of Farley Castle and Heytesbury, and Sir John Hungerford and Sir Anthony his son, both of Down

Ampney, whose wives had other names, and are otherwise accounted for.'

No other Alice Lady Hungerford identifiable with the culprit could be discovered but the second of the three wives of Sir Walter, who was summoned to Parliament as Lord Hungerford of Heytesbury in 1536; and considering that the extreme cruelty of that person to all his wives is recorded in a letter written by the third and last of them, and that his career was eventually terminated with the utmost disgrace in 1540, when he was beheaded (suffering at the same time as the fallen minister Thomas Cromwell, Earl of Essex), it was deemed not improbable that the unfortunate lady might have been condemned for some desperate attempt upon the life of so bad a husband, which had not actually effected its object, or even that her life and character had been sacrificed to a false and murderous accusation. In the survey of his lands he is described as Sir Walter Hungerford, Knight, late Lord Hungerford, 'of *hyge treason* attaynted' (Hoare's *Modern Wiltshire*). It is also stated that part of his offence was maintaining a chaplain named William Bird, who had called the king a heretic, and that he had procured certain persons by conjuration to know how long the king should live (Dugdale's *Baronage*, ii. p. 242). Holinshed states that 'at the hour of his death he seemed unquiet, as manie judged him rather in a frenzie than otherwise.'

In the above state the mystery remained until the discovery, a few years since, of an 'Inventory of the goods belonging to the king's grace by the forfeiture of the Lady Hungerford, attainted of murder in Hilary term, anno xiiij. Regis Henrici VIII.;' where, although the particulars of the tragedy remain still undeveloped, we find that the culprit must have been a different person from the lady already noticed; and the murdered man, if her husband, of course not the Lord Walter.

It is ascertained by the inventory before us, that the Lady Hungerford who was hung at Tybourn on the 23d of February 1523, was really a widow, and that she was certainly convicted of felony and murder; moreover, that her name was Agnes, not Alice, as stated in the Grey Friars Chronicle. This inventory further shows, by the mention it contains of Heytesbury, Farleigh Castle, and other places, as well as by the great amount of personal property described, that the parties were no other than the heads of the Hungerford family. The initials E. and A. placed upon some of the articles point to the names of Edward and Agnes. In short, it is made evident that the lady was the widow of Sir Edward Hungerford, the father of Walter Lord Hungerford already mentioned; and we are led to infer that it was Sir Edward himself who had been poisoned or otherwise murdered by her agency.

It is a remarkable feature of the inventory, that many items of it are described in the first person, and consequently from the lady's own dictation; and towards the end of it is a list of 'the rayment of my husbond's, which is in the keping of my son-in-law.' By this expression is understood that the person so designated was Sir Walter Hungerford, Sir Edward's son and heir.

From this conclusion it follows that the lady was not Sir Walter's mother, who appears in the pedigree as Jane, daughter of John Lord Zouch of Horryngworth, but a second wife, whose name has not been recorded by the genealogists of the family.

To this circumstance must be attributed much of the difficulty that has hitherto enveloped this investigation. The lady's origin and maiden name are still unknown; but the Rev. Mr. Jackson has favoured Mr. J. G. Nichols with some particulars which clearly identify her as the widow of Sir Edward Hungerford. His observations are as follow:

'That Agnes Lady Hungerford was the second wife of Sir Edward Hungerford of Heytesbury, may now be safely declared upon the evidence following. Of this Sir Edward very little is known. But it is quite certain that he was twice married, and that his first wife was a Zouch. The pedigrees uniformly call her Jane; and the arms of Hungerford impaling Zouch were found some years ago on stained glass in a cottage near Farleigh Castle, and were transferred to the church of that parish. By this first wife Sir Edward had only one son, Walter, afterwards created Lord Hungerford of Heytesbury. The date of the first wife's death is not known. The name of the second wife is found in Sir Edward's last will. He resided chiefly at Heytesbury; and from the circumstance of the eleven witnesses' names all belonging to that immediate neighbourhood, it is most likely that he died there. After bequeathing small legacies to various churches and friends, the will concludes thus: "The residue of all my goodes, debts, catalls, juells, plate, harnesse, and all other moveable, whatsoever they be, I freely give and bequeth to *Agnes Hungerforde, my wife.* And I make, ordeyn, and constitute, of this my present last wille and testament, the said Agnes, my wife, and sole executrice." Sir Edward must have died soon afterwards, as the will was proved on the 29th of January 1521-2.

'After an interval of twelve months comes the fact, supplied by the heading of the present inventory, that "Lady Agnes Hungerford, *wydowe*, was attaynted of felony and murder in Hillary Term xiiij. Henry VIII.," *i.e.* between January 11 and January 31, A.D. 1523. And on the 20th February following (as the Grey Friars Register and Chronicle state), Lady Hungerford, whom those documents call *Alice*, was executed at Tybourn. Five months after, Walter Hungerford, only son and heir of Edward Hungerford, Knight, obtained the royal licence to enter upon all lands and tenements of which the said Sir Edward was seised in fee, or which *Agnes*, late wife of Sir Edward, held for term of her life.

'The inventory agrees with the will in another point. By the will, all goods, debts, chattels, jewels, plate, harness (*i.e.* armour), and all other moveables whatsoever, were "freely given" to Agnes the wife. These are precisely the articles specified in the inventory; and that they were the absolute property of the widow is clear, from their being forfeited to the Crown, which would not have been the case had they been hers only for life.

'But though this inventory assists materially in clearing up three points in this transaction—viz., 1*st*, the lady's Christian name; 2*d*, whose wife she had been; and 3*d*, that her crime was "felony and murder"—the rest of the story remains as much as ever wrapped in mystery. It is not yet certain who was the person murdered; and of the motive, place, time, and all other particulars, we are wholly ignorant. John Stow, the chronicler, who repeats what he found in the Grey Friars Chronicle, certainly adds to that account the words, "for murdering her *husband*." But as Stow was not born until two years after Lady Hungerford's execution, and did not compile his own chronicle until forty years after it, and as we do not know whether he was speaking only from hearsay or on authority, the fact that it *was* the husband still remains to be proved.

'Excepting on the supposition that the Lady Agnes was a perfect monster among women, it is almost inconceivable that she should have murdered a husband who, only a few weeks or days before his death, in the presence of eleven clergymen and gentlemen known to them both, signed a document by which he made to her (besides the jointure from lands above alluded to) a free and absolute gift of all the personal property, including the accumulated valuables of an ancient family; and this to the entire exclusion of his only son and heir! When the character of that son and heir, notoriously cruel to his own wives, and subsequently sent to the scaffold for an ignominious offence, is considered, and when it is further recollected that he was not the son, but only step-son of this lady, certain suspicions arise which more than ever excite one's curiosity to raise still higher the curtain that hides this tragedy. We have also yet to learn of what family this lady was; for so far we have only just succeeded in obtaining accurately her Christian name. It is to be hoped that the particulars of the trial may hereafter come to light among the public records.'

The Inventory describes an extraordinary accumulation of valuable property, and is therefore proportionally curious in illustration of the manners and habits of the times. It commences with a list of plate and jewels. Much of the former was adorned with the Hungerford arms, and with the knot of three sickles interlaced, which was used as the family badge or cognizance. A spoon was inscribed with the motto, '*Myn assuryd truth;*' which same motto, under the form '*Myne trouth assured,*' occurs also on the beautiful seal of Margaret Lady of Hungerford and of Bottreaux, who died in 1476.[1]

---

[1] The ancient badge of the Hungerfords was a single sickle, or handled gules (*Collectanea Topograph. et Geneal.* iii. 71). The sepulchral brass in Salisbury Cathedral of Walter Lord Hungerford (*ob.* 1449) and his wife, and another supposed to be that of his grandson Robert Hungerford (*ob.* 1463), were both *semé* of sickles (see their despoiled slabs or matrices engraved in Gough's *Sepulchral Monuments*, vol. ii. plate lvii.). The Hungerford knot was formed by entwining

THE HUNGERFORD FAMILY.

Among the plate we notice 'forks with spones, to ete grene gynger with all,' the usual destination of the forks mentioned in English inventories. Thus, in an inventory of plate belonging to Edward III. and Richard II., we find these forks set with sapphires, pearls, etc. The forks are mentioned also as spoons: they may have either had prongs at one end and a bowl at the other, or have been made like the folding spoons of a more recent period, where a bowl fits over the prongs of the fork.

The vestments and ornaments of the chapel are next described; and then the furniture of the hall, parlour, an adjoining chamber, the nursery, the queen's chamber, the middle chamber, the great chamber, the chapel chamber, the lily chamber, the knighton chamber, the wardrobe chamber, the gallery, the chamber within the gallery, the women's chamber, the cellar, the buttery, the kitchen, the

three sickles in a circle. Three sickles and as many garbs, elegantly disposed within the garter, formed one of the principal bosses of the cloisters to St. Stephen's Chapel, Westminster. The standard of Sir John Hungerford of Down Ampney (temp. Hen. VIII.) was as follows: Red and green in the first compartment out of a coronet, or a garb of the same (charged with a mullet), between two sickles, crest argent, handled gules, banded or; and in the same compartment three similar sickles, each charged on the blade with a mullet; in the second compartment, three sickles interlaced around a mullet; in the third, three like knots of sickles between two single sickles charged as before. The Hungerford crest was a garb between two sickles, all within a coronet: the garb is supposed to have come from the family of Peveril, one of whose co-heirs married Walter Lord Hungerford, K.G., who died 1449. By that alliance the silver sickle met the golden wheatsheaf.

storehouse, and the brewhouse. In the parlour furniture we notice 'a joined cubeboard'—a joined cupboard. It must be remembered that cupboards were not, as they are now, closets set even into the walls, but literally a board or table on which plate was set out, more like the modern sideboard. A considerable list of cupboard clothes may be found in the inventory of the wardrobe stuffs of Catharine of Aragon.

Then follows a list of the agricultural stock 'belonging to the Grange Place,' and the particulars of some parcels of armour 'left in the Castle of Farley,' including brigandine, formed of small plates of metal quilted with linen or other tissue. Among the curious items is boyde money, or bent money. In the will of Sir Edward Howard, Knight, Admiral of England, 1512, occurs: 'I bequeath him [Charles Brandon] my rope of bowed nobles that I hang my great whistle by, containing ccc. angels.' Money was often bent or bowed when intended to serve as love tokens, a custom perpetuated to the days of Butler:

> 'Like commendation ninepence bent,
> With "from and to my love" he went.'

In the present instance it appears to have been bowed for offerings to saints.

A long and curious catalogue of the lady's own dress and personal ornaments is next given, with a list of some obligations or bonds for money, some items of household stuff remaining in her husband's house at Charing Cross (where the Hungerford name still lingers); and lastly, the raiment of her husband, which was in the keeping of her son-in-law.

The particular dwelling-house at which the principal part of the goods and furniture here described lay, is not positively mentioned by name; but as, from the expression above quoted regarding the arms and armour, it would seem not to have been Farleigh Castle, there is every probability that the document chiefly relates to the manor-house of Heytesbury, where Sir Edward Hungerford died. The manor is thus described in a survey made upon the attainder of Walter Lord Hungerford in 31 Henry VIII.: 'The sayde lordship standeth very pleasauntly, in a very swete ayer, and there ys begon to be buylded a fayre place, whiche, if it had bene fynyshed, had bene able to have receyved the kynges highnes; a fayre hall, with a goodly new wyndow mad in the same; a new parlor, large and fayre; iiij. fayre chambers, wherof one is gyhted, very pleasant; a goodlie gallerie, well made, very long; new kitchen; new larder; and all other houses of office belonging unto the same; moted round aboute; whereunto doth adjoyne a goodly fayre orchard, with very pleasaunte walkes in the same' (Sir R. C. Hoare's *Modern Wiltshire*).

This account seems to describe a house that had been erected by Walter Lord Hungerford within the space of the last five years. However, it is certain that his father Sir Edward had also resided at Heytesbury, and the present document shows that in his time the manor-place was already out of 'good receipt' and ample furniture.

THE HUNGERFORD FAMILY.

The reader will not be surprised at further scandal being attached to the family of the Hungerfords, instances of whose degradation we have just recorded. Hence has arisen the popular story of the device of a toad having been introduced into their armorial bearings; but we are assured that this report is in every way nonsensical. 'Argent, three toads sable,' says the Rev. Mr. Jackson, 'is certainly one of their old quarterings, as may be seen upon one of the monuments in the chapel at Farley Castle. But it was borne by the Hungerfords for a very different reason. Robert the second Lord, who died in 1459, had married the wealthy heiress of the Cornish family of *Bottreaux;* and this was one of the shields used by *her* family, being in fact nothing more than an allusion, not uncommon in heraldry, to the name. This was spelled variously, *Bottreaux* or *Botterelles;* and the device was probably assumed from the similarity of the old French word *Botterel*, a toad (see Cotgrave), or the old Latin word *Botterella*,—the marriage with the Bottreaux heiress, and the assumption of the arms, having taken place *many years before* any member of the Hungerford family was attainted or executed (as some of them afterwards were), so that the toad story, which is in Defoe's *Tour*, falls to the ground.'

The town house of the Hungerfords, and which we have already mentioned, was one of the stately mansions which formerly embellished the north bank of the Thames, and stood between York House, and Suffolk, now Northumberland House. The estate had now devolved to Sir Edward

Hungerford, who was principally noted as a spendthrift. He sat in Parliament many years, sold in the same time twenty-eight manors, and ran through a fortune of thirty thousand pounds per annum. Malcolm is therefore correct in his conjecture as to Sir Edward's waning fortunes inducing him to convert his house and gardens into a public market. One of his extravagant freaks was to give five hundred pounds for a wig which he first wore at the coronation of Charles II. Malcolm tells us that, 'influenced by the same motives that prompted his illustrious eastern neighbours, he determined to sacrifice the honours of his ancestors at the shrine of Plutus, and obtained an Act of Parliament in the reign of Charles II. to make leases of the site of his mansion and grounds, where a market was soon afterwards erected.' This privilege was granted in 1679; the market rights were fully established in 1685, when they were granted to Sir Stephen Fox and Sir Christopher Wren, who became proprietors of the market estate. The vainglory of the Hungerfords was not, however, forgotten in the market-house; for in a niche on the north side was placed a bust of Sir Edward Hungerford in the 500-guinea wig. Beneath was this inscription:

> 'Forum utilitatæ publicæ per quam necessariam,
> Regis Caroli secundi inuente Majestatæ propriis
> Sumptibus erexit, per fecitque D. Edvardus
> Hungerford, Balnei Miles, Anno MDCLXXXII.'

Sir Edward did not, however, retrieve his fallen fortunes: he is said to have lived for the last thirty years of his life on charity, and died at the advanced age of 115! By him Farleigh was sold in 1686 to the Bayntons, and it next came into the possession of the Houltons, in which family it still remains. They did not, however, take up their abode in the old castle of the Hungerfords, but at a house in a different part of the parish, adding a park and picturesque grounds.

The next record of the Hungerford family shows a member of it in a more favourable light than his predecessors, but strikingly illustrates the transitoriness of human existence. The spendthrift Sir Edward had an only son, Edward, to whom is dedicated the volume entitled *Humane Prudence*, consisting of quaint maxims and sentences, edited by 'W. de Britaine.' Edward Hungerford was not only heir to a noble fortune, but by a very early marriage, at the age of nineteen, with Lady Alathæa Compton, became entitled, had they both lived, to still larger possessions. 'You have,' says the dedication, 'made a fair progress in your studies *beyond your years.*' 'The *nobleness of your stock* is a spur to virtue.' 'As much as you excel others *in fortune,*' etc. Such phraseology could only be addressed to some young man of good family and great prospects. But Sir Edward's son died in September 1681, aged twenty, and the *Humane Prudence* did not appear till 1682, which renders it doubtful whether Sir Edward's son was the person to whom the book was dedicated.

Here our glances at the chequered fortunes of the Hungerfords must end. Aubrey has this quaint regret for this family decadence. In his *Miscellanies* he points to the place for its 'local fatality,' telling us : ' The honourable family of the Hungerfords is probably of as great antiquity as any in the county of Wilts. Hungerford (the place of the barony) was sold but lately by Sir Edward Hungerford, Knight of the Bath, as also the noble and ancient seat of Farleigh Castle. But that this estate should so long continue is not very strange ; for it being so vast, 'twas able to make several withstandings against the shock of fortune.'

John Britton, in his *Autobiography*, tells us the Hungerford family possessed numerous estates, manors, and mansions, in the counties of Wilts, Berks, Somerset, Gloucester, etc. 'Though, at the zenith of its prosperity, the Hungerford genealogical tree spread its branches over a wide tract of territory, it had dwindled almost to nothing in my boyish days, and was said to have had one of its last distant female representatives in Chippenham, near the end of the last century.' Mr. Jackson, in the *Wiltshire Magazine*, describes two chapels founded by the Hungerfords in the cathedral of Salisbury; a redeeming record wherewith to close our *Hungerfordiana*.

THE HOUSE OF FERRERS.

THE very ancient and honourable family of Shirley, of whom Earl Ferrers is the head, has had the good fortune to be illustrated by an historical narrative, compiled by a distinguished member of its own house. Sir Thomas Shirley of Botolph's Bridge composed three distinct MS. histories of the Shirleys, all of which are preserved in the British Museum. From these records it appears that the Shirleys derive descent from Sasnallo or Sewallus de Etington, whose name, says Dugdale in his *Antiquities of Warwickshire*, argues him to be of old English stock. He resided at Nether Etington, in the county of Warwick, about the reign of King Edward the Confessor, which place had been the seat of his ancestors, there is reason to believe, for many generations before that period. 'After the Conquest,' says Sir Bernard Burke, 'the lordship of Etington was given to Henry Earl of Ferrers, in Normandy, who was one of the principal adventurers with the Norman Duke William, and was held under him by this Sewallus, with whose posterity in the male line it has continued to the present reign; the late Hon. George

Shirley, who died in 1787, having been owner thereof.' This long continuance of ownership is mentioned by Dugdale, who says, in his *Warwickshire*, that 'Etington is the only place in the county which could glory in an uninterrupted succession of its owners for so long a space of time.' The above-mentioned Sewallus founded and endowed the Church of Nether Etington. He had large possessions; his estate in this place only amounting to seventeen hides of land, whence he must have been no less than a thane in the time of the Saxons, which was the same degree of honour among them as a baron or peer of England after the Norman Conquest.

Sir Thomas Shirley, Knt., M.P. for the county of Warwick, in the fourteenth year of Edward III., is said to be 'the great founder of the family of Shirley, famous in his time for his valour, and for the many services he rendered to the Kings of England against the French.' His son and successor, Sir Hugh Shirley, Knt., was made grand falconer to Henry IV. in 1400. He was killed fighting on the side of the same monarch at the battle of Shrewsbury, being one of those who were habited as the king, and taken for him by the opposite party. Shakspeare, in the first part of King Henry IV. Act v. sc. 4, makes Douglas, when fighting and nearly worsting the king, thus accosted by Prince Henry:

'Hold up thy head, vile Scot! or thou art like
Never to hold it up again. The spirits
Of *Shirley*, Stafford, Blount, are in my arms;

It is the Prince of Wales that threatens thee,
Who never promiseth but he means to pay.'

Sir Ralph Shirley, son and successor of Sir Thomas, was one of the chief commanders under Henry v. at Agincourt.

By the marriage of Sir Henry Shirley, Bart., with the Lady Dorothy, youngest daughter and co-heir of Robert Devereux, Earl of Essex and Lord Ferrers of Chartley (the favourite minister of Queen Elizabeth), the present Earl Ferrers enjoys Chartley and twelve other manors in the county of Stafford. By this alliance the Earls of Ferrers quarter the arms of France and England with their own; the Earl of Essex having descended maternally from Richard Plantagenet, Earl of Cambridge, grandson of Edward III. (*Burke*).

Sir Robert Shirley, who founded the church at Staunton Harold in 1653, was the youngest son by the above marriage. He was a zealous royalist, who was committed to the Tower by the usurper Cromwell, May 4, 1650. He was condemned to close imprisonment; and having remained there for some months, but nothing being proved against him to warrant his detention, after several petitions he was set at liberty, that he might be able to furnish the thirteen horses and arms charged by the Parliament on his estate. Sir Robert's building of the church was in those fanatic times hypocritically made a fault; for Beck says: 'It being told the usurping power then reigning that Sir Robert Shirley had built a church, they directed an order of council to him to fit out a *ship*, saying, he that could afford to build a church could no doubt afford to equip a man-of-war.' Sir Robert appears to have been altogether imprisoned in the Tower seven times, where he died November 6, 1656, in his twenty-eighth year, not without a suspicion of having been poisoned by his enemies. A funeral sermon was preached from Luke vii. 5, 'He loved our country much, and hath built us a synagogue.' In a book at Staunton, wherein are kept a number of official letters signed by Charles I. to one of his lordship's ancestors, is a letter of condolence written by Charles II. to Dame Catherine Shirley after the death of her husband. All that Charles, however, did for the family on his restoration, to recompense their losses sustained in the cause of his father, was to create the next heir Master of the Horse and Steward of the Household to his Queen Catherine of Spain; and to make him a present of his own portrait (a small full length, highly finished), and five other pictures (King Charles's Beauties), being duplicates of ladies of his Court, by Sir Peter Lely. The last-mentioned nobleman was, September 13, 1711, advanced to the dignity of Viscount Tamworth and Earl Ferrers.

Some years after this, the annals of the family were stained by the records of a foul and brutal murder, committed by Laurence fourth Earl of Ferrers on the body of his aged land-steward, named Johnson, in January 1760. Lord Ferrers, who was a man of violent and ungovernable temper, and of whose brutality there are many instances on record, had behaved to his wife with such cruelty as to oblige her to apply to Parliament for redress, when was passed an Act for allowing her a separate maintenance, to be raised out of his lordship's estates, and Johnson was appointed receiver of the rents. At this time he stood high in Lord Ferrers' opinion; but he, suspecting that Johnson had combined with the trustees to disappoint him in a contract for coal mines, thenceforth spoke of him as a villain. He gave him warning to quit a farm which he held of his lordship; but finding that the trustees under the Act of Separation had already granted a lease of it, he was annoyed, and from that moment meditated cruel revenge.

However, the Earl so craftily dissembled, that Johnson imagined he was never on better terms with his master; and having arranged with him to come to Staunton on Friday, January 18, 1760, he went, and was admitted into the presence of the Earl, who had contrived to send all the persons from the house except three female servants. When the Earl and Johnson were together, his lordship ordered him to settle an account, and soon after presented him a paper purporting to be a confession of his villany, which he required him to sign. This Johnson refused; and on expostulating with his lordship, the latter drew a pistol from his pocket, and bade him kneel down. He knelt on one knee, when Lord Ferrers cried out so loudly as to be heard by a servant at the kitchen-door, 'Down on your other knee. Declare what you have acted against Lord Ferrers. Your time is come; you must die!' And immediately firing the pistol, the ball entered his body under the last rib. He did not fall; but expressing both by looks and words the sensations of a dying man, the Earl, though he had intended to shoot Johnson, felt involuntary remorse, and ordered the servants to assist him into bed. A surgeon was sent for; but not arriving till the evening, the Earl had himself applied a pledget dipped in Arquebusade water. On the arrival of the surgeon, the Earl told him Johnson was a villain who deserved to die; but as he had spared his life, he desired him to do all he could for him.

From this time, Lord Ferrers, who had been sober when he shot Johnson, continued to drink strong beer till he became drunk; and giving way to violent fits of rage, he came into the room where the dying man lay, and pulled him by the wig, calling him 'Villain,' and again threatening to shoot him, while he was with difficulty prevented tearing off the bedclothes to strike him. Nor would he consent to his being removed to his own house at Lount, declaring that he would keep him there to plague him. In the night, however, Johnson was removed to his own house, where he died at nine o'clock next morning. Horace Walpole relates the circumstances with some difference, telling us 'the Earl sent away all his servants but one, and, like that heroic murderess Queen Christina, carried the poor man through a gallery and several rooms, locking them after him, and then bade the man kneel down, for he was determined to kill him. The poor creature flung himself at his feet, but in vain, was shot, and lived twelve hours. Mad as this action was from the consequences, there was no frenzy in his behaviour. He got drunk, and at intervals talked of it coolly, but did not attempt to escape till the colliers beset his house, and were determined to take him alive or dead.' Another account states: As soon as he (Johnson) was dead, the neighbours set about seizing the murderer, and on reaching Staunton they found him on his way to the stable, half dressed. He, however, returned to the house, fastened the doors, and stood on the defence; but the people still loitering about, he was seen by one Curtis, a collier, on the bowling-green, armed with a blunderbuss, two or three pistols, and a dagger; but Curtis, far from being intimidated, walked up to the Earl, who was so struck with his determined resolution, that he suffered himself to be seized without resistance. He was thence committed to the gaol at Leicester, and thence to the Tower of London.

Lord Ferrers was tried by his peers in Westminster Hall, April 16, and two following days, 1760. Horace Walpole was present, and describes Lord Ferrers to have behaved rationally and coolly; though it was a strange contradiction to see a man trying, by his own sense, to prove himself out of his senses. It was more shocking to see his two brothers brought to prove the lunacy in their own blood, in order to save their brother's life. Many peers were absent. Never was a criminal tried more literally by his own *peers;* for the three persons who interested themselves most in the examination were at least as mad as he—Lord Ravensworth, Lord Talbot, and Lord Fortescue: indeed, the first was almost frantic. The seats of the peeresses were not near full. After Lord Ferrers was condemned, he made an excuse for pleading madness, to which he was forced by his family. He was condemned to be hanged, and to be anatomized, according to the new Act of Parliament.

The night he received the sentence he played at picquet with the Tower warders, would play for money, and would have continued to play longer than he did, but they refused. The governor of the Tower shortened his allowance of wine after his conviction, agreeably to the recent Act of Parliament. This he much disliked, and at last pressed his brother the clergyman to intercede that at least he might have more porter. His brother protested against it; but at last consenting (and he did obtain it), then, said the Earl, 'Now is as good a time as any to take leave of you—adieu!'

The night before his death he made one of his keepers read to him the play of *Hamlet*. He paid all his bills in the morning, after he was in bed, as if leaving an inn; and half an hour before the sheriff fetched him, corrected some verses he had written in the Tower, in imitation of the Duke of Buckingham's epitaph, '*Dubius sed non improbus vixi.*' These verses were found in his apartment in the Tower, and were as follows:

> 'In doubt I lived, in doubt I die,
> Yet stand prepared the vast abyss to try,
> And, undismayed, expect eternity!'

A minute journal of Lord Ferrers's whole behaviour was kept, to see if there was any madness in it. Dr. Munro, after the trial, made an affidavit of his lunacy. 'The Washingtons,' says Walpole, 'were certainly a very frantic race, and I have no doubt of madness in him, but of a very pardonable sort.' Two petitions from his mother and all his family were presented to the king, who said, as the House of Lords had unanimously found him guilty, he would not interfere. The Lord Keeper presented another: the king would not hear him.

The Earl received sentence to be hung on April 21, but he was, in consideration of his rank, respited till the 5th of May. On the last morning he dressed himself in his wedding-clothes, and said he thought this at least as good an occasion of putting them on as that for which they were first made. This marked the strong impression on his mind. His mother wrote to his wife in a weak, angry style, telling her to intercede for him as her duty, and to swear to his madness. But this was not so easy: in all her cause before the Lords, she had persisted that he was not mad. His courage rose where it was most likely to fail. Even an awful procession of about two hours—from the Tower to Tyburn—with that mixture of pageantry, shame, and ignominy, nay, and of delay, could not dismount his resolution. He set out from the Tower at nine, amidst crowds—thousands. First went a string of constables; then one of the sheriffs in his chariot and six, the horses draped with ribands; next, Lord Ferrers in his own landau and six, his coachman crying all the way; guards at each side; the other sheriff's chariot followed empty, with a mourning-coach and six, a hearse, and the Horse Guards. The other sheriff, Vaillant, the French bookseller in the Strand, was in the coach with the prisoner. Lord Ferrers at first talked on indifferent matters, and observing the prodigious confluence of people, he said, 'But they never saw a lord hanged, and perhaps will never see another.' One of the dragoons was thrown by his mare's leg entangling in the hind-wheel. Lord Ferrers expressed much concern, and said, 'I hope there will be no death to-day but mine,' and was pleased when Vaillant told him the man was not hurt. Vaillant made excuses to him on his office. 'On the contrary,' said the Earl, 'I am much obliged to you. I feared the disagreeableness of the duty might make you depute your under-sheriff. As you are so good as to execute it yourself, I am persuaded the dreadful apparatus will be conducted with more expedition.' He told the sheriff he had written to the king to beg that he might suffer where his ancestor the Earl of Essex had suffered, and was in great hopes of obtaining that favour, as he had the honour of quartering part of the same arms, and of being allied to his Majesty; and that he thought it was hard that he must die at the place appointed for the execution of common felons. The chaplain of the Tower talked to the Earl on religion, but he received it impatiently; and all he could obtain was permission to repeat the Lord's Prayer on the scaffold.

The House of Ferrers.

The procession was stopped by the crowd, when the Earl said he was dry, and wished for some wine-and-water; which being refused, he replied, 'Then I must be content with this,' and took some pigtail tobacco out of his pocket. As they drew nigh, the Earl, taking out his watch, gave it to Vaillant, desiring him to accept it as a mark of gratitude for his kind behaviour, adding, 'It is scarce worth your acceptance, but I have nothing else: it is a stop watch, and a pretty accurate one.' He then gave five guineas to the chaplain, and took out as much for the executioner.

When they came to Tyburn, his coach was detained some minutes by the crowd; but as soon as the door was opened, he stepped out and readily mounted the scaffold. It was hung with black at the expense of the family. Under the gallows was a newly-invented stage, to be struck from under him. He showed no fear or discomposure, only just looking at the gallows with a slight motion of dissatisfaction. He said little, kneeled for a moment to the prayer; said, 'Lord have mercy upon me, and forgive me my errors,' and immediately mounted the upper stage. He had come pinioned with a black sash, and was unwilling to have his hands tied or his face covered, but was persuaded to both. When the rope (said to be a silken one) was put round his neck, he turned pale, but recovered instantly; and but seven minutes elapsed from leaving the coach to the signal given for striking the stage. He was quite dead in four minutes. Here the decency ended. The sheriffs fell to eating and drinking on the scaffold as he was still hanging, which he did for above an hour. The executioners fought for the rope, and the one who lost it cried. The mob tore off the black as relics; 'but,' adds Walpole, 'the universal crowd behaved with great decency and admiration, as they well might, for no exit was ever made with more sensible resolution and with less ostentation.'

After execution the body was conveyed to Surgeons' Hall to undergo the remainder of the sentence, and was there publicly exposed to view. There is a print of 'Earl Ferrers as he lay in his coffin at Surgeons' Hall.' On the evening of the 8th of May the body was delivered to the Earl's friends for interment. This, it is said, was in a grave fourteen feet under the tower of old St. Pancras' Church; but upon the removal of the latter in 1848, we did not hear of the finding of the remains. The bill of expenses for the execution is said to have been found at Staunton, and among the articles enumerated is the silken rope. The landau in which the Earl rode to Tyburn was afterwards locked up in a coach-house at East Acton, and never again used. There it remained until it fell to pieces.

Neither within Westminster Hall nor without, on the days of trial, was there the least disturbance, though the hall was full, and the whole way from Charing Cross to the House of Lords was lined with crowds. 'The foreigners,' says Walpole, 'were struck with the awfulness of the proceeding. It was new to their ideas to see such deliberate justice, and such dignity of nobility mixed with no respect for birth in the catastrophe, and still more humiliated by anatomizing the criminal.' During the trial in the Hall, the cell to which the prisoner retired was on fire, which, by sawing away some timbers, was put out without any alarm to the Court.[1]

A singular tradition is current in the Ferrers family. The park of Chartley, in Staffordshire, is a wild, romantic spot, and was formerly attached to the Royal Forest of Needwood and the Honour of Tutbury, of the whole of which the ancient family of Ferrers were the puissant lords. Their immense possessions, now forming part of the Duchy of Lancaster, were forfeited by the attainder of Earl Ferrers after his defeat at Burton Bridge, where he led the rebellious Barons against Henry III. The Chartley estate being settled in dower, was alone reserved, and has been handed down to its present possessor. In the park is preserved the indigenous Staffordshire cow, small in stature, of sand-white colour, with black ears, muzzle, and tips at the hoofs. In the year of the battle of Burton Bridge a black calf was born; and the downfall of the great house of Ferrers happening at the same period, gave rise to the tradition, which to this day has been current among the common people, that the birth of a parti-coloured calf from the wild breed in Chartley Park is a sure omen of death within the same year to a member of the lord's family; and by a noticeable coincidence, a calf of this description has been born when-

[1] The Countess of Ferrers, who, after his lordship's death, was married to Lord Frederick Campbell, brother to John fourth Duke of Argyll, was unfortunately burnt to death at her seat, Coomb Bank, Kent, in 1807.

ever a death has happened in the family of late years. The decease of the Earl and his Countess, of his son Lord Tamworth, of his daughter Mrs. William Joliffe, as well as the deaths of the son and heir of the eighth Earl and his daughter Lady Frances Shirley, were each preceded by the ominous birth of a calf. In the spring of 1855, an animal, perfectly black, was calved by one of this weird tribe in the park of Chartley, and it was soon followed by the death of the Countess. (Abridged from the *Staffordshire Chronicle*.) This curious tradition has been cleverly wrought into a romantic story, entitled *Chartley, or the Fatalist*.

THE HOUSE OF TALBOT.

THE noble family of Talbot, of which the Earl of Shrewsbury is generally regarded as the head, though his right was disputed by the Talbots of Malahide, and those of Bashall, in Yorkshire (now extinct in the male line), is of Norman extraction, and from the Conquest has held a foremost place in the annals of English history and of chivalry. The first upon record is Richard de Talbot, who is mentioned in *Domesday Book* as holding 'nine hides of land under Walter Gifford, Earl of Buckingham.' His son Hugh, having been governor of the King's Castle at Plessey, or Pleshey, in Essex, assumed the monastic cowl late in life, and died a monk in the Abbey of Beaubeck, in Normandy. His grandson Gilbert was warder of the Castle of Ludlow, and attended the coronation of Richard I. in a distinguished capacity; and his grandson, another Gilbert, having been placed in command over the 'marches' of Herefordshire, married Gwendoline, daughter of the Prince or King of South Wales, whose arms his descendants have borne heraldically ever since. His grandson, a third Sir Gilbert, who had been involved in the execution of Piers Gaveston, Earl of Cornwall, received the king's pardon, and was summoned to Parliament as a baron in 1331. His son and successor, Sir Richard Talbot, was summoned as a baron to Parliament in 1332-55; and being an eminent officer under Edward III., was made by the king a knight-bannaret on the field of battle. He owned large estates on the borders of Wales; among others, Gooderich Castle on the Wye, where he resided in great state and splendour. It was this nobleman's grandson, John Talbot, whom Shakspeare terms 'the great Alcides of the field,' who became the first Earl of Shrewsbury.

Gooderich Castle, though not of large dimensions, contained all the different works which constitute a complete ancient baronial castle. The general design forms a parallelogram, defended by a round tower at each of the angles, with an Anglo-Saxon keep. The entrance through a dark vaulted passage is the most striking feature. The chapel is graceful, and the hall stately, of the time of Edward I. Another room of almost equal size leads to the Ladies' Tower. The ruin is mantled with ivy and clematis. A castle, which belonged to one Goodric, stood here before the Conquest; the structure underwent alteration down to the reign of Henry VI.

Born towards the close of the thirteenth century, and having married the heiress of the proud house of Furnival, John Talbot was summoned to Parliament in 1409 as 'Johannes Talbot de Furnyvall.' In 1412 he was appointed

THE HOUSE OF TALBOT. 137

Lord Justice of Ireland, and two years later Lord-Lieutenant. This post he held for seven years. But it was not on the narrow theatre of Ireland that he manifested his great military capacity. It was in France, where he took the field under Henry V., that he displayed those great qualities which made him the terror of the French nation. His earlier feats of arms were shown at the siege and capture of Meaux. He was with Henry V. when he died, and he seems to have inherited the spirit of his royal master. Equally valiant and faithful was he to that master's successor, Henry VI., for whom he gained so many battles on French soil, that the peasant mothers of Normandy hushed their children to rest by the bare mention of 'the dogge Talbot' being near. Checked for a moment at Patay by the Maid of Orleans, he was once taken prisoner; but being speedily exchanged, he soon retrieved the honour of the English arms. In reward, he was created Earl of Shrewsbury in England, and Waterford in Ireland; reappointed to his old viceregal post; and made High Steward of Ireland,—the highest honours which at that time were open to a subject.

After this, he went once more to fight in France. We find him in command of the fleet, landing and taking Falaise, and as Lieutenant of the Duchy of Aquitaine, marching to the south, and forcing Bordeaux and other towns in that part to surrender to English arms. Thence he advanced to the relief of Chatillon, and giving the besieging French army battle, 17th July 1453, in the eightieth year of his age, he received a wound in the thigh which proved immediately mortal.

Talbot had been victorious in no less than forty battles and dangerous skirmishes; and his death proved fatal to the English rule in France, which never flourished afterwards. He was buried at Whitchurch, in Shropshire, where a fine recumbent monument records his honours in terms very nearly coincident with the well-known lines of Shakspeare:

> 'Valiant Lord Talbot, Earl of Shrewsbury,
> Created for his rare success in arms,
> Great Earl of Wachford, Waterford, and Valence;
> Lord Talbot of Goodric and Urchinfield;
> Lord Strange of Blackmere; Lord Verdun of Alton;
> Lord Cromwell of Wingfield; Lord Furnival of Sheffield;
> The thrice victorious Lord of Falconbridge;
> Knight of the noble order of St. George,
> Worthy St. Michael, and the Golden Fleece;
> Great Mareschal to Henry the Sixth
> Of all his wars within the realm of France.'

In rebuilding the church at Whitchurch about a century and a half ago, the urn was found which contained the heart of the Earl of Shrewsbury, carefully embalmed, and wrapped in a covering of what was once handsome crimson velvet.

John second Earl of Shrewsbury, true to his family's devotion to the Lancastrian cause, fell, with his brother Sir Christopher, at the battle of Northampton, 10th July 1460, fighting under the Red Rose. His third son, Sir Gilbert Talbot, who was High Sheriff of Shropshire in the reign of

Richard III., but proved a staunch adherent to the Earl of Richmond at Bosworth, commanded the right wing of his army on that memorable field, and received knighthood, with a grant of lands, for his valiant conduct, from the victor. In two years afterwards, Sir Gilbert had a command at the battle of Stoke, and was made a knight-banneret; and George, the fourth Earl of Shrewsbury, was installed as Knight of the Garter for his valiant conduct at the same battle.

George, the sixth Earl of Shrewsbury, had the custody of Mary Queen of Scots, and assisted at her execution. His lordship married secondly Elizabeth of Hardwick, who had already been thrice married. 'She was a woman of masculine understanding and conduct; proud, furious, selfish, and unfeeling. She was a builder, a buyer and seller of estates, a money-lender, a farmer, a merchant of lead, coals, and timber. She died immensely rich.'

The fortunes of the Duke of Shrewsbury present a remarkable instance of the attainment of the highest honours of rank and state, but limited to his own individual enjoyment of them. He was the elder son of the eleventh Earl of Shrewsbury, who died of a wound received in his duel with George Villiers, second Duke of Buckingham, at Barnes. He was born in the year of the Restoration, and had Charles II. for his godfather. In 1694 he was created Marquis of Alton and Duke of Shrewsbury, and installed a Knight of the Garter. His Grace was a prominent statesman in the reigns of William and Mary, Queen Anne, and

George I. He had quitted the Church of Rome and become a Protestant in 1679, and by his steady adherence to the Protestant cause had incurred the displeasure of James II. He was one of the seven who in June 1688 joined the celebrated Association, inviting over the Prince of Orange. At the demise of Queen Anne (who delivered to him the Treasurer's staff on her death-bed), the Duke of Shrewsbury was at the same time Lord-Lieutenant of Ireland, Lord High Treasurer of Great Britain, and Lord Chamberlain,—a circumstance, says Sir Bernard Burke (*Peerage*, edit. 1862), previously unparalleled in our history. His Grace on this occasion secured the Hanoverian accession by at once signing the order for proclaiming George I. The Duke married the daughter of the Marquis of Palliotti, but died without issue; when the dukedom and marquisate expired, and the earldom, etc., reverted to his cousin.[1]

In August 1857, died Bertram seventeenth Earl of Shrewsbury, without leaving any cousin or male kinsman to succeed him in his honours and estates; and it was not until the month of June in the following year that the

[1] When Addison was on his travels in Italy, at Florence he spent some days with the Duke of Shrewsbury, 'who, cloyed with the pleasures of ambition, and impatient of its pains, fearing both parties and loving neither, had determined to hide in an Italian retreat talents and accomplishments which, if they had been united with fixed principles and civil courage, might have made him the foremost man of his age. These days, we are told, passed pleasantly, and we can easily believe it; for Addison was a delightful companion when he was at his ease, and the Duke, though he seldom forgot that he was a Talbot, had the invaluable art of putting at ease all who came near him' (*Macaulay*).

House of Lords was satisfied that Earl Talbot had made out his claim to the Earldom of Shrewsbury and the Irish honours which had always belonged to that ancient and noble title. On the 10th of June 1858 he took his seat in the House of Peers as Premier Earl of England, being the only nobleman in that grade of the peerage who takes precedence of Edward Earl of Derby. 'The Great Shrewsbury Case,' as it was called, not without good reason, involved the inheritance not only of a title celebrated in the pages of Shakspeare, and closely interwoven with the thread of English and French history, but also the possession of the costly seat, Alton Tower, and other large landed estates, to the extent of £50,000 or £60,000 a-year, all of which had been bequeathed by Earl Bertram to an infant of the Howard family, with the hope and intention that they should never pass into Protestant hands. The case created great interest in the higher circles of society, and no small amount of religious bigotry was evoked on both sides. Eventually, after a long and expensive suit, it was ruled that the estates ought to pass with the titles. Earl Talbot had the Earldom of Shrewsbury adjudged to him, as being descended through William Talbot, Bishop of Durham, and John Talbot of Salwarp, from Sir John Talbot of Allbrighton, county of Salop, and of Grafton, county of Worcester; he lived in the reigns of Henry VII. and Henry VIII., and his father, Sir Gilbert Talbot of Grafton, was the youngest son of John second Earl of Shrewsbury, who fell fighting in the cause of the Red Rose of the House of Lancaster, on the bloody field of Northampton, July 10, 1460. This peerage case, therefore, was singular in one respect,—namely, that in order to prove a common ancestor to Bertram seventeenth Earl, and Henry John eighteenth Earl, it was necessary to go back to a period of nearly 400 years.

A copy was given in evidence of an inscription from an ancient monument in the Church of Bromsgrove, Worcestershire, erected to the memory of Sir John Talbot of Allbrighton and his two wives. This inscription, as far as related to Sir John's issue, was in the following words: 'The Lady Margaret, hys first wyfe, bare to him three sonnes and five daughters, and ye Lady Elizabeth bare to him four sonnes and four daughters.' Major Talbot of Castle Talbot, county Wexford, who was brother of the late Countess of Shrewsbury, opposed Earl Talbot's claim in the House of Lords, and grounded that opposition upon his descent, as he alleged, from one of these younger sons of Sir John Talbot of Allbrighton by his first wife.—*Sir Bernard Burke's Peerage*, 1865.

GEORGE VILLIERS, DUKE OF BUCKINGHAM, ASSASSINATED BY JOHN FELTON.

THE murder of the Duke of Buckingham by Felton was the first great home event in one of the most eventful reigns recorded in English history. The prime favourite of two sovereigns, James I. and Charles I., for many years Buckingham had so conducted himself as to give great umbrage to the people; and the opinion generally held of him is expressed in this strong and coarse comment, current towards the end of his career:

> 'Who rules the kingdom? The King!
> Who rules the King? The Duke!!
> Who rules the Duke? The Devil!!!!'

George Villiers (afterwards Duke of Buckingham) first appeared at the court of James I. in 1614, and the political intriguers of the day set him up in opposition to the declining favourite Somerset. He was a man of attractive personal appearance, had been educated at the French Court, and at once fascinated the weak monarch, and rapidly made way in his affections. He heaped honours on him and his family; and Villiers rose as fast as Somerset fell; ultimately becoming more powerful than the latter nobleman, and as great a favourite with Prince Charles as he was with the king. He bore himself with great *hauteur* even to such men as the Lord Chancellor Bacon, who was compelled to dance attendance for days together in his ante-chamber among his servants, 'sitting upon an old wooden chest, with his purse and seal lying by him on that chest.' His brothers and male relatives were married to heiresses (sometimes compulsorily), and the female branches to the richest and noblest of the aristocracy; while all alike trafficked in titles and places, lodging about the court, and making the most of their lucrative interest.

But though this excited the jealousy of the courtiers, the people in general were not thoroughly roused against the favourite, until he had fomented the Quixotic expedition of Prince Charles into Spain, and accompanied him thither. The popular dislike to the Spanish match was intense, and the fear of popish innovation excessive: the favourite was therefore loudly condemned by all. At the same time, he was on the most intimate terms with his sovereign and prince, and the letters which passed between them evince a familiar intimacy which has scarcely a parallel in history. James addressed him as 'My sweet hearty,' 'My sweet Steenie [1] and gossip,' 'My only sweet

[1] This was no Christian name of the Duke's, but is a Scotticism for Stephen, bestowed on him by the king, who is said to have done so because the favourite's good looks reminded him of representations of St. Stephen, depicted with beautiful features, in accordance with Acts vi. 15.

and dear child;' and tattled about the favourite's family affairs more like an old nurse than a king. Charles addressed him as 'Steenie,' and consulted him on every subject of importance; while Buckingham returned the familiarity by addressing the king as 'Your sowship;' or, 'Dear dad and gossip;' and subscribing himself, 'Your humble slave and dog, Steenie;' with, 'I kiss your warty hands,' etc.

Buckingham was raised to the dukedom while at Madrid, in order that he might be elevated in the eyes of the Spaniards; but his dissipation and insolence disgusted them, as much as his freedom of speech and manners before the prince.

The infirmities of James, and the strong friendship of his son, kept Buckingham at the head of affairs until the death of the king. On the accession of Charles to the throne, the favourite assumed a still more powerful position; but this favouritism, and Buckingham's mal-administration, rendered him very unpopular; while the public plunderings of the favourite and his family knew no bounds. On the very day that the Duke was denounced in the House of Commons, his physician, Dr. Lambe—generally termed 'the Duke's devil'—who was believed to deal in the black art, and instigate the Duke's worst acts, was attacked in the streets of London, and so ill-treated that he died during the same day. A doggerel rhyme of fearful import then became current:

'Let Charles and George do what they can,
The Duke shall die, like Dr. Lambe.'

K

A paper was affixed to a post in Coleman Street, upon which were the three lines quoted at p. 143, and this addition: 'Let the Duke look to it; for they intend shortly to use him worse than they did the doctor; and if things be not shortly reformed, they will work a reformation for themselves.'

The Duke's life had been attempted at Rhé by a Jesuit armed with a three-edged knife; and an account of the event, with a woodcut of the knife, had been published on his return, to endear the Duke to all good Protestants. Popular feeling, however, ran counter to this. Sir Symonds D'Ewes relates that 'some of his friendes had advised him how generally he was hated in England, and how needfull it would bee, for his greater safetie, to weare some coate of maile, or some secret defensive armour; but the Duke slighting, saied, "It needs not; *there are no Roman spirits left.*"' Lady Davis, who had become celebrated for the foretelling of events, had confidently predicted the death of the Duke in 1628. A Latin distich was also in very general circulation. A copy, preserved in the Ashmolean MS., states it to have been 'made some few monthes before he (the Duke) was murthered, by John Marston.' An apparition was also stated to have announced the Duke's fate; but Clarendon considers this story was planned by the Countess and the person to whom it was said to have appeared, to inspire the Duke with a livelier regard to his own safety.

The following week the King and Duke journeyed in the same coach to Deptford. He parted with the king, and proceeded to Portsmouth, where a more sudden fate than

Lambe's awaited him, and is thus described in a letter sent by Sir Dudley Carleton to the Queen on the afternoon : ' This day, betwixt nine and ten of the clock in the morning, the Duke of Buckingham, then comming out of a parlor into a hall, to goe to his coach, and soe to the king (who was four miles off), having about him diverse lords, colonells, and captains, and many of his owne servants, was by one Felton (once a lieutenant of this our army) slaine at one blow with a dagger knife. In his staggering he turn'd about, uttering onely this word " Villaine !" and never spake word more ; but presently plucking out the knife from himselfe, before he fell to the ground, hee made towards the traytor two or three paces, and then fell against a table, although he were upheld by diverse that were neere him, that (through the villaine's close carriage in the act) could not perceive him hurt at all, but guess'd him to be suddenly overswayed with some apoplexie, till they saw the blood come gushing from his mouth and the wound so fast, that the life and breath at once left his begored body.'

The house in which the murder was committed is now standing in Portsmouth (No. 10, High Street), but has been so repeatedly altered, both within and without, in converting it first into an inn and then into a private house, that it retains scarcely any of its old features.

Howell says that Felton 'had thought to have done the deed' in the room where the Duke was being shaved, after rising from bed, 'for he was leaning upon the window all the while.'

Wotton thus describes the murder: 'The Duke came with Sir Thomas Fryer close at his ear; in the very moment as the said knight withdrew himself from the Duke, the assassin gave him, with a back blow, a deep wound into his left side, leaving the knife in his body, which the Duke himself pulling out, on a sudden effusion of spirits, he sank down under the table in the next room, and immediately expired.'

Sir Symonds D'Ewes, who was related to the Duchess of Buckingham, in his account of the murder, says: 'The Duke having received the stroake, instantlie clapping his right hand on his sword-hilt, cried out, "God's wounds! the villaine has killed me!"'

Felton had sewed in the crown of his hat, half within the lining, a written paper, which ran as follows: 'That man is cowardly base, and deserveth not the name of a gentleman o^r souldier, that is not willinge to sacrifice his life for the honor of his God, his kinge, and his countrie. Lett noe man commend me for doinge of it, but rather discommend themselves as the cause of it; for if God had not taken away o^r harts for o^r sinnes, he would not have gone so longe unpunished.—JNO. FELTON.'

At the death, the paper was not found, and what had become of it was not known for a certainty. It was long in the possession of Mr. Upcott, and had been found among the Evelyn papers at Wotton, endorsed twice over in John Evelyn's handwriting, 'A note found about Felton when he killed the Duke of Buckingham, 23 Aug. 1628.' Sir Edward

Nicholas, Secretary of State, who had the first possession of it, was one of the persons before whom Felton was examined at Portsmouth. His daughter married Sir Richard Browne, and the learned and philosophic Mr. John Evelyn married the only daughter of Sir Richard Browne. Lady Evelyn, the widow of his descendant, presented it to Mr. Upcott.

King Charles had parted but the day before from Buckingham, and was staying at Southwick Park, a seat of the Norton family a few miles from Portsmouth, from which place Carleton's letter is dated, he having probably posted there with the news. The King was at prayers, when Sir John Hippesly immediately went up to him and whispered the tidings in his ear. The King is reported to have heard it without visible emotion; but when the service was ended, he hastily went to his chamber, and bewailed his death passionately, casting himself on his bed with abundance of tears.

Felton had been bred a soldier, and came of a good family in Suffolk. During his imprisonment he was visited by the Earl and Countess of Arundel and their son, ' he being of their blood.' Sir Henry Wotton terms Felton ' a younger brother of mean fortune, by nature of a deep, melancholy, silent, and gloomy constitution.' Felton stated his inducements to the crime to be the imputations thrown out against the Duke in a pamphlet, and his denunciation by the people and Parliament. The latter was no doubt the real cause, inasmuch as, when Felton was exhorted by the royal chaplain to confess his motives, he answered, ' Sir,

I shall be brief: I killed him for the cause of God and my country.' It was this feeling which probably induced Felton to take so little interest in his own fate, when he might have escaped so easily, as is narrated in Carleton's letter.

Suspicion at first was excited towards the Frenchmen about the Duke, who were with difficulty saved from the vengeance of the Duke's attendants. Felton meanwhile walked quietly into the kitchen of the house, and remained there unnoticed until the first stupor of amazement had passed away, and the real murderer was sought for. He had expected a sudden death at the hands of the Duke's servants when he struck the blow, and it was this which induced him to fasten the written paper in his hat; he wished not to avoid the death he expected, and on the loud outcry of 'Where is the murderer?' he coolly confronted the enraged inquirers with 'I am the man!' His life was with difficulty saved, and he was conveyed under guard to the house of the governor of Portsmouth.

He had performed his journey to Portsmouth 'partly on horseback and partly on foot,' says Wotton; 'for he was indigent, and low in money.' But before leaving London, 'in a bye cutler's shop on Tower Hill, he bought a ten-penny knife (so cheap was the instrument of this great attempt), and the sheath thereof he sewed to the lining of his pocket, that he might at any moment draw forth the blade alone with one hand, for he had maimed the other.'[1]

---

[1] A different tale is told by the historians of Sheffield, who say: 'In 1626, Thomas Wild, cutler, living in the Crooked-bill Yard, High

ASSASSINATED BY JOHN FELTON.   151

Felton was conveyed to the Tower in September; and Charles would have had him put upon the rack to discover if he had any accomplices, but that the judges decided that 'torture was not justifiable according to the law of England.' He constantly affirmed that he did it of his own will, 'not maliciously, but out of an intent for the good of his country.' He was hanged at Tyburn, and his body conveyed to Portsmouth, and hung there in chains.

Buckingham was buried at Westminster secretly on the 17th of September, and a public funeral, with an *empty coffin*, paraded on the next night, guarded by soldiers with *raised* pikes and muskets, as if the people's well-known dislike was expected to be vented on his remains. His heart is affirmed to have been placed in the marble urn which forms the centre of the monument in Portsmouth church. It was at first, 'greatly in contravention of religious decorum,' erected within the communion rails, but has been removed to the north aisle of the chancel.

That Buckingham's unpopularity outlived him, is evident from the fears of the Court at his funeral; and the sympathy of the populace was more with Felton than with the murdered Minister. Such was his love of truth and rigid honour,

Street, made Lieutenant Felton the knife with which he stabbed the Duke of Buckingham. The knife was found in the Duke's body, and had a corporation mark upon it, which led to the discovery of the maker, who was immediately taken to the Earl of Arundel's house in London, when he acknowledged the mark was his, and that he had made Lieutenant Felton two such knives when he was recruiting at Sheffield, for which he charged him tenpence.'

that Felton obtained amongst his acquaintances the nickname of 'honest Jack,' one which, after his assassination, became extremely popular throughout the nation.

D'Israeli remarks: 'The assassination was a sort of theoretical one; so that when the king's attorney furnished the criminal with an unexpected argument, which appeared to him to have overturned his own, he declared that he had been in a mistake; and lamenting that he had not been aware of it before, from that instant his conscientious spirit sank into despair.' Meade also tells us that Sir Robert Brook and others who were present at the murder 'affirm, that when Felton struck the Duke, he exclaimed, "God have mercy upon thy soule;" which occasioned a friend of mine wittily to say, There was never man murdered with so much gospell.'

The strong public feeling in favour of Felton may be gathered from another anecdote. On the departure of the fleet, which Buckingham came to Portsmouth to command, in September 1628, after the king had made 'a gratious speech, they shouted, and, for a farewell, desired his Majestie to be good to John Felton, their once fellow-souldier.'

But it was not the rude populace and rough sailors only who lauded the act of the assassin. Meade, in a letter dated November 15, 1628, says: 'On Friday sennight was censured in the Star Chamber, Alex. Gill, B.D., at Oxford, and usher in Paul's school under his own father, for saying in Trin. Coll. that our king was fitter to stand in a Cheapside shop with an apron on, and say, "What lack you?" than to governe a kingdome; 2*d*, that the Duke was gone down to hell to meet King James there; 3*d*, for drinking a health to Felton, saying he was a sorry fellow, and had deprived him of the honour of doing that brave action, etc. His censure was, to be degraded both from his ministrie and degrees taken, to lose one ear in London and the other at Oxford, and be fined £2000.' In another letter, dated November 22, we are told, 'Gill is degraded;' but the fine there was mitigated, etc.

A collection of poems and songs relating to Buckingham and his assassination has been printed for the Percy Society, edited by the careful hand of the late Mr. Fairholt, F.S.A. Buckingham was so despised by the large majority of Englishmen, that his foul murder was hailed as a national deliverance; and the condemnatory poems which followed the Duke to the grave could only be exceeded by the laudations which were showered on Felton. In one of these poems, 'Felton's Epitaph,' the ignominy of his fate is most ingeniously construed into a triumph by the author of the lines ensuing. There is another copy of this poem in Ashmole MS., where it is said to have been 'made by D. Donn.' It varies a little in words, and is less pure than the following from the Sloane MS.; but the sense is the same. This is one of the best and most remarkable poems in the collection :

> 'Here uninterr'd suspends (though not to save
> Surviving frends th' expences of a grave)
> Felton's dead earth, which to the world must bee
> It's owne sadd monument, his elegie;

> As large as fame, but whether badd or good
> I say not: by himselfe 'twas writt in blood;
> For which his body is entomb'd in ayre,
> Archt o'er with heaven, sett with a thousand faire
> And glorious diamond starrs. A sepulchre
> That time can never ruinate, and where
> Th' impartiall worme (which is not brib'd to spare
> Princes corrupt in marble) cannot share
> His flesh; which if the charitable skies
> Embalme with teares, doeing those obsequies
> Belong to men, shall last, till pittying fowle
> Contend to beare his bodie to his soule.'

While the vicious character of the Duke held him up to popular odium, his mismanaged and crooked dealings as a politician made him amenable to the denunciations of the satirists, who were unsparing in their coarsest lampoons. The whole is a strongly coloured picture of popular feeling, which can only be reproduced to the modern eye in the apologetic words of the transcriber of the *Visions of Tundale:*

> 'Be it trowe, or be it fals,
> It is as the copie was.'

An addition to this strange eventful history will be found in Mr. Forster's *Life of Sir John Eliot;* namely, that on the day preceding Felton's attack there had been a mutiny among the seamen at Portsmouth, of which the stir had not yet subsided. In an unpublished letter of Nethersole's, Mr. Forster found: 'At Portsmouth, the day before, a sailor was certainly killed in a kind of mutiny there; some say by a servant of the Duke, others by his own hand.' Rous's *Diary* (Camden Society, 1856) gives from a letter of the Captain of the Guard, to whose custody Felton was committed after killing the Duke, an account of the above mutiny, when a sailor who had offended Buckingham was by a court-martial condemned to die. A rescue was attempted, when the Captain of the Fleet drew upon the sailors with great fury; and next the Duke himself, with a great company on horseback, drove the sailors on the port point, when many were dangerously hurt, and two killed outright. The captain saw the first mutineer carried with a guard to the gibbet, where he was hanged by another mutinous sailor. Thus Buckingham personally superintended the execution of the man who had merely 'affronted him,' and who could have had no part in the subsequent outbreak. That a long course of unbridled power and profligacy had produced insanity in Buckingham, is suggested as the only solution of his profanity and grossness. Retribution was but unworthily represented in the individual vengeance of Felton; but there can be little doubt that, had Buckingham evaded or survived the attack of the assassin, the long defied justice of England would at no distant period have consigned him to the executioner. (See *Notes and Queries*, 3d series, No. 189.)

DRAGON LEGENDS.

THERE is a curious class of household tales, the genuine appendices to the history of ancient families, long occupying the same ground and stations; and perhaps no other certain deduction can be drawn from such legends, except that the families to which they relate are of ancient popular repute, against whose gentle condition 'the memory of man runneth not to the contrary.'

'As to the matter-of-fact contained in these legends,' says Sir Bernard Burke, 'it is impossible to deny that, when a great part of England lay in moor, morass, and forest, wolves and bears must have been troublesome neighbours.' Wolves were by no means exterminated by King Edgar. The monks of Fors, in Wensleydale, about 1180, had a dangerous grant from Alan Earl of Richmond, of the flesh of all wild animals torn by wolves within their own dale. King James I. and VI. sometimes took the diversion of wolf-hunting in Scotland, in which kingdom the last wild wolf was killed as late as 1680; and in Ireland proclamations were issued against wolves in Antrim in the reign of Anne.

It is, however, much more difficult to account for serpents of a magnitude to require the intervention of a hero to rid the country of their terrors. These became magnified into dragons, which are thought to have been an exaggeration of the crocodile by old naturalists; for the pictured dragon resembles a huge lizard more than any other animal. In the *Apocalypse* the devil is called the dragon, on which account St. George, the patron saint of England, is usually painted on horseback, and killing at a dragon under his feet, as emblematical of the saint's faith and fortitude. The term Dragon was often applied allegorically, as to a Danish rover, a domestic tyrant, or, as in the well-known case of the Dragon of Wantley, a villanous overgrown lawyer, endowed with all the venom, maw, and speed of a flying eft, whom the gallant More of More Hall ' slew with nothing at all' but the aid of a good conscience, and a fair young maid of sixteen, 'to 'noint him o'ernight when he went to fight, and to dress him in the morning.' Of him we shall presently speak more at length.

How the idea of the crocodile could reach our villages centuries ago is a mystery; but it has been surmised that the real history of these crocodiles or alligators, if they are such, may be, that they were brought home by crusaders as specimens of dragons, just as Henry the Lion Duke of Brunswick brought from the Holy Land the antelope's horn, which had been palmed upon him as a specimen of a griffin's claw; and that they should be afterwards fitted with appropriate legends, is not surprising. At the west door of the

Cathedral of Cracow are hanging some bones said to have belonged to the dragon which inhabited the cave at the foot of the rock (the Wawel) on which the cathedral and royal castle stand; and this creature is said to have been destroyed by Kratz, the founder of the city. Others think that the dragon of the Crusaders must have been the boa constrictor. St. Jerome mentions the trail of a dragon seen in the sand in the desert, which appeared as if *a great beam* had been dragged along. Now, it is not likely that a crocodile would have ventured so far from the bank of the Nile as to be seen in the desert.

Recently an ingenious attempt has been made to identify the dragon with the crocodile. M. de Freminville cites many known facts of natural history, to prove that there is no reason to believe that crocodiles never inhabited Western Europe, merely because we do not now find them there. And, above all, he adduces the fact that, in the sand at the mouth of the Seine, at Harfleur, and Quillebœuf, entire skeletons of crocodiles have been found in a state only half fossilized. From all which he concludes, that the continual battles of the heroes of the middle ages were, in truth, real encounters with crocodiles.

A correspondent of *Notes and Queries*, No. 61, passing through the city of Brünn, in Moravia, had his attention drawn to the *Lindwurm*, or Dragon, preserved there from a very remote period. This monster, according to tradition, was invulnerable, like his brother of Wantley, except in a few well-guarded points; and from his particular predilection in favour of veal and young children, was the scourge and terror of the neighbourhood. The broken armour and well-picked bones of many doughty knights, scattered around the entrance to the cave he inhabited, testified to the impunity with which he had long carried on his depredations, in spite of numerous attempts to destroy him. The lindwurm at length fell a victim to the craftiness of a knight, who, to deceive his opponent, stuffed, as true to nature as possible, with unslaked lime, the skin of a freshly killed calf, which he laid before the dragon's cave. The monster, smelling the skin, is said to have rushed out instantly, and to have swallowed the fatal repast; and feeling afterwards, as may be readily expected, a most insatiable thirst, hurried off to a neighbouring stream, where he drank, until the water, acting upon the lime, caused him to burst. The inhabitants, on learning the joyful news, carried the knight and the lindwurm in triumph into the city of Brünn, where they have ever since treasured up the memento of their former tyrant. The animal or reptile thus preserved is undoubtedly of the crocodile or alligator species, though any attempt to count the distinguishing bones would be fruitless, the scaly back having been covered too thickly with pitch as protection from the weather. May not the legendary dragons have their origin from similar circumstances to those of this Brünn lindwurm?

Of all dragons, that of Wantley is the most celebrated. 'This famous monster had, according to old story, forty-four teeth of iron; and some historians say he used to swallow up churches full of people, fat parson and all, and pick his teeth with the steeple; but this was probably only scandal. Little children, however, it is certain, he used to munch up as we would an apple. He had eyes like live coals, with a long sting in his tail; and his sulphurous breath poisoned the country for ten miles round. The knight who went to fight this monster very wisely got himself a suit of armour stuck all over with iron spikes, so that he looked like a great hedgehog; and when the dragon tried to worry him, he was obliged to leave go again. Then the knight gave him some proper kicks in the ribs with the spikes at the end of his iron boots, and once ran his sword right into him, and killed him; but the dragon, forgetting he was dead, still fought on, till a great part of his tail being lopped off, and his blood pouring out by bucketsful, he cried out "Murder!" most lustily, and afterwards fainted away, and groaned, and kicked, and died. But, after all, the knight ran his sword into him several times, rightly conceiving that such a villain could never be too dead! If this story should not be true, it's founded on truth, and that's all the same thing. An overgrown rascally attorney at Wantley, near Rotherham, in Yorkshire, cheated some children out of a large estate; but a gentleman in the neighbourhood, arming himself with the spikes of the law, recovered their property for them; and the attorney having lost it and his character for ever, sickened, grieved, and died. But what would such a dry, every-day story of villany be worth without some poetical flourishes about it? or, as

Flutter says, "Really the common occurrences of this little dirty world are hardly worth relating without some embellishment."'[1]

'Old Wortley Montague (Lady Mary's husband),' says Walpole, 'lived on the very spot where the dragon of Wantley did,—only, I believe, the latter was much better lodged: you never saw such a wretched hovel—lean, unpainted, and half its nakedness barely shaded with harateen stretched till it cracks. Here the miser hoards health and money—his only two objects; he has chronicles in behalf of the air, and battens on tokay, his single indulgence, as he has heard it is particularly salutary. But the savageness of the scene would charm your Alpine taste: it is tumbled with fragments of mountains, that looked ready laid for building the world. One scrambles over a huge terrace, on which mountain ashes and various trees spring out of the very rocks; and at the brow is the den, but not spacious enough for such an inmate. However, I am persuaded it furnished Pope with this line, so exactly it answered to the picture:

"On rifted rocks, the dragon's late abode."'

St. Leonard's Forest had, some two centuries and a half since, a prodigy which ranks amongst Sussex traditions. Concerning this monster there was published a tract, entitled '*True and Wonderful:* a discourse relating to a strange and monstrous serpent or dragon lately discovered,

[1] Percy's *Reliques of Ancient Poetry.*

and yet living, to the great annoyance and divers slaughters both of men and cattle, by this strong and violent Poyson, in Sussex, two miles from Horsham, in a wood called St. Leonard's Forest, and thirtie miles from London, this present month of August 1614, with the true generation of serpents.'

The monster was 'nine feet or rather more in length, and shaped almost in the form of an *axle-tree of a cart*, a quantitie of thickness in the middest, and somewhat smaller at both ends!' He was blackish upon the back, and red under the belly; and besides having large feet, he was furnished with two large bunches 'so big as a footeball, which, as some think, will grow to wings.' 'I hope,' adds the narrator, 'that God will so defend the poor people in the neighbourhood, that he shall be destroyed *before he growe to fledge.*' He left a track behind him, 'as by a small similitude we may perceive in a snail.' His 'former part' he could 'shoote forth as a necke, supposed to be about an ell long.' He was 'of countenance very proud,' and carried himself 'with great arrogancie.' He cast his venom 'about four roddes,' thereby killing a man, a woman, and two mastiffs. He did not, however, devour his victims, either human or canine, but lived chiefly upon the conies of a neighbouring warren, which was found to be 'much scanted and impaired in the increase it had been wont to afford.'

This monster was perhaps, after all, nothing more than some misshapen log of wood that superstition had converted into a dragon.

A more romantic legend makes St. Leonard himself, after the pattern of the earlier saints Michael and George, the slayer of the dragon; and it may be reckoned as the prettiest relic of the legendary lore of Sussex, that wherever the blood of the saint was spilled during the dread encounter, there sprang up abundance of 'lilies of the valley,' which still adorn and perfume various spots in the forest. The legend goes on to state that the saint, on being asked what reward he would like for his meritorious service, demanded the eternal silence of the nightingale, which was granted; and hence it was predicted of the forest, that in it

> 'The Adders neber stynge,
> Nor ye Nyghtingales synge.'

The belief in monstrous serpents lurking among the woods of the Weald of Sussex was not quite extinct in the writer's boyhood, and it might very possibly be traced up through the middle ages to the period of Scandinavian and Teutonic romance; and when a great part of the county yet remained in a condition of forest, it would always be the interest of smugglers, gamekeepers, woodmen, and such like, to invest their several spheres with terrors for the young and the weak-minded, and to 'breathe a browner horrour o'er the woods' (M. A. Lower—*Old Speech and Words*).

It is curious to find that the district wherein we have been tracing these Dragon legends, has in our time yielded to the geologist gigantic evidences of a former world. In the beds of the Wealden series, in Tilgate

Forest, Dr. Mantell has found fragments of the most remarkable reptilian fossils yet discovered. In the grounds of the Crystal Palace at Sydenham are réstorations of these animals, sufficiently perfect to illustrate this reptilian epoch. They include the Iguanodon, a herbivorous lizard, exceeding in size the largest elephant, accompanied by the equally gigantic and carnivorous great Saurian (*Megalosaurus*), and by the two yet more curious reptiles, the forest or Weald Saurian (*Pylæosaurus*), and the Pterodactyl, an enormous bat-like creature, now running upon the ground like a bird; its elevated body and long neck not covered with feathers, but with skin, naked or resplendent with glittering scales, its head like that of a lizard or crocodile, and of preposterous size, with its long fore extremities stretched out, and connected by a membrane with the body and hind legs. Suddenly this mailed creature rose in the air, and realized or even surpassed in strangeness *the flying dragon of fable;* its fore-arms and its elongated wing-finger furnished with claws; hand and fingers extended, with the interspace filled up by a tough membrane; and its head and neck stretched out like that of the heron in its flight. When stationary, its wings were probably folded back like those of a bird; though perhaps, by the claws attached to its fingers, it might suspend itself from the branches of trees. In times when the belief in dragons was strong, these colossal remains, when unearthed, were not understood, and philosophers had yet to learn how to reconstruct an extinct animal, starting with a single bone.

It would therefore be a stretch of speculation to identify the dragons of the Sussex peasantry with the above fossil remains; but the association is very suggestive of the axiom, that truth is stranger than fiction.

A curious legend lingers about 'Tees-seated Sockburn, county Durham, where, by long descent, Conyers was lord.' The hall has disappeared, and the legend alone connects the deserted spot with a recollection of its early owners. Sir John Conyers, a doughty knight, is recorded to have slain a venomous wyvern, which was the terror of the country round, and to have been requited by a royal gift of the manor of Sockburn, to be held by the service of presenting a falchion to each bishop of Durham on his first entrance into the Palatinate. Truly could the Conyers say:

'By this sword we hold our land.'

The Norman name of Conyers may not be, as thought, the veritable style of the dragon-slaying knight of Saxon times; much less probable is it that the falchion of Cœur-de-Lion's days, still preserved in the modern house at Sockburn, belonged to him. But the sword of the Conyers was the title-deed to their estate. In compliance with the tenure, when each new bishop of Durham first comes to his diocese, the lord of Sockburn, meeting him in the middle of Neashamford or Croft Bridge, presents him with a falchion, addressing him in these words: 'My Lord Bishop, I here present you with the falchion wherewith the champion Conyers slew the worm, dragon, or fiery-flying serpent, which destroyed man, woman, and child; in memory of which, the king then reigning gave him the manor of Sockburn to hold by this tenure, that, upon the first entrance of every bishop into the county, this falchion should be presented.' The bishop returns it, wishing the Lord of Sockburn health and long enjoyment of the manor.

THE WORM OF LAMBTON HALL.

THIS strange story has often been told, but by none so well as by Surtees, the able historian of the county, in these words:

'The heir of Lambton fishing, as was his profane custom, in the Wear on a Sunday, hooked a small worm or eft, which he carelessly threw into a well, and thought no more of the adventure. The worm (at first neglected) grew till it was too large for its first habitation, and, issuing from the Worm Well, betook itself to the Wear, where it usually lay a part of the day coiled round a crag in the middle of the water. It also frequented a green mound near the well (the Worm Hill), where it lapped itself nine times round, leaving vermicular traces, of which grave living witnesses depose that they have seen the vestiges. It now became the terror of the country; and, amongst other enormities, levied a daily contribution of nine cows' milk, which was always placed for it at the green hill; and in default of which, it devoured man and beast.

'Young Lambton had, it seems, meanwhile totally repented him of his former life and conversation, had bathed himself in a bath of holy water, taken the sign of the cross, and joined the Crusaders. On his return home, he was extremely shocked at witnessing the effects of his youthful imprudences, and immediately undertook the adventure. After several fierce combats, in which the Crusader was foiled by his enemy's *power of self-union*, he found it expedient to add policy to courage; and not perhaps possessing much of the former, he went to consult a witch, or wise woman. By her judicious advice he armed himself in a coat of mail, studded with razor-blades; and thus prepared, placed himself on the crag in the river, and awaited the monster's arrival. At the usual time the Worm came to the rock, and wound himself with great fury round the armed knight, who had the satisfaction to see his enemy cut to pieces by his own efforts, whilst the stream, washing away the severed parts, prevented the possibility of reunion.

'There is still a sequel to the story. The witch had promised Lambton success only on one condition—that he should slay the first living thing which met his sight after the victory. To avoid the possibility of human slaughter, Lambton had directed his father, that as soon as he heard him sound three blasts on his bugle, in token of the achievement performed, he should release his favourite greyhound, which would immediately fly to the sound of the horn, and was destined to be the sacrifice. On hearing his son's bugle, however, the old chief was so overjoyed that he forgot the injunction, and ran himself with open arms to meet his son. Instead of committing a parricide, the conqueror again repaired to his adviser, who pronounced, as the alternative of disobeying the original instructions, that no chief of the Lambtons should die in his bed for seven or (as some accounts say) for nine generations,—a commutation which, to a martial spirit, had nothing probably very terrible, and which was willingly complied with.'

It is hardly worth while to add anything as to the verification of the alleged prophecy. Some thirty years ago, it was shown that both the father and the grandfather of the then Lord Durham died in their beds, when it was remarked that 'the period embraced in the supposed prediction must long since have expired.'

The Lambtons were a family of good and valorous repute long before the date of their family legend (which only ascends to the fourteenth century); and it does not appear that the hero of the tale reaped anything from his adventure, except the honour of the achievement, and a very singular curse on his descendants till the ninth generation.

The Worm Hill is not within the domain of Lambton in the county of Durham, but on the north bank of the Wear, in the estate of North Biddick, a mile and a half from *old* Lambton Hall. The hill is a small artificial cone of common earth and river gravel. The Worm Well lies between the hill and the Wear. Half a century ago the Worm Well was in repute as a *wishing well*, and was one of the scenes dedicated to the festivities and superstitions of Midsummer Eve. A *crooked pin* may sometimes be still discovered sparkling amongst the clean gravel at the bottom of the basin.

This legend and its traditions are thought to have been represented under the form of a gigantic snail. Mr. Halliwell records having seen, in Pynson's edition of *Kalender of Shepherdes*, a curious woodcut representing a snail defying the attacks of armed men. It was accompanied by the following lines:

> 'I am a beast of right great mervayle,
> Upon my backe my house reysed I here;
> I am neyther flesshe ne bone to auvayle:
> As well as a great oxe two hornes I were:
> If that these armed men approche me nere,
> I shall then soone vaynquysshe every chone;
> But they dare not, for fere of me alone.'

Upon this Mr. Riley observes that the above words 'may bear reference to the *Laidly Worm*, a fabulous monster which in remote times is said to have devastated the county of Durham, slaughtering men, women, and children, and setting armed troops at defiance. It is, I believe, supposed by antiquaries at the present day, that by the word *worm* a serpent or dragon was meant; but it is not improbable that the author of the *Kalender of Shepherdes* may have understood the word in a somewhat more literal sense, and, by a stretch of the imagination, adapted the story to a snail' (*Notes and Queries*, 2d series, Nos. 53, 62). Snails, we know, have been used in love divinations, and in various other forms of superstition.'

'The Serpent in the Sea' was at one time a very general superstition among the heathens; for we find it in Isaiah xxvii. 1 : 'In that day the Lord, with His sore, and great, and strong sword, shall punish leviathan the piercing serpent, even leviathan that crooked serpent; and He shall slay *the dragon that is in the sea.*'

LEGENDS OF 'THE RED HAND.'

HERALDRY has been stigmatized as 'the science of fools with long memories;' but it should rather be designated as a science which, properly directed, would make fools wise, for it is a key to history which may yet unlock stores of information. Its study has been so confused with the fantastic absurdities of its professors, that in the lapse of centuries it has become clogged with popular errors as to the significance of its badges and other distinctions.

The badge of Ulster King-at-Arms in Ireland is a *red hand*, the origin of which is as follows :—

In an ancient expedition of some adventurers to Ireland, their leader declared that whoever first touched the shore should possess the territory which he reached. *O'Neil*, from whom descended the princes of Ulster, bent upon obtaining the reward, and seeing another boat likely to land, cut off his hand and threw it on the coast. Hence the traditionary origin of 'The Red Hand of Ulster.' 'The Red Hand' was assigned to King James I. as the badge of the baronets, the design of the institution of the order being the colonization of Ulster and Ireland. The arms of that province were deemed the most appropriate insignia.[1]

But there is a superstition connected with this honourable badge of baronetcy, which is too deeply rooted in the minds of the vulgar to be eradicated without great difficulty, as the following instance will show: In the year 1856, Mr. C. J. Douglas being at Hagley, and conversing with a villager about the Lyttelton family, was gravely informed that, on account of the misdeeds of Thomas Lord Lyttelton (concerning whom the story is told that he foretold his own death, being informed thereof in a dream), the Lord Lytteltons were compelled to have a 'bloody hand' in their arms, and that their arms being painted on a board, with the bloody hand very conspicuous thereon, were placed over the door of the hall at Hagley; and Mr. Douglas was moreover informed that his lordship dare not remove it for twelve months. This board, which was placed there just after the death of the late lord, was nothing more or less than a *hatchment*; and Mr. Douglas was told that the hand was to be smaller every generation, until it entirely disappeared.

Mr. Douglas adds another instance of this absurd belief. In one of the windows of Aston Church, near Birmingham, are the arms of the Holts, baronets of Aston; and there, unfortunately, the hand has been painted *minus* one finger; to explain which, it is told that one of the Holts, having committed some evil deed, was compelled to place the

---

[1] Communication from Sir Bernard Burke, Ulster, to *Popular Errors Explained and Illustrated*, new edition, 1858.

bloody hand in his arms, and transmit the same to his descendants, who were allowed to take *one finger off* for each generation, until all the fingers and thumb being *deducted*, it might at length be dispensed with altogether (*Notes and Queries*, 2d series, No. 12).

The tradition to which this strange insertion is said to refer is, that one of the family 'murdered his cook, and was afterwards compelled to adopt the red hand in his arms.' The tradition adds, that Sir Thomas Holt murdered the cook in a cellar at the old family mansion, by 'running him through with a spit,' and afterwards buried him beneath the spot where the tragedy was enacted. In 1850, the ancient family residence where the murder is said to have been committed, was levelled with the ground; and among persons who, from their position in society, might be supposed to be better informed, considerable anxiety was expressed to ascertain whether any portion of the skeleton of the murdered cook had been discovered beneath the flooring of the cellar, which tradition, fomented by illiterate gossip, pointed out as the place of his interment.

The ancient family residence was situated at Duddeston, a hamlet adjoining Birmingham. Here the Holts resided until May 1631, when Sir Thomas took up his abode at Aston Hall, a noble structure in the Elizabethan style of architecture, which, according to a contemporary inscription, was commenced in April 1618, and completed in 1635. Sir Thomas was a decided royalist, and maintained his allegiance to his sovereign, although the men of Birmingham were notorious for their disaffection, and the neighbouring garrison of Edgbaston was occupied by Parliamentarian troops. When Charles I., of glorious or unhappy memory, was on his way from Shrewsbury to the important battle of Edgehill, on the confines of Warwickshire, he remained with Sir Thomas as his guest from the 15th to the 17th of October; and a closet was long pointed out to the visitor where he is said to have been concealed. A neighbouring eminence is to the present day called 'King's Standing,' from the fact of Charles having stood thereon while addressing his troops. By his acts of loyalty, Sir Thomas Holt acquired the hostility of his rebellious neighbours. Accordingly, we learn that on the 18th of December 1643 he had recourse to Colonel Levison, who 'put forty muskettiers into the house' to avert impending dangers; but eight days afterwards, on the 26th of December, 'the rebels, 1200 strong, assaulted it, and the day following took it, kill'd 12, and ye rest made prisoners, though with lose of 60 of themselves.' The grand staircase, deservedly so entitled, bears evident marks of the injury occasioned at this period, and an unoffending cannon-ball is still preserved.

Edward, the son and heir of Sir Thomas, died at Oxford on the 28th of August 1643, and was buried in Christ Church. He was an ardent supporter of the king. The old baronet was selected as ambassador to Spain by Charles I., but was excused on account of his infirmities. He died in 1654, in the eighty-third year of his age. His excellence and benevolence of character would afford presumptive evidence of the falsehood of the Red-Hand tradition, if it were not totally exploded by the absurdity of the hypothesis upon which it is grounded. Sir Thomas was succeeded in the baronetcy by his grandson Robert, who, in compliance with his will, built an almshouse, or hospital, for five men and five women. It is unnecessary to trace the family further, except to state that nearly at the close of the last century the entail was cut off. The family is now unknown in the neighbourhood, except in its collateral branches. The mansion was next occupied by James Watt, Esq., son of the eminent mechanical philosopher.

With reference to the former residence of the Holts at Duddeston, it will be sufficient to state, that in the middle of the last century the house and grounds were converted into a tavern and pleasure-gardens, under the metropolitan title of Vauxhall, and for a century continued to afford recreation to the busy inhabitants of Birmingham; but in 1850 the house was taken down, and the site and the gardens cleared for building purposes.

Here we may mention that the Red Hand in a hatchment at Wateringbury Church, Kent, and on the table in the hall of Church-Gresley in Derbyshire, has found explanation similar to the preceding. Indeed, there is scarcely a baronet's family in the country respecting which this Red Hand of Ulster has not been the means of raising some tale, of which murder and punishment are the leading features.

In the case of the armorial bearings of Nelthorpe of Gray's Inn, Middlesex, a sword erect in the shield, a second sword held upright in the crest, and a red hand held up in the angle of the shield, would, as naturally expected, in the absence of better information, lead to the supposition of some sanguinary business in the records of the family.

Of interest akin to the preceding is the Legend of Sir Richard Baker, surnamed 'Bloody Baker,' who lies interred in the Church of Cranbrook, in Kent, where a handsome monument is erected to his memory. The gauntlet, gloves, helmet, and spurs, were (as is often the case in monuments of Elizabeth's date) suspended over the tomb. The colour of the gloves was *red*, denoting the blood Baker had shed in his lifetime, of which the following strange tale is told.

The Baker family had formerly large possessions in Cranbrook, but in the reign of Edward VI. great misfortunes fell on them: by extravagance and dissipation they gradually lost all their lands, until an old house in the village (afterwards used as the poorhouse) was all that remained to them. The sole representative of the family remaining at the accession of Queen Mary was Sir Richard Baker. He had spent some years abroad, in consequence of a duel; but when Queen Mary reigned, he thought he might safely return, as he was a Papist. On coming to Cranbrook, he took up his abode in his old house; he only brought with him a foreign servant, and these two persons lived alone. Very soon strange stories began to be whispered of unearthly shrieks having been heard frequently to issue at nightfall from his house. Many persons of importance were stopped and robbed in the Glastonbury woods; and many unfortunate travellers were missed, and never after heard of.

Richard Baker still continued to live in seclusion, but he gradually repurchased his alienated property, although he was known to have spent all he possessed before he left England. But wickedness was not always to prosper. He formed an apparent attachment to a young lady in the neighbourhood, remarkable for always wearing a great number of jewels. He often pressed her to come and see his old house, telling her he had many curious things he wished to show her. She had hitherto always evaded fixing a day for her visit; but happening to walk within a short distance of the house, she determined to surprise Baker with a call. Her companion, a lady older than herself, endeavoured to dissuade her from doing so; but she would not be turned from her purpose. They knocked at the door, but no one answered them: they, however, discovered it was not locked, and determined to enter. At the head of the staircase hung a parrot, which, on their passing, cried out:

> 'Peapot, pretty lady, be not too bold,
> Or your red blood will soon run cold.'

And cold did run the blood of the adventurous damsel, when on opening one of the room doors she found it nearly filled with the bodies of murdered persons, chiefly women. Just then they heard a noise, and on looking out of the window saw Bloody Baker and his servant bringing in the body of a lady. Paralyzed with fear, they concealed themselves in a recess under the staircase.

As the murderers with their dead burden passed by them, the hand of the murdered lady hung in the baluster of the stairs: with an oath Baker chopped it off, and it fell into the lap of one of the concealed ladies. They ran away, having the presence of mind to carry with them the dead hand, on one of the fingers of which was a ring. On reaching home, they told the story, and, in confirmation of it, displayed the ring. All the families in the neighbourhood who had lost relatives mysteriously were then told of what had been found out; and they determined to ask Baker to a party, apparently in a friendly manner, but to have constables concealed ready to take him into custody. He came unsuspectingly, and then the lady told him all she had seen, pretending it was a dream. 'Fair lady,' said he, 'dreams are nothing; they are but fables.' 'They may be fables,' replied she; 'but is this a fable?' And she produced the hand and ring! Upon this the constables rushed in, and took Baker into custody; and the tradition further says that he was burnt, notwithstanding Queen Mary tried to save him on account of his professing the Roman Catholic religion.

A somewhat similar legend is connected with a monument in the Church of Stoke d'Abernon, Surrey, the appearance of a 'bloody hand' upon which is thus accounted for. Two young brothers of the family of Vincent, the elder of whom had just come into possession of his estate, were out shooting on Fairmile Common, about two miles from the village. They had put up several birds, but had not been able to get a single shot, when the elder swore with an oath that he would fire at whatever they next met with. They had not gone much further before the miller of a mill near at hand (and which was standing a few years ago) passed them, and made some trifling remark. As soon as he had passed by, the younger brother jokingly reminded the elder of his oath, whereupon the latter immediately fired at the miller, who fell dead upon the spot. Young Vincent escaped to his home, and through the influence of his family, backed by large sums of money, no effective steps were taken to apprehend him. He lay concealed in the 'Nunnery' building on his estate for some years, when death put a period to the insupportable anguish of his mind. To commemorate this rash act, and his untimely death, the 'bloody hand' was placed on his monument in Stoke Church; but the narrator of the story conjectures that the hand might be only the Ulster badge.

Legend of the Bodach Glass.

Among the warnings or notices of death to be found in the dark chronicle of superstition, the omens peculiar to certain families are not the least striking. Pennant tells us that many of the great families in Scotland had their demon or genius, who gave them monitions of future events.

Thus, the family of Rothmurchan had the Bodac au Dun, or Ghost of the Hill; and Kinchardines, the Spectre of the Bloody Hand; Gartnibeg House was haunted by Bodach Gartin; and Tulloch Gorus by Manch Monlach, or the Girl with the Hairy Left Hand. *Bodach* signifies, from the Saxon, Bode, a messenger, a tidings-bringer.

The Bodach Glass is introduced in the novel of *Waverley* as the family superstition of the MacIvors, the truth of which has been traditionally proved by three hundred years' experience. It is thus described to Waverley by Fergus:

'You must know, then, that when my ancestor, Ian nan Chaistel, wasted Northumberland, there was appointed with him in the expedition a sort of Southland chief, or captain of a band of Lowlanders, called Halbert Hall. In their return through the Cheviots they quarrelled about the division of the great booty they had acquired, and came from words to blows. The Lowlanders were cut off to a man, and their chief fell the last, covered with wounds, by the sword of my ancestor. Since that time his spirit has crossed the Vich Ian Vohr of the day when any great disaster was impending. My father saw him twice: once before he was made prisoner at Sheriff Muir, another time on the morning of the day on which he died.'

Fergus then relates to Waverley the appearance of the Bodach: 'Last night,' said Fergus, 'I felt so feverish that I left my quarters, and walked out, in hopes the keen frosty air would brace my nerves. I cannot tell how much I dislike going on, for I know you will hardly believe me.

However, I crossed a small foot-bridge, and kept walking backwards and forwards, when I observed, with surprise, by the clear moonlight, a tall figure in a grey plaid, such as shepherds wear in the south of Scotland, which, move at what pace I would, kept regularly about four yards before me.'

'You saw a Cumberland peasant in his ordinary dress, probably.'

'No; I thought so at first, and was astonished at the man's audacity in daring to dog me. I called to him, but received no answer. I felt an anxious throbbing at my heart; and to ascertain what I dreaded, I stood still, and turned myself on the same spot successively to the four points of the compass. By heaven, Edward, turn where I would, the figure was instantly before my eyes at precisely the same distance! I was then convinced it was the *Bodach Glass*. My hair bristled, and my knees shook. I manned myself, however, and determined to return to my quarters. My ghastly visitor glided before me (for I cannot say he walked) until he reached the foot-bridge; there he stopped, and turned full round. I must either wade the river, or pass him as close as I am to you. A desperate courage, founded on the belief that my death was near, made me resolve to make my way in despite of him. I made the sign of the cross, drew my sword, and uttered, "In the name of God, evil spirit, give place!" "Vich Ian Vohr," it said, in a voice that made my very blood curdle; "beware of to-morrow.' It seemed at that moment not half a yard from my sword's point; but the words were no sooner spoken than it was gone, and nothing appeared further to obstruct my passage.'

THE WHITE-BREASTED BIRD OF THE OXENHAM FAMILY.

HOWELL, the letter-writer, relates that he saw, in a stone-cutter's shop in Fleet Street, a marble slab, with the epitaphs of four persons of the Oxenham family; when at or near death, 'a bird with a white breast was seen fluttering about their beds.' The last appearance of this kind is stated to have been in 1794. In 1641 there was published a tract, with a frontispiece, entitled 'A True Relation of an Apparition, in the Likeness of a Bird with a White Breast, that appeared hovering over the Death-bed of some of the Children of Mr. James Oxenham,' etc. And in an account of Sydenham is a statement of a similar appearance at the death of one of the family of Oxenham, in that parish. The inscription upon the marble seen by Howell was: 'Here lies John Oxenham, a goodly young man, in whose chamber, as he was struggling in the pangs of death, a bird with a white breast, was seen fluttering about his bed, and so vanished.'

DONINGTON CASTLE AND CHAUCER.

F the castle of Donington, near Newbury, in Berkshire, only a small ruin remains. Of the castle of Donington, in Leicestershire, the remains are more extensive. In its entirety, this stronghold, situated on a commanding eminence, rose abruptly from the valley of the Trent, which it proudly looked over and threatened. The character of this fortress was unquestionably castellated, of the eleventh century; and the ballium or court is still distinctly defined. Each of these castles has been assigned as the abode of Chaucer.

The castle in Leicestershire, built by Eustace Baron of Haulton and Constable of Chester, was demolished by order of King John about the year 1216; its owner, John de Laci, having taken too prominent a part with the rebel barons. But the castle was evidently rebuilt by his grandson, Henri Laci Earl of Lincoln, who died in 1360. The fortress then came into the possession of Thomas Earl of Lancaster, who married Alice, Lincoln's daughter. This prince was cousin to Edward II.; and he joined a confederacy of barons who took up arms against the king because of the profligacy of his favourites. After the battle of Borough Bridge, being taken prisoner, he was beheaded in the year 1322; and, immediately afterwards, the castle was given to the favourite Despencer. Speed thus alludes to this transaction: 'He had not long before created the elder Spencer Earl of Winchester, and deckt the plume of his fortunes with a toppe-feather taken out of the said late Earl of Lancaster's estate, that is to say, with the castle and honour of Donington, parcell of the earldome of Lincoln.' However, the Despencers did not wear this 'toppe-feather' long, for in 1325 they were both executed by the capricious Edward's command.

In 1327, Edward Earl of Kent, uncle of Edward III., was owner of the castle; but in 1330, through the base machinations of Mortimer and the infamous Queen Isabella, this good Earl was put to death. An old historian speaks of this event as follows: 'From noone till five at night he [the Earl] stood at the place of death without the castle gates, none being found to behead him, till a base wretch of a marschal-sea was sent and did it; so little conscience did the malice and ambition of his potent adversaries make of shedding the royal blood, which, by God's juster judgment, was not long unavenged.'

In 1352 the castle belonged to John Plantagenet Earl of Kent, and Joan his sister was his heir. This Joan was daughter of Earl Edmund, who was brother by the father's side to Edward II. She is reputed to have been the most beautiful woman of the age, and the troubadours and minstrels of the time celebrated her beauty in their songs. She married three times: first the valiant Earl of Salisbury, from whom she was divorced (this first marriage being nothing more than a contract of betrothal); secondly, Lord Thomas Holland, who in 1352, in right of his wife, was created Earl of Kent; third, after his death, the Prince of Wales, her cousin. 'Edward the Black Prince,' says Speed, 'passionately loving her, did marry her, and by her issue had two sons,' one of whom, Richard, afterwards became King of England. In 1385, Joan, Richard the Second's mother, held the town and castle of Donington, with the *et cetera* of the king, as of the honour of Chester.

Towards the latter part of the reign of Richard II., and about 1396, according to some historians, Geoffrey Chaucer, the prince of English poetry, resided at Castle Donington. This statement is, however, open to discussion, as there is another Castle Donington which claims the like distinction. John of Gaunt, the powerful Duke of Lancaster, married, for his third wife, Lady Catherine Swinford. This took place in 1396, and her sister Philippa had been previously married to the poet in 1369. 'Shortly after this marriage,' says Clarke (*Riches of Chaucer*), 'we find Geoffrey in possession of Castle Donington Park and Castle, the noble presentation for life of his princely brother-in-law.' Ashmole the antiquary says of Donington Castle that it was built by a general of King Stephen's, and in course of time became the residence of Geoffrey Chaucer. Camden, in his *Britannia*, who calls it Dennington or Dunnington, describes it as a small but elegant castle, on the top of a woody hill, commanding a pleasant prospect, and lighted by windows on every side; the ruins are visible on the right hand of the road from London to Bath.

It is quite probable that, if Chaucer did not reside here during much of the last four years of his valuable life—namely, from 1396 to 1400—he repeatedly visited the place. Evelyn says, in his *Sylva*, that at Castle Donington is a famous oak called 'Chaucer's Oak,' under which he wrote several poems; and, moreover, that Chaucer planted three oaks—'The King's Oak,' 'The Queen's Oak,' and 'Chaucer's.' Osterre says that Chaucer and Wickliffe frequently met, and that the abbot and monks of Leicester dreaded Chaucer's poetry more than Wickliffe's preaching; that a famous hunter was abbot in those days at Leicester, Sir William de Clowne by name, and that his skill as a hare-hunter was so great that the king and his nobles paid him an annual pension that they might hunt with him, and that he is one of the characters intended in *The Monk and the Friar*.

The subject is surrounded with obscurity. We find Chaucer in 1359 at Woodstock—at that time a royal residence, and the birthplace of the Black Prince. He was banished there because of his Lollard tendencies; and in that pleasant retreat he wrote the *Romaient of the Rose*, containing bitter invectives against priestcraft. There he resided upwards of thirty years, and during that time must have had frequent opportunities of meeting the Princess

Joan. Both her sons by Thomas Holland were then residing at Castle Donington, where she herself, no doubt, would occasionally resort after the death of the Black Prince in 1376, as she is described by an old chronicle 'passionately fond of her first-born sons.' What so likely as that she would invite Chaucer to Castle Donington, and thereby facilitate his intercourse with Wickliffe, whose convert she was, and who at that time preached all over the country? Wickliffe died in 1384, the Princess Joan in 1385, and the poet Chaucer in 1400; and after a lapse of nearly five hundred years, the recollection of these three personages, who occupy such distinguished and prominent places in the page of history, as the greatest reformer, the greatest beauty, and the greatest poet of that age, imparts an interest to the spot they may all have inhabited or visited together.

Godwin, in his *Life of Chaucer*, in two quarto volumes (1803), improves upon the several details of his abode at Castle Donington, by telling us that the Duke of Lancaster purchased the castle, and bestowed it upon Chaucer, being 'determined in the feudal sense to ennoble him!'—although he elsewhere suggests that 'the circumstances of Chaucer himself might be considered as rendering it somewhat improbable that he had made such an acquisition toward the close of his life.'

Mr. Robert Bell, in his annotated edition of the poet, says that, 'even if Chaucer's necessities throughout the period when he is supposed to have kept up the costly establishment at Castle Donington were not conclusive against its probability, it is discredited by other circumstances. Donington Castle became the property of Sir John Phelip, the first husband of Chaucer's granddaughter. This gentleman died in 1415; and there is no evidence of any previous connection of any member of Chaucer's family with Donington Castle; nor is there any ground for supposing that Sir John Phelip's tenure commenced till after Chaucer's death. Upon the subsequent marriage of Sir John Phelip's widow, it passed into the possession of her second husband, the Duke of Suffolk.

'The story of his residence in Berkshire is further shown to be groundless, by the ascertained fact that Chaucer was unquestionably living in London during the last three years of his life; and that on Christmas Eve, 1399, he entered upon the lease of a house in Westminster for a term of fifty-three years, at the annual rent of £2, 13s. 4d. Had he been residing in Berkshire, it is not likely that at his advanced age he would have come up to London and encumbered himself with another establishment. The tenement was situated in the garden of the Chapel of the Blessed Mary of Westminster, said to be very nearly the same spot on which Henry VII.'s chapel stands; and it was devised to Chaucer by Robert Hermodesworth, a monk, with the consent of the abbot and convent of that place.'

Chaucer died here, 25th October 1400. Soon after Chaucer's death, Sir Hugh Shirley was appointed governor of the castle, and it was incorporated with the Duchy of

Lancaster. During the Wars of the Roses, the castle and town were true to the Red Rose, and the Lancastrian party held it. Edward IV., being in peaceable possession of the throne, granted the stewardship, in 1461, of the castle and manor to Sir William Hastings for distinguished services: he was chamberlain to Edward IV.

After passing through various hands, a descendant of this Sir William Hastings (George Hastings, Earl of Huntingdon) purchased, in 1505, from Robert Earl of Essex and others, the Castle and Park of Donington, with all the herbage, pannage, and agistments thereof. The castle 'he quite ruined,' but built a 'fair house' in the neighbourhood. Many martial trophies have been found at different times among the ruins, such as chain-armour, daggers, a battle-axe, cannon-balls, etc.

In Domesday Book, there was 'at Dunitone' a mill of 10s. 8d. value, and a wood twelve furlongs long and eight broad. No doubt the present park and king's mills are a portion of the property thus named in the Conqueror's survey. Many of the early Saxon writers refer to immense forests of oak-trees which covered this part of England; and there are individual trees standing in Donington Park which must have formed part of these forests. One which goes by the name of 'Daniel Lambert' is fifteen yards in circumference fifteen feet above its base. This giant of the forest has no doubt flourished in vigour and beauty for a thousand years.

The offices of constableship, etc., of Donington Castle

appear to have been hereditary in the family of De Staunton. Thomas de Staunton, in the time of Richard II., was high steward. His descendant Robert de Staunton, it is probable, was slain in battle. His granddaughter, and sole heiress of his son, was married in 1423 to Ralph Shirley, Esq., son of Sir Ralph Shirley, Knight, a distinguished commander at the battle of Agincourt; and from this union of the Stauntons and Shirleys have sprung many mighty men of renown, amongst the rest Sir Robert Shirley, Baronet,

> 'Whose singular praise it is
> To have done the best things in the worst times,
> And hoped them in the most calamitous.'

The son of this Sir Robert, in reward for his special services rendered to King Charles by his father, was in 1677 created Lord Ferrers, and in 1711 Viscount Tamworth and Earl Ferrers.[1]

[1] See Dr. Wilson Pearson; in the *Journal of the British Archæological Association*, 1863.

THE HOUSE OF HOWARD.

THE calamities which befell the ducal House of Howard, within the lapse of a century, may be cited as impressive instances of the instability of pride and place and human grandeur ; and these in the history of a house whose greatness has almost passed into the proverbial distich :

> ' What can ennoble sots, or slaves, or cowards?
> Alas! not all the blood of all the Howards.'

This ducal house stands next to the blood-royal, at the head of the peerage of England, and is the chief of the honourable and large-spreading family of Howard. Sir John Howard was an eminent Yorkist, not only on account of his princely birth (maternally) and magnificent fortune, but from the stations of high trust which at different periods had devolved upon him. After distinguishing himself very early in life in the French wars of Henry vi., Sir John was constituted by Edward iv., in 1461, Constable of the Castle of Norwich, appointed Sheriff of the counties of Norfolk and Suffolk, and granted some of the forfeited manors of James Butler, Earl of Wiltshire, in England, and of Ormonde in

Ireland. In 1468, being treasurer of the king's household, Sir John Howard obtained a grant of the whole benefit that should accrue to the king by the coinage of money in the City and Tower of London, or elsewhere in the realm of England, so long as he should continue in that office. In 1470, when he was summoned to Parliament under the title of Lord Howard, he was made captain-general of all the king's forces at sea for resisting the attempts of the Lancastrians, then rallying under Nevil Earl of Warwick, the Duke of Clarence, and others. In 1471 his Lordship was constituted Deputy-Governor of Calais and the marches adjacent; and his summons to Parliament as a Baron continued until he was created Earl Marshal of England and Duke of Norfolk, 28th June 1483, when his son and heir, Thomas Howard, was created Earl of Surrey. The Duke had previously been invested with the insignia of the Order of the Garter. As Earl Marshal his Grace was empowered (in the king's presence or absence) to bear a golden staff, tipped at each end with black, the upper part thereof to be adorned with the royal arms, and the lower with those of his own family; and for the better support of the dignity of this office, he obtained a grant to himself and his heirs for ever of £20 annually, payable half-yearly, out of the fee-farm rent of Ipswich, in Suffolk. His Grace was subsequently constituted Lord Admiral of England, Ireland, and Aquitaine for life, and obtained grants of divers manors and lordships.

But he did not long enjoy these great possessions; for

the next year, being with Richard at Bosworth Field, he fell in leading the van of that prince's army. His Grace was urged by some of his friends to refrain from attending his sovereign on the field; and the night previous to the battle, this doggerel warning was found in his tent:

> 'Jockey of Norfolk, be not too bold,
> For Dickon thy master is bought and sold.'

Yet he would not desert his royal master; but as he had faithfully lived under him, so he manfully died by his side.

Next, Catherine Howard, niece of the second Duke of Norfolk, became the fifth wife of Henry VIII. In this marriage Henry considered himself perfectly blessed: the agreeable person and disposition of Catherine had entirely captivated his affections; and in the height of his transport, he publicly in his chapel returned solemn thanks to Heaven for the unspeakable felicity the conjugal state afforded him. His bliss was soon fated to terminate; and in the bitter disappointment he experienced in Catherine, Heaven seemed to revenge upon him the cruelty with which he had sacrificed his former wives. Her transition from the throne to the scaffold occupied but eighteen months (*Kings of England*).

Next, Thomas Howard, aspiring to the hand of Lady Margaret Douglas, daughter of Margaret Queen of Scotland, and niece of Henry VIII., was attainted of treason, and died a prisoner in the Tower of London in 1536.

Henry Earl of Surrey, son of the third Duke, was one of the brightest ornaments of the House of Howard; and as statesman, poet, and warrior, he is thus characterized by

Sir Egerton Brydges: 'Excellent in arts and in arms, a man of learning, a genius, and a hero, of a generous temper and a refined heart, he united all the gallantry and unbroken spirit of a rude age with all the elegance and grace of a polished era. With a splendour of descent, in possession of the highest honours and abundant wealth, he relaxed not his efforts to deserve distinction by his personal worth. Conspicuous in the rough exercises of tilts and tournaments, and commanding armies with skill and bravery in expeditions against the Scots under his father, he found time, at a period when our literature was rude and barbarous, to cultivate his mind with all the exquisite spirit of the models of Greece and Rome, to catch the excellences of the revived muses of Italy, and to produce in his own language compositions which, in simplicity, perspicuity, graceful ornament, and just and natural thought, exhibited a shining contrast with the works of his predecessors, and an example which his successors long attempted in vain to follow.' The iniquitous execution of this gifted nobleman was the last tyrannical act of Henry VIII. The Earl of Surrey underwent the penalty of his unjust sentence during the lifetime of his father (whom the death of the king preserved from the same fate), 21st January 1547.

Thomas, the fourth Duke, shared the fate of his distinguished father, being implicated in the affairs of Mary Queen of Scots. Partly from accident, and partly from the treachery of the Duke's secretary, the conspiracy was discovered. It was soon traced by the terror of *the rack;*

and there is in existence a warrant from the queen for putting two of the Duke's servants to this torture. The body of the warrant is in the handwriting of Lord Burghley, and the torture was actually inflicted.

The Duke was arraigned for high treason, 16th January 1571; and being condemned, his execution was deferred until June 2 following, when he was beheaded upon a scaffold on Tower Hill. There can be little doubt that efforts then making to procure the liberty of the Queen of Scots, and re-establish the supremacy of Catholicism, had much influence over his fate; for it is known that no fewer than four warrants which had been issued for his execution were successively revoked by Elizabeth. Her last revocation, entirely in her own handwriting, is preserved in the Ashmolean Museum at Oxford. Elizabeth wrote, soon after her discovery of the Duke's entanglement in the Queen of Scots' scheme, the following lines :

'The doubt of future woes exiles my present joy;
And wit me warns to shun such snares as threaten mine annoy;
For falsehood now doth flow, and subjects' faith doth ebb,
Which would not be, if reason ruled, or wisdom weaved the web.
But clouds of toys untry'd do cloak aspiring minds,
Which turn to rain of late repent, by course of changed winds.
The top of hope supposed, the root of ruth will be ;
And fruitless all their graffed guiles, as shortly ye shall see.
Those dazzled eyes with pride, which great ambition blinds,
Shall be unsealed by worthy wights, whose foresight falsehood binds.
The daughter of Debate, that eke Discord doth sow,
Shall reap no gain, where former rule hath taught still peace to flow.
No foreign banish'd wight shall anchor in our port :
Our realm it brooks no stranger's force ; let them elsewhere resort.

Our rusty sword with rest, shall first the edge employ
To poll their tops that seek such change, and [thereto] gape with joy.'

Granger mentions an extremely rare print of the above nobleman, in which he is represented under an arch, whilst under a correspondent arch are displayed thirty coats of arms quartered in one shield. All his honours became forfeited; but his eldest son Philip inherited, in right of his mother, the feudal Earldom of Arundel, as owner of Arundel Castle in Sussex, and was summoned to Parliament as Earl of Arundel; but being attainted in 1590, he was committed to the Tower in 1595. He was styled 'the Renowned Confessor;' and we find of his life an impressive narrative, edited from the original MSS. by Henry Granville, fourteenth Duke, and published in 1857. The Earl's piety was remarkable. He constantly rose in the morning at five o'clock; and 'as soon as he was risen out of bed, he fell down upon his bare knees, and breathed forth in secret his first devotions to Almighty God, his eyes and hands lifted up to heaven. With his kneeling in that manner then and at other times, his knees were grown very hard and black.' . . . . In those times which were allotted to walking or other recreation, his discourse and conversation either with his keeper or the lieutenant, or his own servants, was either tending to piety or some profitable discourse, as of the lives of holy men, of the sufferances and constancy of the martyrs of ancient times, from which he would usually deduce some good document or other, as of the facility of a virtuous life after a man had once overcome his sensuality; of the happiness of those that suffered anything for our Saviour's sake, with such like; to which purpose he had writ with his own hand, upon the wall of his chamber, this Latin sentence: *Quanto plus afflictionis pro Christo in hoc sæculo, tanto plus gloriæ cum Christo in futuro.* [The more affliction we endure for Christ in this world, the more glory we shall obtain with Christ in the next.]

The Earl's last moments are thus pathetically described. The last night of his life he spent, for the most part, in prayer, sometimes saying his beads, sometimes such psalms and prayers as he knew by heart; and oftentimes used these holy aspirations: O Lord, into Thy hands I commend my spirit. Lord, Thou art my hope and life. Very frequently, moreover, indicating the holy names of Jesus and Mary.

'Seeing his servants in the morning stand by his bedside, weeping in a mournful manner, he asked them what o'clock it was. They answered that it was eight, or thereabout. "Why then," said he, "I have almost run out my course, and come to the end of this miserable and mortal life;" desiring them not to weep for him, since he did not doubt, by the grace of God, but all would go well with him. Which being said, he returned to his prayers upon his beads again, though then with a very slow, hollow, and fainting voice, and so continued as long as he was able to draw so much breath as was sufficient to sound out the names of Jesus and the glorious Virgin, which were the last words he was ever heard to speak.

'The last minute of his last hour being now come, lying on his back, eies firmly fixt towards heaven, and his long, lean consumed arms out of the bed, his hands upon his breast laid in cross, one upon the other, about twelve o'clock at noon, in which hour he was also born into this world, arraigned, condemned, and adjudged unto death upon Sunday the 19th of October 1595 (after almost eleven years' imprisonment in the Tower), in a most sweet manner, without any sign of grief or groan, only turning his head a little aside, as one falling into a pleasing sleep, he surrendered his happy soul into the hands of Almighty God, who to His so great glory had created it.

'Some have thought, and perhaps not improbably, that he had some foreknowledge of the day of his death; because, about seven or eight days before making certain notes, understood only by himself, in his calendar, what prayers and devotions he intended to say upon every day of the week following, on Monday, Tuesday, etc., *when he came to the Sunday on which he dy'd, he there made a pause, saying, Hitherto, and no further:* this is enough; and so writ no more, as his servants, who then heard his words and saw him write, have often testified.'

In the chapter following occurs this curious record: 'I forgot to note in the due place, that upon the night precedent to the Earl's arraignment and condemnation, a nitingale was heard to sing with great melody in a jessamine tree all ye night long in the garden of Arundel House [in the Strand, London], where his Countess and children did then remain; the which may seem the more strange, in regard the like was neither before nor since that time ever heard in that place. Another thing as strange did happen in the Tower soon after his death; for two tame stags, which the lieutenant kept there for his pleasure, falling into a fury, never desisted knocking their horns against the wall, till, their brains being beaten out, they dy'd.'

This nobleman's son, best known as the Earl of Arundel, who in 1621 was constituted Earl Marshal of England for life, fell under the displeasure of King Charles I., on account of the marriage of his eldest son, Henry Frederick Lord Maltravers, with the Lady Elizabeth, eldest daughter of Esme Stuart, Duke of Lennox; whose hand, as his own ward, his Majesty had intended to bestow on Lord Lorne, afterwards Marquis of Argyle. For this offence the Earl and his Countess were at first restricted to their seat at Horsley, in Surrey; and afterwards committed to the Tower, but shortly after liberated. This Earl's successor adhered steadily to Charles I. at the time of the Civil Wars, and served in his army as a volunteer until he was sent for to Padua, on the illness of his father in 1646. During his absence the Parliament took possession of his estates; and on his return to England he found it difficult to subsist; the composition of his estates, £6000, was paid for the use of the Navy. The Earl then retired to his mansion in the Strand, and lived there in great privacy until his death in 1652.

At the Deepdene, near Dorking, in Surrey, which for centuries formed a portion of the Howards' possessions, lived the Hon. Charles Howard, son of the above Earl of Arundel. He was an accomplished chemist, and built here a laboratory; 'and in subterranean grots, formed for that purpose, had furnaces of different kinds,' of which some remains existed to our time; he was also styled 'the Christian philosopher,' and built here an oratory. Aubrey was so enchanted with the Deepdene garden, or 'solitaire recess,' that he could 'never expect any enjoyment beyond it, but the kingdom of heaven.' Henry Charles Howard of Greystokes, son and heir of the above, who resided at the Deepdene, is spoken of as having 'a fine taste for the polite arts;' thus inheriting the genius of the famous Earl of Arundel, who presented to the University of Oxford the Arundelian Marbles.[1]

[1] At the classic Deepdene, too, were written *Anastasius*, by Thomas Hope; and *Coningsby*, a novel of political life, by Benjamin Disraeli.

THE TRAGEDY OF SIR JOHN ELAND.

IN the West Riding of Yorkshire, on the southern bank of the Calder, in the district formerly comprising the Forest of Hardwyke, stands, on an eminence, the ancient town of Eland, or more properly Ealand. Opposite to the town, and on the north bank of the river, on the opening of the wood, stands the timber-built mansion of Eland Hall, for several generations the seat of the ancient and honourable family of the Elands; and memorable on account of the deadly feud that arose in the reign of Edward III. between Sir John Eland and some of the neighbouring gentry. The family of Eland was of great antiquity, and had large possessions in this Riding, as also in the townships of Spotland and Whiteworthe, in Lancashire. They were liberal benefactors to the great abbey at Whalley. Sir William de Eland was Constable at Nottingham Castle, and was the same who betrayed Earl Mortimer by showing the secret passage in the rock. Early in the fourteenth century Sir John Eland was the representative of this powerful family, and he resided at Eland Hall, the seat of his ancestors. The origin of the sanguinary quarrel is not very clearly stated. The ballad which relates the story is thought to have been written for the use of the minstrels, and was sung or recited at the entertainments of the gentry in those parts; and Brady, in his *History of the Reign of King Stephen*, says that this mode of taking private revenge was brought by the Normans into England. Those lawless times are glanced at in the ballad:

> 'For when men live in worldlie wealth,
>   Full few can have that grace
> Long in the same to keep themselves
>   Contented with their place.
>
> 'The squire must needs become a knight,
>   The knight a lord would be:
> Thus shall you see no worldlie wight
>   Content with his degree.'

Sir John Eland, being sheriff, was disobeyed in some respect by his neighbour Sir Robert Beaumont of Crossland Hall, who had thus incurred his resentment. Another account states that one Exley, an adjoining proprietor, had killed the nephew of Sir John in a fray; and flying from his vengeance, was received and sheltered by Sir Robert Beaumont. As usual in those days, compensation was accepted; and all might have ended, had not one Lockwood of Lockwood, and Sir Hugh Quarmby, stirred the strife anew. Sir John, having mustered his tenants and friends, came suddenly in the night, and having first met Sir Hugh Quarmby and Sir John Lockwood, friends of Sir Robert Beaumont, at their houses at Quarmby and Lockwood, proceeded with his men to Crossland Hall, the seat of Sir Robert Beaumont; and lying in ambush till the drawbridge over the moat that surrounded the house was let down in the morning, he rushed in and entered the knight's chamber. Sir Robert made a courageous resistance, but being unarmed, was soon overpowered and slain; and with him fell all his servants who had come to his defence. The tradition says: 'The knight was driven back into his chamber, where his faire ladye, hanging upon him, besought for his life, and placed her precious body so as to shield her bleeding lord. But all in vain, for faint with loss of blood, they bound his arms; and heedless of the cries and shrieks of his terrified ladye, drew him into his own hall, and there cut off his head.

'And so, after this wicked deed, they bethought to regale themselves. And the cloth was spread, and the meat was brought, and the cellar furnished abundance of good wine; and that stern knight, Sir John Eland, sitting at the head of the table, on the dais, sent for the two sons of the slain Sir Robert; and when they came, ordered them to eat and drink with them. The younger, who was of a mild and gentle nature, overcome with fear, did as he was bidden; but Adam, the elder, looking angrily at his brother, sturdily refused to eat or drink with the slayers of his father.' Lady Beaumont, stealing away in the dead of the night from Crossland Hall, escaped with her children, and found a secure asylum with the Townleys of Townley. She subsequently took up her residence at Brereton, as most remote from her deadly foe. Thither also retired the young Lockwood and Quarmby, with another youth named Lacie, who was likewise on some account an object of Sir John Eland's resentment. These young gentlemen were brought up at Brereton by Lady Beaumont, where they employed their time acquiring skill and address in the martial exercises of that age, and with a continual sense of the wrong inflicted by the knight of Eland. As we do not find that he was called to any account for these outrages, it seems that he must have obtained the king's pardon. The young brood of Eland's enemies still abode at Brereton Hall:

> 'The feats of fence they practised
>   To wield their weapons well,
> Till fifteen years were finished !
>   And then it so befell.'

Then the young Beaumont, Lockwood, Quarmby, and Lacie having grown up to manhood, resolved to avenge the death of their parents. Having learnt from two of their spies the day on which Sir John Eland held the sheriff's turn at Brighouse, a village on the Calder, about three miles from Eland Hall, they took measures for waylaying him as he returned home:

> 'The day was set, the turn was kept
>   At Brighouse by Sir John:
> Full little wist he was beset
>   Then at his coming home.
> Dawson and Haigh had played their parts,
>   And brought from Brereton Green
> Young gentlemen with hardy hearts,
>   As well were known and seen.'

They gathered such of the retainers of the families as they

could rely upon, to meet them on the previous night in Strangstrighte Wood, on the left bank of the river, and at different places made their way to Cromwellbotham Wood, through which the road ran from Brighouse to Eland Hall. Being near Lacie's house, they rested and refreshed, and then took their station in a glen, close to which the road wound, sometimes on its very margin, and sometimes many yards above, where the smooth front of the cliff, protruding to the water's edge, forced the road over the steep ascent. For so dark a purpose a fitter place could not be conceived. The men, occupying each side of the glen, concealed themselves in the fissures of the rocks behind, or in the hollows of the ancient and decayed oaks :

> 'Adam of Beaumont there was laid,
>   And Lacie with him also ;
> And liegemen who were not afraid
>   To fight against the foe.
>
> And Lockwood, too, so eager was,
>   That close by the road he stood,
> And Quarmby stout, who quailed not
>   To work the deed of blood.'

'The day was far spent,' saith the tradition, 'when Adam Beaumont, from his high seat, saw a distant company wind round the hill, and crossing the river, take the road towards Cromwellbotham Wood. Giving the signal, he hastened down, and planting himself athwart the road awaiting the arrival of the fierce knight, who, little wotting what was prepared for him, had ridden forward apart from his company :

> 'From the lane end then Eland came,
> And spied these gentlemen;
> And wondered he who they could be,
> And val'd his bonnet then.'

Adam Beaumont was the first to speak, rudely seizing the bridle of Sir John Eland's horse, and throwing him back upon his haunches:

> 'Thy courtsey vails thee not, Sir Knight,
> Thou slew my father dear,
> Sometime Sir Robert Beaumont hight,
> And slain thou shalt be here.'

It was a valiant defence that bold knight made; for, throwing himself off his horse when Adam Beaumont seized the reins, he drew his short sword, and laid about him stoutly. 'False loon art thou, and cowardly traitor,' shouted he to Quarmby, who had already wounded him sore; 'had I had thee but single-handed, or even with Beaumont only to back thee, I would send ye both to rot with your fathers.' 'How many swords hadst thou, false knight, to back thee, when thou camest on our kin, and like a craven fox slew them in the night?' quoth Quarmby. As soon as Sir John was slain outright, and his bloody corpse lay in the road, pierced with many wounds, besmeared too with dust and dirt—for in his death-throws he had struggled on the ground with Lockwood, whose foot had slipped in the dreadful fray—the party quickly dispersed. And the retinue of the proud sheriff now found him upon the bare road a stiffened corpse, and conveyed him, upon a bier made hastily of oaken boughs, to Eland Hall. And all his friends and servants resorted thither, and greatly bemoaned him; for, though relentless and fierce to his foes, he was ever generous and kind to those who lived under him, and showed himself at all times a steady and bounteous friend to our Holy Church, as the monkes of Whalley can certify right well :

'They tolled the bell, and the mass was said,
  And the lady sorely wept her lord :
"But, mother," the young heir questioned,
"When may I draw my father's sword ?"

'"Forbear, my child," the mother said,
  "That sword hath brought us ill ;
Four noble heads are now laid low,
  More blood we may not spill."'

The friends of the late Sir John Eland made for many days diligent search for his murderers; but Beaumont and his company had fled, and passing over into Lancashire, had crossed the dangerous sands of Morecambe Bay, and hid themselves among the dark Fells of Furness, where Beaumont had friends. Here they openly boasted of their misdeeds, and how they had avenged the death of their fathers. They also plotted more mischief, had spies to inform them of all that passed, and laid their plans openly.

Meanwhile, the lady of Eland Hall and her family lived a life of quiet, surrounded with her faithful dependants. Years passed on; and as Beaumont and his friends never appeared in the country, it was thought that the feud was now at an end, and nothing further need be feared. The young knight grew up brave and good; he lived in his father's halls and among his father's kin; and he too was a friend of the Holy Church.

But Adam Beaumont and his fierce and relentless company among the dark Fells of Furness, not satisfied with the blood of their powerful and wicked foe, thirsted even more for the blood of his good and knightly son, together with his loving wife and darling babes, living in fancied security in Eland Hall. So many years had now passed away, that much of the former caution was laid aside, and occasionally the young knight and his lady would venture abroad unarmed and unprotected. Their enemies, by means of spies, heard of this:

> 'Adam of Beaumont then truly,
> Lacie and Lockwood eke,
> And Quarmby, came to their countrie,
> Their purpose for to seek.'

They again repaired to their haunt in Cromwellbotham (the foot of the winding spring) Wood, and there lay in that very glen where they had shed the blood of Sir John Eland. And here, receiving food and sustenance from Lacie's house close by, they lay in ambush till the eve of Palm Sunday, having spies to keep a close watch upon the family at Eland Hall, and their movements. On this holy eve they stole from their hiding-places; and it being 'mirke midnight,' made their way to Eland Mill, on the further bank of the Calder stream, just below the hill on which the town stood. Stealthily forcing their way into the mills, they hid themselves there till early dawn; when the miller's wife, going into the mill for some meal, was seized, and bound hand and foot, and her mouth gagged. The miller, vexed at the delay, took his cudgel and went to the mill, where he was soon felled with his own weapon, bound fast and gagged, and laid beside his wife.

We will now return for a while to Eland Hall, where on the eve of Palm Sunday the young knight retired to rest with his fair wife and their family. A fearful storm disturbed their rest, and the young knight had a terrific dream of armed men grinning horribly, and threatening to slay him and those most dear to him. He rose early in the morning, but still disturbed in mind, fearing that some evil accident was about to befall him. His lady bade him take courage, saying, 'It is the morn of Palm Sunday, and to church we must go, as is our wont; and surely no evil can betide good Christians on such a holy day, and going forth, too, for so holy a purpose.' The knight was persuaded to keep his church, as was ever his wont, and left the hall with his fair lady, and his young son and heir closely following, with several of his household. They thus arrived at the river-bank, where a long weir was carried transversely to conduct the waters to the large wheel of the mill. Below this weir was a ford, over which was a passage by large stepping-stones; which road, leading round the back of the mill, conducted the passenger up the hill to the church and to the town. Scarcely had the knight and his lady reached the river-brink, when a sad and fearful scene, thus told in the ballad, met their eyes:

'The drought had made the waters small,
  The stakes appeared dry;
The knight, his wife, and servants,
  Came down the dam thereby.

'When Adam Beaumont this beheld,
  Forth of the milne (mill) came he;
His bown in hand with him he held,
  And shot at him sharply.

'He hit the knight on his breastplate,
  Whereupon the bolt did glide;
William of Lockwood, wroth thereat,
  Said, "Cousin, you shoot wide."

'Himself did shoot, and hit the knight,
  Who nought was hurt with this;
Whereat the knight had great delight,
  And said to them, "I wis

'"If that my father had been clad
  With armour such certaine,
Your wicked hands escaped he had,
  And had not so been slaine.

'"Oh, Eland Town, alack," said he,
  "If thou but knew of this,
These foes of mine full fast would flee,
  And of their purpose miss."

'William of Lockwood was a dread,
  The town would rise indeed;
He shot the knight right through the head,
  And slew him thus with speed.

'His son and heir was wounded there,
  But dead he did not fall:
Into the house conveyed he was,
  And died in Eland Hall.'

But if these vengeful men thought to escape from the second misdeed as they did from the first, they counted their chances ill. The domestics who had escaped the slaughter instantly gave the alarm, and the town and neighbourhood were roused to arms by the sound of the horn, and by the backward ringing of the bells. The whole parish being assembled,

> 'All sorts of men showed their good will;
> Some bows and shafts did bear;
> Some brought forth clubs and rusty bills,
> That saw no sun that year.'

Beaumont, Lockwood, and Quarmby, seeing the Eland men approach, made a halt, and kept them at bay with their arrows, until these being exhausted, they were compelled to betake themselves to flight, and thought to make good their retreat into the thick copse of Aneley Wood: but Quarmby—who was, in truth, the hardiest of them, and one who had never ceased stirring up the less deadly vengeance of his companions—refused 'to turn his face,' and was soon mortally wounded by his foes:

> 'Lockwood, he bare him on his back,
> And hid him in Aneley Wood,
> To whom his purse he did betake
> Of gold and silver good.'

They did not leave Quarmby until the breath was out of his body; they then continued for some time the pursuit of the other assassins in the direction of Huddersfield. The fate of Lacie is not known, as he is not mentioned in the story after his coming with the others from Furness Fells. Adam Beaumont, deprived of his lands, made his escape into foreign parts, became a Knight of Rhodes, and after greatly distinguishing himself, was killed fighting against the Turks. Another version of the story is, that Lockwood took refuge in a solitary retreat, then called Camel, but now Canon Hall, five miles from Barnsley. This retreat becoming known, he fled to Ferrybridge, and next to Crossland Hall. The sheriff with a great company of men beset the house, and summoned him in the king's name to surrender. He refused to obey, and defended himself for a time, but was induced by fair promises to surrender to the sheriff, who no sooner had him in his power than he put him to death. By this catastrophe the ancient family of the Lockwoods of Lockwood was utterly extirpated. The name of Beaumont still continued to exist, as it appears that Adam de Beaumont had a younger brother, from whom descended a race that flourished to the reign of Charles I.

Dr. Bentley has annexed the history of Sir John Eland to his account of Halifax; and from the investigation of MSS., the whole tragedy here related appears not only probable, but supported by collateral evidence. The deadly feud commenced by Sir John Eland, ended in the murder of the knight and his son, and the extinction of the male line of his family. All the broad lands became the inheritance of the sole surviving child and daughter, Isobel, who, being placed under the guardianship of Sir John Saville of Tankersley, afterwards became his wife, and founded the great and puissant house of Saville, now represented by the Earls of Scarborough, who still hold the manor.

The Tragedy of Sir John Eland.

The ballad already quoted concludes with an injunction to this Saville, who married the heiress, as follows:

> 'Learn, Saville, here, I you beseech,
>   That in prosperitie
> You be not proud, but mild and meek,
>   And dwell in charitie.
>
> 'For by such means your elders came
>   To knightly dignitie;
> But Eland he forsook the same,
>   And came to miserie.'

It may be added, that the house where lived Exley, from whose foul deed this tragedy originated, is still standing in the village of the same name. In its style of building, security sets at defiance convenience, but was fitted for those lawless times when might was right.[1]

---

[1] Burke's *Anecdotes of the Aristocracy*, second series, vol. i.

PONTEFRACT CASTLE AND ITS ECHOES.

PONTEFRACT, one of the most notable historic sites of England, lies about two miles south-west from Ferrybridge, nine miles nearly east from Wakefield, and fifteen miles north-west from Doncaster, in Yorkshire. The town was a burgh in the time of Edward the Confessor. Ilbert de Lacy must be regarded as the founder of the castle, which subsequently became the scene of many events which have conferred upon it opprobrious repute in English history. Judging from the character of the position, on an elevated rock, commanding extensive and picturesque views, and the form of the surrounding earthworks, this fortress was evidently the work of that great Earl whose devotion and services had attached him to the Conqueror, by whom Ilbert de Lacy had made to him large grants of land ; and according to the custom of the age, he enriched as well as founded several religious houses. Kirkstall Abbey and St. Oswald's still exhibit in their ruins a testimony of his munificence. Of the castle which he built at Pontefract in twelve years, there exist but slight architectural vestiges.

The remains of his monastic institutions are of greater extent.

We pass over the several possessors of the castle to Henry de Lacy, who built the castle of Denbigh. His son was drowned in a deep well in this castle, when Pontefract devolved upon his daughter Alicia; and by her marriage with Thomas Plantagenet, nephew of Edward I., the vast estates of the De Lacys were transferred to the Earl of Lancaster.

Upon examining the remains of the round towers still visible at Pontefract, it appears that whilst their foundation may belong to Thomas Earl of Lancaster, all the walling above the set-off is later—not unlikely the work of Henry Duke of Lancaster, who died in 1382. The three sieges the castle underwent in the civil war of the Commonwealth, and the work of demolition ordered by the Parliament, have reduced it to a deplorable state of ruin. Originally it must have been a very grand, though never a very extensive structure. It is difficult to show the real intention of the mysterious subterranean passages. A heated imagination would at once mark them as places 'with many a foul and midnight murder fed;' but the more practical ideas of those accustomed to examine those singular contrivances, would rather ascribe their purpose to a secret means of passing under the fosse, or as the approach to a well. The soft stone through which these passages are cut rendered the work easy. One of these passages to the north or upper portion of the castle descends for several feet by steps in a direct line. At the bottom it terminates in three or four small chambers, hollowed out of the solid rock. This work seems to have been executed in the reign of Edward II.

The names of several of the towers have been preserved: as the Round Tower, Clifford Tower, the Treasurer Tower, Gascoyne's Tower, Swillington Tower, the Red Tower, the Queen's Tower, the King's Tower. All these towers have been assigned in old plans of the castle, but the site can now only be traced, as they were taken down in 1649. Originally, Pontefract was built according to the usual plan of a Norman castle. There was a keep at the western end, and a large bailey below it. The towers were built at equal distances in the curtain-wall of the enclosure. There was a barbican and drawbridge at the south-west angle, and the whole was encircled by a deep fosse. At the north-east angle was a chapel, served by five priests. This building, which owes its erection to Ilbert de Lacy, still retains a portion of masonry belonging to his original foundation.

Amongst the records of the Duchy of Lancaster is a roll of household expenses of the Earl of Lancaster rendered (Edward II.) 1315, showing the Earl's magnificent scale of living. Thus, there was expended £604, 17s. 6½d. in 184 casks and 2 pipes of wine, allowances for barrels of sturgeon and stockfish; 1713 pounds of wax, with vermilion and turpentine for making red wax; costs of the Earl's horses, table-cloths, towels, etc.; almonds, figs, pepper, nutmegs, and various spices—the whole allowance, £5230, 18s. 7½d. Then come the livery of cloth, skins, and saddles, and clothes for the knights, £1079, 18s. 3d.; then allowance for the purchase of horses, fees, gifts, alms, jewels, and payment of debts, £1207, 7s. 11¾d. From these entries it is abundantly clear that the Earl of Lancaster lived sumptuously, spending more than £100,000 a-year, according to the present value of money.

There are great differences of opinion as to the justice of beheading Thomas Earl of Lancaster. Those who hurried on this bloody deed can scarcely find in the official document of his arraignment, words sufficiently strong to express his misdemeanours and crimes. We must recollect that the wretched King Edward's attachment to Gaveston, and his affection for the Despencers, rendered him contemptible in the eyes of the people, and encouraged the Earl of Lancaster to endeavour to check the misgovernment of the country; thus he became the leader of a popular cause, and the instrument by which reforms were eventually established. The turf upon Blacklow Hill was still moist with the blood of Gaveston. His death continued to rankle in the heart of Edward. It was unavenged. Though the favourite's end was alike cruel and contrary to the law as then established, few—perhaps none but the king himself —looked upon it as an illegal act. Yet, without question, such was the eagerness for Gaveston's death, that the formal proceedings of justice were set aside. He had a kind of judicial trial; but the officers of justice authorized by the Crown were not summoned to it. He was condemned without the full assent of Parliament. These proceedings must always leave a stain upon the Earl of Lancaster's character; though his enemies have loaded his memory with many unfounded charges, as shown by the high reputation he obtained immediately after his death. Queen Isabella believed him to be deserving of canonization, which she sedulously besought the Pope to grant, pleading in recommendation the numberless miracles that were wrought at his tomb, and being fully impressed, as people were in the middle ages, with these supernatural works.

Attempts were made to effect a reconciliation between the king and the confederate barons, at the head of whom was Lancaster. The friendship was renewed, but the king was detected in breaking the conditions. A knight who had once served the Earl of Lancaster, was taken near Pontefract with a blank charter under the royal seal, directed to the King of Scotland, offering him any conditions he pleased, provided he would compass the death of his relative. Both parties now flew to arms, but Lancaster soon found himself ill supported by his compeers; and marching northward for reinforcements from Bruce King of Scotland, the king in the meantime sent the Earl of Surrey and Kent to besiege the castle at Pontefract, which surrendered at the first summons. Lancaster was next closely pursued by the king with great superiority of numbers. The Earl, endeavouring to rally his troops, was taken prisoner at Boroughbridge, with ninety-five barons and knights, and carried to the castle of Pontefract, where he was imprisoned in a tower which Leland says he had newly made. This tower had a wall 10½ feet thick and 25 feet square: the only entrance was by a hole or trap-door in the floor of the turret; so that the prisoner must have been let down into this abode of darkness, from whence there could be no possible mode of escape.

A few days after, the king being at Pontefract, ordered Lancaster to be arraigned in the hall before a small number of peers, among whom were the Despencers, his mortal enemies. A series of articles of impeachment was drawn up. The process was exaggerated and diffuse; the accusation feebly made; and the sentence unjust, and wickedly executed. Lancaster was condemned to be hanged, drawn, and quartered; but the punishment was changed to decapitation. After sentence was passed, he said, 'Shall I die without answer?' He was not, however, permitted to speak; but a certain Gascoygne took him away, and having put an old hood over his head, set him on a lean mare, without a bridle. Attended by a Dominican friar as his confessor, he was carried out of the town amidst the insults of the people, and there beheaded. Thus fell Thomas Earl of Lancaster, the first prince of the blood, and uncle to Edward II., who condemned him to death. Several of the Earl's adherents were hanged at Pontefract. The rolls of Parliament, and the wretched king's subsequent conduct, show how the Earl's accusers endeavoured to repair the wrong they had committed. The self-reproaches of the monarch proved his remorse. The Parliament revoked their judgment, and restored the son the estates and honours of which the father had been unjustly deprived. 'It is pitiable to contemplate at this moment the abject state of the king in consequence of the Earl of Lancaster's death. He was keeping his Christmas at York the year following, when a retainer of his late noble relative was taken and condemned to die. One of those about the court, knowing he had formerly occupied a place similar to his own, being touched with compassion at his fate, offered to speak on his behalf to the monarch. He had, however, no sooner begun to implore for his life, than Edward broke into a violent passion, and exclaimed, "Begone, wicked and malicious detractors! you can plead for this worthless fellow, but none of you would so much as open your mouth in behalf of my cousin of Lancaster, who, if he had lived, might have been useful both to myself and to the whole kingdom." Whilst this incident proves that Edward II. was not naturally cruel, it also shows that he repented the crime he had been urged by his advisers to commit.' [1]

After this fearful tragedy, it might be supposed that the walls of Pontefract could never again become so deeply stained with crime; but we are detained by the recital of other deeds, less unprovoked, and perhaps more atrocious. It was on the 23d of October 1399, that Arundell Archbishop of Canterbury, acting on the behalf of Henry of Lancaster, took the first steps for deposing King Richard II.

[1] 'The Honour and Castle of Pontefract,' by the Rev. C. H. Hartshorne; *Journal of the British Archæological Association*, 1864.

He began by charging the Lords Spiritual and Temporal to keep his propositions regarding his dethronement a profound secret; and this might have been directly carried out, had not Percy Earl of Northumberland put some questions to the assembled Parliament, which, interfering with the projected plan, caused it to be deferred a little longer. When the unhappy monarch tendered his resignation of the crown, he showed that if he had failed to discharge them with ability, he was nevertheless fully conscious of the duties a sovereign owes to his people. He declared that he would rather that 'the commonwealth should rise by his fall, than that he should stand upon its ruins.' So that whatever his private faults may have been, it can never be truly laid to his charge that he oppressed his subjects.

At the Parliament which held its sitting in October, it was decreed that the king should be perpetually imprisoned; that a place should be selected which should be unfrequented by any concourse of people; that none of his friends should be permitted to visit him; and that he should be under secret and unknown restraint. The dungeons of 'London's lasting shame' were deemed too cheerful for the captive monarch.

In the 'dolorous castell' of Flint was Richard deposed. Thither he was inveigled by the Earl of Northumberland, with the assurance that Bolingbroke wished no more than to be restored to his own property, and to give the kingdom a Parliament. Northumberland with a small train first met Richard at Conway, then on his return from Ireland. The king distrusted the Earl, who, to remove all suspicion, went with him to mass, and at the altar took an oath of fidelity. The king fell into the snare, and proceeded with the Earl for some time, till he perceived about the precipice of Renmaen Rhôs a large band of soldiers with the Percy banners. Richard would then have retired; but Northumberland, seizing hold of his bridle, forcibly directed his course onward. Richard was hurried to Rhuddlan, where he dined, and reached Flint the same night. The mock homage of Bolingbroke there, the devotion of the king's favourite greyhound, which fawned on his rival, must be in recollection. The king's prison was one of the rooms of the upper floor. As the railway traveller proceeds along the Holyhead line from Chester to Rhyl, the keep of Flint Castle is conspicuous. A portion of the fortress has been pulled down for building a county jail on the castle lands: it is a mercy that any of this interesting historic memorial was spared. Even its cold chambers were deemed too comfortable a place for Richard's wasting life; and the council decreed that he should slowly pine away in the Castle of Pontefract.

Richard had been, however, previously conveyed to the Tower of London, where the formal deposition took place.[1]

---

[1] In Act v. sc. i. of Shakspeare's *Richard the Second*, the line, 'You must to Pomfret, not unto the Tower,' says Mr. Staunton in his *Illustrative Comments*, is not historically correct. In the prose manuscript preserved in the National Library of Paris, is an extremely interesting and characteristic narrative of an interview which took place between the king and Henry of Lancaster while the former was confined in the

There is a tradition that it was merely given out that Richard had starved himself to death, and that he escaped from Pontefract to Mull, whence he shortly proceeded to the mainland of Scotland, where for nineteen years he was entertained in an honourable but secret captivity. This tradition has been wrought into a tale, entitled 'The White Rose in Mull,' in the *Chameleon,* 1832. Here we may remark that a large mass of contradictory evidence has exercised the ingenuity of many historical writers concerning the death of Richard II. The question is full of difficulty, as may be seen in the *Chronicque de la Traison et Mort de Richart deux Roy Dengleterre,* published by the Historical Society in 1846.

The Rev. Mr. Hartshorne observes, upon the vague and

Tower. This manuscript records that when the Dukes of Lancaster and York went to the Tower to see the king, Lancaster desired the Earl of Arundel to send the king to them. When this message was delivered to Richard, he replied: 'Tell Henry of Lancaster from me that I will do no such thing, and that, if he wishes to speak with me, he must come to me.' On entering, none showed any respect to the king except Lancaster, who took off his hat, and saluted him respectfully, and said to him, 'Here is our cousin the Duke of Aunarle, and our uncle the Duke of York, who wish to speak to you.' To which Richard answered, 'Cousin, they are not fit to speak to me.' 'But have the goodness to hear them,' replied Lancaster; upon which Richard uttered an oath, and turning to York, 'Thou villain, what wouldst thou say to me? And thou traitor of Rutland, thou art neither good nor worthy enough to speak to me, nor to bear the name of earl, duke, or knight; thou and the villain thy father have both of you foully betrayed me; in a cursed hour were ye born; by your counsel was my uncle of Gloucester put to death.' The Earl of Rutland replied to the king, that in what he said he lied, and threw down his bonnet at his feet; on which the king said, 'I am king and thy lord, and will conflicting accounts of Richard's death: 'It is perhaps hopeless to expect that we shall gain any fresh information. Under the deficiency of any circumstantial narrative of the king's last few days, we must accept for our guidance the statement of those persons who took a leading part in the transactions of the time. Thus it has been stated by some that Richard was brutally murdered by Sir Piers of Exton; and this story has obtained almost general belief. On the other hand, we have the credible testimony of Archbishop Scroop, an eye-witness of what was passing in public affairs. From his elevated position he must have been cognizant of what measures were adopted; whilst, living at no great distance from Pontefract, he must have become acquainted with what was actually going on. By way of palliating the

---

still continue king, and will be a greater lord than I ever was, in spite of all my enemies.' Upon this Lancaster imposed silence on Rutland. Richard, turning then with a fierce countenance to Lancaster, asked why he was in confinement, and why under a guard of armed men. 'Am I your servant or your king? What mean you to do with me?' Lancaster replied: 'You're my king and lord, but the council of the realm have ordered that you should be kept in confinement till full decision (*jugement*) in Parliament.' The king again swore, and desired he might see his wife. 'Excuse me,' replied the Duke; 'it is forbidden by the council.' Then the king, in great wrath, walked about the room, and at length broke out into passionate exclamations and appeals to Heaven; called them 'false traitors,' and offered to fight any four of them; boasted of his father and grandfather, his reign of twenty-two years; and ended by throwing down his bonnet. Lancaster then fell on his knees, and besought him to be quiet until the meeting of Parliament, and then every one would bring forward his reason.—See Notes by the Rev. John Webb, to his translation of the *French Metrical History*, etc.; *Archæologia*, vol. xx.

mode of the king's death, it has been stated that it was his voluntary act. But there is no reason to dispute the Archbishop's account, which positively declares that Richard lingered for a space of fifteen days, and died under starvation. He perished, says this prelate, by hunger, thirst, and cold; he died the basest death any one in England had ever undergone. Doubtless, if divine vengeance would follow this holy man's excommunication, those who instigated this merciless act would not escape a just reward for their guilt. In the succeeding reign of Henry IV., Archbishop Scroope being taken prisoner, was in Pontefract Castle condemned to death.

Yet again we are compelled to listen, and to shudder as we listen, to other tragic acts that stained the walls of Pontefract with blood. The next noble victim who suffered a violent death within the castle was Anthony Woodville, the gallant Earl of Rivers. He was the most accomplished person of the age, himself an author, and the liberal patron of that illustrious artisan who first practised the art of printing in England. No ostensible reason has been assigned for his execution; and it was the more unjust, because the Protector, afterwards Richard III., hurried Lord Rivers, his uncle, and his half-brother Sir Richard Grey, with Sir Thomas Vaughan, to the scaffold, without the usual form of a trial. Shakspeare makes Richard III. to whine forth these lines:

'O Pomfret, Pomfret! O thou bloody prison!
Fatal and ominous to noble peers!

P

> Within the guilty closure of thy walls
> Richard the Second here was hack'd to death;
> And for more slander to thy dismal seat,
> We give to thee our guiltless blood to drink.'

'In reviewing the three great tragedies that we have witnessed at Pontefract, we must have been struck with the immunity under which these flagrant acts of barbarity and injustice were perpetrated. Even the person of the sovereign was as little respected as that of the nobility. The principles of sound government were in their infancy. The obedience due to monarchical power was little regarded, or indeed understood; whilst the nobility on their part coerced, as they had the opportunity, the sovereign and their vassals alike. There was no real security for property or life; the exigencies of the crowd excited it to violence, and the fear of opposition from the barons first led the Plantagenets to appeal to the people in their own defence. Thus, step by step, our constitution became formed out of the pressure of circumstances.'[1]

We now pass over matters of minor importance in the history of Pontefract to the time of Charles I. In the king's contest with his Parliament, this was the last fortress that held out for the unfortunate monarch. At Christmas 1644 Sir Thomas Fairfax laid siege to the castle, and on 19th January following, after an incessant cannonade of three days, a breach was made. The brave garrison would not surrender; the besiegers mined, but the besieged

[1] The Rev. Mr. Hartshorne, *ut ante*.

countermined, and the work of slaughter went on till the garrison were greatly reduced. At length, the Parliamentarians were attacked and repulsed by a reinforcement of Royalists from Oxford; and thus ended the first siege of Pontefract.

In March 1645 the enemy again took possession of the town; and after three months' cannonade, the garrison, being reduced almost to a state of famine, surrendered the castle by an honourable capitulation on 20th June. Sir Thomas Fairfax was appointed governor; and he, thinking the Royal party to be subdued, appointed a colonel as his substitute, with a garrison of 100 men. The Royalists next by stratagem recovered Pontefract, of which Sir John Digby was appointed governor.

The third and final siege of this fine castle commenced in October 1648. General Rainsborough was appointed to the command of the army; but he being previously intercepted at Doncaster, Oliver Cromwell undertook to conduct the siege. After having remained a month before the fortress without making any impression upon its massive walls, Cromwell joined the grand army under Fairfax; and General Lambert, being appointed commander-in-chief of the forces before the castle, arrived at Pontefract on the 4th of December. He raised new works, and vigorously pushed the siege: but the besieged held out. On 30th January 1649 the King was beheaded; and the news no sooner reached Pontefract than the Royalist garrison proclaimed his son Charles II., and made a vigorous and slaughtering sally against their enemies. The Parliamentarians, however, prevailed; and on 25th March 1649, the garrison, being reduced from 500 or 600 to 100 men, surrendered by capitulation. Six of the principal Royalists were excepted from mercy: two escaped, but were retaken, and executed at York; the third was killed in a sortie; and the three others, concealing themselves among the ruins of the castle, escaped after the surrender; two of the last lived to see the Restoration.

This third siege was most destructive to the castle: the tremendous artillery had shattered its massive walls; and its demolition was completed by order of Parliament. Within two months after its reduction, the buildings were unroofed, and all the materials sold. Thus was this princely fortress reduced to a heap of ruins. During the siege the fine church of All Saints was greatly damaged: the roof was almost destroyed, and the fine lantern surmounting the tower was battered down. The lantern was, however, rebuilt in its present form, in consequence of a vote of Parliament, which allotted £1000 for that purpose out of the money accruing from the sale of the materials of the castle.

Pontefract Castle, by its situation as well as by its structure, was rendered almost impregnable. It was not commanded by any contiguous hills, and could only be taken by blockade. The whole area occupied by the fortress was about seven acres.

The north-west prospect from the castle heights takes

in the beautiful vale watered by the Aire, skirted by woods and plantations; it is bounded only by the hills of Craven. The north and east prospects are more extensive; the scenery is less striking, but the towers of York Minster are distinctly seen. To the east, whilst the eye follows the course of the Aire towards the Humber, the fertility of the country, the spires of churches, and the hills Brayton, Barf, and Hambleton Haugh, one covered with wood, add to the beauty and variety of the scene. The south-east view includes part of the counties of Lincoln and Nottingham. To the south and south-west the towering hills of Derbyshire, stretching towards Lancashire, form the horizon; while the foreground is a picturesque country, variegated with handsome residences. In a *Topographical Excursion in the Year* 1634, Pomfret is described as 'a high and stately, famous and princely, impregnable castle and cittadel, built by a Norman upon a rock; which, for the situation, strength, and largenesse (?), may compare with any in the kingdom.' The highest of the seven towers is the Round Tower, in which that unfortunate prince (Richard II.) was 'enforc'd to flee round a poste till his barbarous butchers inhumanly depriv'd him of life. Upon that poste the cruell hackings and fierce blowes doe still remaine. We view'd the spacious hall, which the gyants kept, the large fayre kitchen, which is long, with many wide chimneys in it,' etc.

The origin and etymology of the name of the town are alike unknown. According to Camden, its name was changed to Pontefract by the Romans. The place was called Kirkby in the time of the Saxons, and it is not improbable that it was one of the first places in England at which a church was erected and Christianity preached. William the Conqueror is said to have called the name of the town *Pomfrete*, from some fancied resemblance to a place so called in Normandy, where he was born. For 600 years, the castle was the ornament and terror of the surrounding country. At the present day, little even of its ruins remains. The area is now chiefly occupied by gardens, and a quarry of filtering stones, which are in great request in all parts of the kingdom.

Pontefract must be numbered in our recollections of childhood; since here were grown whole fields of liquorice root, from the extract of which were made *Pontefract cakes*, impressed with the town arms—three lions passant gardant, surmounted with a helmet, full-forward, open-faced, and garde-visure. We have likewise seen these cakes impressed with the celebrated castle, and the motto, '*Post mortem patris, pro filio*' (after the death of the father, for the son)—bespeaking the loyalty of the Pontefract royalists in proclaiming Charles II. after the death of his father.

THE RADCLIFFES OF DERWENTWATER.

THE Radcliffes of Derwentwater were one of the oldest families in Cumberland. In that county, through the mountains called Derwent Falls, the river Derwent spreads itself into a spacious lake, wherein are three islands: one was the seat of the family of Radcliffe, knight, *temp.* Henry v., who married Margaret, daughter of Sir John de Derwentwater, knight; another island was inhabited by miners; and the third is supposed to be that wherein Bede mentions St. Herbert to have led a hermit's life. James, the Earl of Derwentwater, who died the victim of his stedfast though misguided loyalty in 1716, was greatly lamented. He was a perfect cavalier, and a fine exemplar of an English nobleman; he was amiable, brave, open, generous, hospitable, and humane. He gave bread to multitudes of people whom he employed on his estate: the poor, the widow, the orphan, rejoiced in his bounty. He was only twenty-eight years of age when he was brought to the scaffold; and he left a young and beautiful widow, Anne Maria, the daughter of Sir John Webb, baronet, and two infant children, to lament his death, and suffer by his attainder. That exquisitely touching ballad, 'Farewell to Lochaber,' is said to have been written by the Earl, and addressed to his wife on the eve of his departure for the miserable venture wherein he forfeited life, lands, and nobility.

The end of the ill-starred Charles Radcliffe, titular Earl of Derwentwater, was summary. After his conviction for treason in 1716, he received several reprieves from time to time on account of his youth; and the Government wishing to shed no more of the blood of his house, he would have been pardoned; but he and thirteen others made their escape from Newgate, 11th December 1716, and thus placed themselves beyond the benefit of the general Act of Grace, which was passed about that time.

Radcliffe, on reaching the Continent, went to Rome, and obtained a small pension from the Chevalier. He then settled in Paris, and there married Lady Newburgh. He twice during his exile came to London; and though his presence was known to the Government, his visits passed unmolested. The rising of 1745 brought him again into action. He sailed from Calais in the November of that year on board a French man-of-war, with his son and other officers, and a quantity of ammunition of war. The vessel, no doubt bound for Scotland in aid of the insurgents (though there was no legal proof given of the fact), was seized in the open sea by the Sheerness man-of-war, and brought to Deal. Radcliffe and his son were committed to the Tower. The son being deemed a foreigner, was exchanged on the first cartel; but Radcliffe himself was confined until the rebellion was over, when, in Michaelmas term 1746, he was brought to the bar of the Court of King's Bench, to have execution awarded against him on his former sentence. He pleaded that he was not the same person as the party convicted, and prayed time to bring witnesses; but as he would not deny, in his affidavit relative to the absence of witnesses, that he was the attainted Charles Radcliffe, the court proceeded, and decided against his plea. He then wished to plead the general pardon of 1716; but the court (one judge, Sir Michael Forster, dissenting) would hear no further plea, and the prisoner was ordered for execution. Though then legally no nobleman, regard was so far paid to the rank and station of his family, that he did not undergo the then ordinary punishment for treason; but, like his brother the Earl of Derwentwater, he was decapitated on Tower Hill. He died, as he had lived, one of the most devoted and unbending adherents of the house of Stuart, and behaved at his execution with dignified calmness and courage. Charles Radcliffe was the mainspring of the support his house gave to the Chevalier: he and his brother, besides their lives, lost in the cause £300,000 in real value. (Notes to Burke's *Peerage*, 1865.)

Walpole writes to Sir Horace Mann, November 29, 1745: 'A small ship has taken the *Soleil*, privateer from Dunkirk, going to Montrose, with twenty French officers, sixty others, and the brother of the beheaded Lord Derwentwater, and his son, who at first was believed to be the second boy.

News came yesterday of a second privateer, taken with arms and money; of another lost on the Dutch coast, and of Vernon being in pursuit of two more. All this must be a great damp to the party, who are coming on fast, fast to their destruction. Last night they were to be at Preston. The country is so far from rising for them, that the towns are left desolate on their approach, and the people hide and bury their effects, even to their pewter. Warrington bridge is broken down, which will turn them some miles aside.'

In another letter, dated December 9, Walpole describes the advance of the rebels to Derby, where they got £19,000, plundered the town, and burnt a house of the Countess of Exeter. Though they marched thus into the heart of the kingdom, there was not the least symptom of a rising. In London the aversion to them was amazing. 'But the greatest demonstration of loyalty appeared on the prisoners being brought to town from the *Soleil* prize. The young man is certainly Mr. Radcliffe's son; but the mob, persuaded of his being the youngest Pretender, could scarcely be restrained from tearing him to pieces all the way on the road, and at his arrival. He said he had heard of English mobs, but could not conceive they had been so dreadful, and wished he had been shot at the battle of Dettingen, where he had been engaged. The father, whom they call Lord Derwentwater, said, on entering the Tower, that he never expected to arrive there alive. For the young man, he must only be treated as a French captive; for the father, it is sufficient to produce him at the Old Bailey, and prove that he is the individual person condemned for the last rebellion, and so for Tyburn.'

Amidst the romantic scenery of Hexham in Northumberland, near the Devil-water stream, are the remains of Dilston, or Devilstone Hall, the desolate appearance of which is sadly in unison with the brief and melancholy history of the devoted and unfortunate Earl of Derwentwater. Dilston, the baronial seat of the ancient family of Devilstone, is about two miles distant from Hexham. It stands on an eminence at the entrance to a deep, woody dell, near the confluence of the Devil-water and the river Tyne. The hall was rebuilt in 1768, but has fallen to ruin, except the chapel belonging to it, which is kept in repair, and whose vault contains the remains of the Radcliffe family. The baronial tower of the ancient lords of Devilstone still exists near the ruins of the comparatively modern edifice of the Radcliffes. About two miles higher up the stony course of the river, is a spot called the Linnels, where the Lancastrian army encamped previously to the battle of Hexham; and not far from this historic site, opposite a farm called the Black Hill, is 'The Queen's Cave,' traditionally the place where the fugitive Queen Margaret and her infant son were protected by the robber after the disastrous battle of Hexham. It is a recess in the rock, 31 feet long and 14 feet broad, but so low as scarcely to allow a person of ordinary height to stand upright within it.

The barony of the Devylstounes passed from the family of that name in succession to the Tyndales,—a family which produced William Tyndale, one of the first translators of the Scriptures into the English language, and who was burnt for heresy at Antwerp in 1536. Another member of the family is recorded under the remarkable denomination of 'Jock Fitz Jolilock,' otherwise 'John about the Pan.' From this family the barony was transmitted to the Claxtons, one of whom married Sir Edward Radcliffe, a knight of the body to Henry VIII., and who became heir in remainder to the estates, failing issue of his brother Sir Richard.

The fortunes of the ill-fated Earl, who devoted himself to a forlorn cause, urged by a principle of romantic honour, and paid the penalty upon the scaffold at Tower Hill, have scarcely at this day ceased to be deplored in Northumberland, where his gracious and amiable qualities have endeared his memory to popular remembrance. Strange tales have been narrated of the superstitions of the simple inhabitants of the Devil-water and the neighbourhood of Corbridge, relating to the portents which preceded the death of the unfortunate nobleman and the downfall of an ancient family; and the aurora borealis, which made an extraordinarily vivid appearance in Northumberland on the night of the execution, is still called by old persons *Lord Derwentwater's Corpse Lights.*

The Earl was denied his last request, to be laid with his ancestors, embodied in a ballad well known in the north country as 'Derwentwater's Farewell:'

> 'Albeit that here, in London town,
> It is my fate to die,

THE RADCLIFFES OF DERWENTWATER. 237

> Oh, carry me to Northumberland,
> In my father's grave to lie.
> There chant my holy requiem
> In Hexham's holy towers,
> And let six maids of fair Tynedale
> Scatter my grave with flowers.'

His remains were ostensibly interred in the churchyard of St. Giles-in-the-Fields, where is a stone to his memory, bearing his arms and an inscription, both nearly obliterated. It is on the north side of the churchyard, not far from the tomb of the Pendrells, famous for their devotion to an earlier member of the Stuart family, in whose cause the Earl fell a sacrifice. But either the above funeral was a mock ceremony, or the corpse was subsequently disinterred; for, on an examination of the family vault in 1805, made by the Commissioners of Greenwich Hospital, the body was capable of being recognised, not only by the mark of decapitation, but also, from being remarkably preserved, by the open countenance and regular features, which were still found to correspond with the portrait of the ill-starred nobleman.[1] It is traditionally said that the Earl's body was conveyed privately by night to this place, and that by day it was deposited in different houses on the road belonging to persons of the Roman Catholic Church, where solemn obsequies were performed over it. The chapel at Dagen-

---

[1] We may here add, that among the funds by means of which Greenwich Hospital is supported are the forfeited estates of the Earl of Derwentwater, given by Act of Parliament in 1735, deducting an annual rent-charge of £2500 to the Earl of Newburgh and his heirs-male.

ham Park, in Essex, is said to have been one of those resting-places; and at Ingatestone, in the same county, there was, some twenty years ago, in an almshouse, an aged woman, whose mother, as she stated, assisted in sewing on the Earl's head. At Thorndon, the seat of Lord Petre, is preserved an oaken chest, bearing an inscription in brass, engraved by Lady Derwentwater's order: it contains the dress worn by the Earl at his execution, the neck of the shirt being cut away; also the black serge which covered the block, stiffened with blood, and cut through by the fatal blow which severed the head.[1]

These interesting details possess additional value from their being contributed by one familiar with the locality, namely Mr. Wykeham Archer, the sound antiquary and topographer, especially of the historic ground of Northumberland, where sites of Roman fame are better remembered by their association with stirring scenes and events in our own history.

[1] The fourth Earl of Derwentwater, John, son of the decapitated Earl, married Elizabeth Countess of Walsten, in her own right, in the Cathedral of Frankfort-on-the-Maine, 1740. He attained the age of 86, and died 1798. His body was buried at Ashaffenburg, but in 1799 his heart was conveyed by his two sons secretly, to be placed below the body of his decapitated father, in the little ruinous family chapel at Devilstone in Northumberland. These two sons served with distinction at Waterloo. The fifth Earl died without issue. The sixth Earl married Princess Sobiesky; he died in 1833. His son, the seventh Earl, died in 1854, unmarried. The representative of this old, distinguished, noble family, is Amelia, the present Countess of Derwentwater, so well known for her artistic talents.—*Communication to the 'Times' by 'A Genealogical Historian,'* 1868.

THE BRAVE EARL OF LEVEN.

THIS renowned person, one of the most noted soldiers of his time, remarkable for his coolness and courage, and his great knowledge of the military art, was of high birth, his family being a branch of the very ancient and historic house of Lesley, or Leslie, Earls of Rothes. He was the only son of George Lesley, a brave soldier, who had the command of the garrison in the Castle of Blair in the reign of King James VI. He (Sir Alexander Lesley) first acted as a volunteer in Lord Vere's regiment in Holland, where he soon rose to the degree of a captain. He then went to Sweden, and entered into the service of Gustavus Adolphus, and behaved so gallantly, that that warlike monarch raised him to the rank of a lieutenant-general, and then to that of field-marshal of his armies. In 1628, when the town of Stralsund was besieged by a victorious army under the command of Count Walsten, and reduced almost to the last extremity, the king sent General Lesley to take upon him the command of the garrison; and he there acted with such singular resolution and conduct, that he obliged the Count to raise the siege. The burghers were so sensible of the service Lesley had done them, that they struck several medals in his honour, some of which have been preserved in the family. In 1630, Lesley drove the Imperialists entirely out of Rugen. He continued in the Swedish service with high distinction, until the troubles in Scotland brought him home. He was in 1638 invited by the Covenanters to take upon him the command of their army, which he accepted; and he was made governor of the Castle of Edinburgh in March 1639. In 1640 he invaded England at the head of the Scotch army, and defeated a party of the king's troops under the command of Lord Conway at Newburn, and took possession of Newcastle. At the treaty with the king at Ripon, General Lesley was one of the Parliament's commissioners; and the king was so well pleased with the General's behaviour, that he created him Lord Balgony and Earl of Leven by patent dated 1641. After going in 1642 to Ireland to suppress the insurrection there, Lesley Earl of Leven had again in 1643 the command of the Scotch army that was sent to the assistance of the Parliament's forces against the king; and the victory of Marston Moor in 1644 was chiefly ascribed to him. He was appointed in 1647 Lord-General of Scotland.

Notwithstanding his support of the Parliamentarians, Lesley showed himself afterwards more loyal than otherwise, owing to his disapproval of the king's murder. After that event, none appeared more forward than the Earl of Leven in raising an army and restoring King Charles II.

The Brave Earl of Leven.

He served as a volunteer against Oliver Cromwell at the battle of Dunbar, and heartily joined and concurred with the Royalists in every measure for the Restoration; but when he, with others of the royal party, had a meeting in Angus to concert matters for their future conduct, General Monk, who then besieged Dundee, having got intelligence of their meeting, sent a strong party in the night, surprised and took them prisoners at Alyth, in Angus, and transferred the veteran Leven, with several others, prisoners to London, where they were confined in the Tower. The Earl remained incarcerated there, and suffered sequestration and many other hardships, till, by the mediation of the Queen of Sweden, he obtained his liberty; and was so sensible of the service her Majesty had done him, that he went over to Sweden to make his acknowledgments, and was there received and entertained with great respect in honour of his former services. He at last returned to his own country, retired to his seat, Balgony, in Fife, and died there at a very advanced age in 1662.

FYNDERN AND THE FYNDERNES.

THE picturesque little village of Fyndern, about five miles south-west of Derby, was for many centuries the seat of the Fyndernes, probably from the time of the Norman Conquest. There they continued until the family became extinct in the middle of the sixteenth century, when the sole heiress, Jane Fynderne, became the wife of Chief-Justice Harpur of Swarkestone, the ancestor of the present owner of the estates, Sir John Harpur Crewe, Bart., of Calke Abbey. The name of Walter Fynderne occurs as one of the attesting witnesses to a charter of Ranulph sixth Earl of Chester, to Repton Priory, about 1190, which shows their early connection with this place. The Fyndernes were also of Staffordshire, Warwickshire, Essex, Berkshire, etc.

One sad episode in the history of the family of the Fyndernes—and it is not the only one—is brought to light by the singular will of Henry, the last Lord Gray of Codnor, in Derbyshire. By this document it appears that one of the daughters of this honourable house, Katherine Fynderne, had fallen from the path which the others had trodden so virtuously and so well, and had become the mistress of this nobleman, and borne him several sons, who survived him. There is, however, reason to believe that she belonged to the Nottinghamshire branch of the Fyndernes, and was not a daughter, but a cousin, of the Fyndernes of Fynderne. By this will it appears that Henry Lord Gray of Codnor (who, being much devoted to chemistry, procured a licence for the transmutation of metals, and had grants of lands for his great services from Edward IV. and Richard III.) was thrice married: first, to Margaret ———; secondly, to Katherine, daughter to the Duchess of Norfolk; and thirdly, to Katherine, said to be the daughter to the Earl of Devonshire. It would seem that he had a liking for the name of Devonshire, having two wives and a mistress all bearing that name.

Jane Fynderne, the last of the family, in whose lovely person were brought together all the virtues and all the possessions not only of the original Derbyshire stock, but of the Nottinghamshire branch of the Fyndernes, became the wife of Lord Chief-Justice Harpur, to whom she brought the ample estates for so many generations held and enjoyed by her ancestors. She became the mother of two knights, Sir John Harpur of Swarkestone, and Sir Richard Harpur of Littleover, from the first of whom the present family of Harpur-Crewe is lineally descended; the name of Crewe having been taken in 1808, by sign-manual, by the then Sir Henry Harpur.

Mr. Llewellyn Jewitt, F.S.A., in a very interesting paper

in the *Reliquary*, 1863, thus sketches the sad scene of long decay, in one of his visits to the spot :—

The seat of the De Fyndernes was at some little distance from the church, on rising ground, at the other side of the village green. It was once a stately mansion of great extent. In the croft where it stood the foundations of the walls may still be traced, as may also remains of terraces and outer wallings of considerable extent; while on the opposite side of the churchyard are also foundations of other buildings, of 'fish-ponds,' and other appliances, in the midst of these turf-grown remains, which are all that are left to show where the princely hospitality of the Fyndernes had been kept for generation after generation.

From the times of Edward I. to those of Henry VIII., the house of Fyndern was one of the most distinguished in Derbyshire. Members of it had won their spurs in the Crusades, and at Cressy, and at Agincourt. The territorial possessions of the Fyndernes were large. The Fyndernes were High Sheriffs, occasionally Rangers of Needwood Forest, and Custodians of Tutbury Castle;[1] and they matched

---

[1] 'Stout Ferrers there kept faithless ward,
And Gaunt perform'd his castle-guard.
There captive Mary look'd in vain
For Norfolk and her nuptial train;
Enrich'd with royal tears the Dove,
But sigh'd for freedom, not for love.'—
Needwood Forest, by Mundy.

Mary Queen of Scots was a prisoner in Tutbury Castle at the time of

with some of the best families of their times. The present church, then the family chapel, had rows of monumental brasses, and altar-tombs, all memorials of the Fyndernes.

Of the 'Fynderne flowers,' and the poetic tradition which connects them with the Fyndernes, Sir Bernard Burke thus touchingly writes in his *Vicissitudes of Families* :—

'In 1850 a pedigree research caused me to pay a visit to the village. I sought for the ancient hall. Not a stone remained to tell where it had stood! I entered the church. Not a single record of a Finderne was there! I accosted a villager, hoping to glean some stray traditions of the Findernes. "Findernes!" said he; "we have no Findernes here, but we have something that once belonged to them: we have *Findernes' flowers*." "Show me them," I replied. And the old man led me into a field which still retained faint traces of terraces and foundations. "There," said he, pointing to a bank of "garden flowers grown wild," "there are the Findernes' flowers, brought by Sir Geoffrey from the Holy Land; and do what we will, they will never die!" Poetry mingles more with our daily life than we are apt to acknowledge; and even to an antiquary like myself, the old man's prose and the subject of it were the very essence of poetry.

'For more than three hundred years the Fyndernes had been extinct, the mansion they had dwelt in had crumbled

the Duke of Norfolk's intrigues. She listened to his proposals of marriage as the only means of obtaining her liberty, declaring herself otherwise averse to further matrimonial connections.

into dust, the brass and marble intended to perpetuate the name had passed away, and a little tiny flower had for ages preserved a name and a memory which the elaborate works of man had failed to rescue from oblivion. The moral of the incident is as beautiful as the poetry. We often talk of "the language of flowers;" but of the eloquence of flowers we never had such a striking example as that presented in these flowers of Fynderne:

> '"Time, Time, his withering hand hath laid
>   On battlement and tower;
> And where rich banners were displayed,
>   Now only waves a flower."'

'This tradition, which has given inspiration to more than one poet, is very general among the villagers. It is said that the flowers brought from the Holy Land, and planted there by the hands of the Crusader himself, can never die. This belief has, I regret to say, had a sad check in the circumstance to which I have alluded, as related to me by many of the inhabitants of the village. A former tenant of the field where they grew—the flowers I have seen were the narcissus, but other kinds also bloomed there—dug them up wherever seen, and removed them to his garden, where they died away. Their memory, however, will *never die*.'

THE GOLDSMITH OF LEEDS:

A Tragic Tale.

THE mace or civic sceptre of the Leeds Corporation has a very curious historical association. It bears an engraved inscription, which states that it was made by a goldsmith of the name of Maingee: 'Arthur Maingee de Leeds fecit.' This revered emblem of municipal loyalty was made in 1694, and the goldsmith who made it was *hanged for high treason* two years afterwards. The circumstances of his trial and execution are very extraordinary. Mr. Maingee was arraigned at the summer assizes held at York, in 1696, before the Lord Chief-Justice Turton. The charge was for high treason, in counterfeiting the lawful coin of the realm. The chief witness against Maingee was an approver of the name of George Norcross, a supposed accomplice. The late Mr. Norrison Scatcherd, of Morley, has left us a long detailed account of this trial in manuscript. From this document it would appear that the prosecution was conducted as much by the Chief-Justice who tried the case, as by the counsel for the Crown. Norcross proved that he was employed by Maingee as a clipper at 5s. a-day, and that he saw him not only clip the sheets of base metal into the size and form of the intended shilling or half-crown, with shears, but that he also saw him stamp it on both sides by striking it heavily with a forge hammer, on a balk in the roof of his house, in a secret chamber. This witness was supported in his statement by a man and woman whose stories were very incoherent. In summing up, his Lordship concluded thus: 'Gentlemen, if you believe what has been proved against Mr. Maingee to be true, you are to find him guilty. But, on the contrary, if you believe what Maingee and his witnesses tell you, and discredit the evidence for the king, you are to find him not guilty. But as far as I see, gentlemen, it appears otherwise. Still it is not I, but you, who must be his judges in this case. I have no more to say to you, gentlemen.' Most persons will agree in thinking that his Lordship had said quite enough. The jury, of course, under such direction brought in a verdict of guilty, and Maingee was sentenced the same evening (26th August) to be drawn on a hurdle to the common place of execution, and there to be hanged as a traitor. Urgent applications were made in Maingee's behalf to the Government, and he was actually twice reprieved. But in the end the Chief-Justice's influence prevailed, and the unfortunate jeweller was executed on the 3d of October following. Norcross then accused Alderman Ibbetson, Mr. Blayds, Mr. Totty, Mr. Walker, and several other respectable burgesses, of being concerned in this extensive system of coining base money, and selling clippings to Maingee. But in these cases his testimony was unsupported and discredited, and the bills were thrown out by the grand jury. After this break-down Norcross disappeared from Leeds. It was reasonably supposed that Maingee was most unjustly convicted upon such disreputable testimony, especially as he made a solemn asseveration of his innocence, after receiving the sacrament on the morning of his execution. At the same time he entirely exonerated those fellow-citizens who were included in the same accusation by Norcross. Maingee, in fact, was universally considered a murdered man, if not a martyr.

Now comes a curious sequel to this tragic story. It happened that it became necessary to pull down Maingee's old house in Briggate in 1832, just 136 years after his execution. The site of this house is at present occupied by three new houses, a few doors below Kirkgate, nearly opposite to Green and Buck's, the grocers. Well, in stripping off the roof of this old house, the workmen came upon a small secret chamber; and on the floor of this chamber they found these two pairs of shears or clippers, these being the very tools with which Norcross swore Maingee and himself used to clip the coins. Here we have two dumb witnesses brought forward after this long lapse of time to corroborate the discredited evidence of this approver of infamous reputation. How very fortunate for the worthy Alderman Ibbetson, Messrs. Blayds, Totty, Walker, and Co., that this concealed chamber was not more carefully examined before their indictments were quashed by the grand jury at York; for it is otherwise quite possible (with the sanguinary laws by which especially forgeries were punished in those days—indeed, even up to the present century) that Alderman Ibbetson, and several other respectable burgesses, before whom this identical mace was often borne in imposing civic procession to the old parish church, might have been all hanged as accomplices of the unlucky goldsmith.

The guilt of the goldsmith has, however, been questioned. The finding of common tools, without the discovery of dies, coins, base or otherwise, effects of hammering on a balk, etc., 136 years after the occurrence, can scarcely, it is thought, be deemed sufficient evidence to confirm his iniquity. The whole appears to rest upon the value of the testimony of the principal witness, who swore to having seen the operations performed.

A COUNTRY GENTLEMAN OF THE SEVENTEENTH CENTURY.

IN the year 1638 lived Mr. Henry Hastings, by his quality son, brother, and uncle to the Earl of Huntingdon. He was peradventure an original in his age, or rather the copy of our ancient nobility in hunting, not in warlike times. He was low, very strong and very active, with a reddish flaxen hair; his clothes always green cloth, and never worth, when new, five pounds.

His house was perfectly of the olden fashion, in the midst of a large park well stocked with deer; and near the house, rabbits for his kitchen; many fish-ponds; great store of wood and timber; a bowling-green in it long but narrow, full of high ridges, it being never levelled since it was ploughed. They used round sand-bowls, and the green had a banqueting-house like a stand, a large one built in a tree. He kept all manner of sport-hounds that ran buck, fox, hare, otter, and badger; and hawks, long and short winged. He had all sorts of net for fish. He had a walk in the New Forest and manor of Christchurch:

this last supplied him with red deer, sea and river fish; indeed, all his neighbours' grounds and royalties were free to him, who bestowed all his time on these sports, but what he borrowed to caress his neighbours' wives and daughters. This made him very popular; always speaking kindly to the husband, brother, or father, who was, to boot, very welcome to his house. Whenever he came there, he found beef, pudding, and small-beer in great plenty; the house not so neatly kept as to shame him or his dirty shoes; the great hall strewed with marrow-bones; full of hawks, perches, hounds, spaniels, and terriers; the upper side of the hall hung with fox-skins of this and the last year's killing; here and there a polecat intermixed; game-keepers' and hunters' poles in great abundance.

The parlour was a large room as properly furnished; on a great hearth, paved with bricks, lay some terriers, and the choicest hounds and spaniels. Seldom but two of the great chairs had litters of cats in them, which were not to be disturbed,—he having always three or four attending him at dinner,—and a little white stick of fourteen inches long lying by his trencher, that he might defend such meat that he had no mind to part with to them. The windows, which were very large, served for places to lay his arrows, cross-bows, stone-bows, and such like accoutrements. The corners of the room full of the best chosen hunting or hawking poles. His oyster table at the lower end, which was of constant use twice a day all the year round; for he never failed to eat oysters at both dinner and supper time all seasons. The neighbouring town of Poole supplied him with them.

The upper part of the room had two small tables and a desk, on the one side of which was a church Bible, and on the other side the *Book of Martyrs*. On the table were hawks' hoods, bells, and such like; two or three old hats, with their crowns thrust in so as to hold ten or a dozen eggs, which were of the pheasant kind of poultry: these he took much care of, and fed himself. Tables, dice, cards, and bones were not wanting. In the hole of the desk were stores of tobacco-pipes that had been used. One side of this end of the room was the door of a closet: therein stood the strong beer and wine, which never came from thence but in single glasses, that being the rule of the house, exactly observed; for he never exceeded in drink, or permitted it. On the other side was the door of an old chapel, not used for devotion. The pulpit, as the safest place, was never wanting of a cold chine of beef, venison pasty, gammon of bacon, or a great apple-pie with thick crust, extremely baked. His table cost him not much, though it was good to eat at. His sports supplied all but beef and mutton, except Fridays, when he had the best of salt fish, as well as other fish he could get; and this was the day his neighbours of best quality visited him. He never wanted a London pudding, and always sung it in with 'My part lies therein.' He drank a glass or two of wine at his meals, very often put syrup of gillyflowers in his sack, and had always a tunglass without feet placed by him, holding a pint of small beer, which he often stirred with rosemary. He was well-natured, but soon angry. He lived to be a hundred, and never lost his eye-sight, but always wrote and read without spectacles, and got on horseback without help. Until past fourscore he rode to the death of a stag as well as any. He died on the 5th of October 1650. (*Extracted from the Works of Lord Chancellor Cooper, Earl of Shaftesbury.*)

A FOUNDLING KNIGHT.

Sir William de Sevenoake, a person of distinction in the fifteenth century, rose from beggary to opulence. According to Lambarde, in his *Perambulation of Kent*, De Sevenoake was deserted by his parents when a boy, and found lying in the street of the town of Sevenoaks. By some charitable persons he was brought up and apprenticed to a grocer in London, and became alderman of Tower Ward, and 'maior and chief majistrate of that citie' in 1418. He was knighted by Henry VI., and represented the city in Parliament. After accumulating great wealth, he died in 1432, and was buried in the old church of St. Martin, Ludgate, which was taken down in 1436. Sir William de Sevenoake has perpetuated his name and philanthropy by founding and endowing a grammar school and almshouse in the town wherein he was found as above.

THREE EARLS STANHOPE.

THE barony of Stanhope has been filled in succession by three remarkable men of independent character and eminent public services. The first Earl was the eldest son of the Honourable Alexander Stanhope, a distinguished diplomatist in the reigns of King William and Queen Anne. His son became eminent as a soldier, and carried arms under King William in Flanders, and under the Duke of Schomberg and Earl of Peterborough. He was appointed to the command of the British forces in Spain in 1708, and obtained considerable renown by the reduction of the celebrated Port Mahon, in the island of Minorca. At the close of his military career he became an active Whig leader in Parliament, took office under Sunderland, and soon after was raised to the peerage. His death was very sudden. He was of a constitutionally warm and sensitive temper. In the course of the discussion of the South Sea Company's affairs, which so unhappily involved some of the leading members of the Government, the Duke of Wharton (Feb. 4, 1721) made some severe remarks in the House of Lords, comparing the conduct of

Ministers to that of Sejanus, who made the reign of Tiberius hateful to the old Romans. Stanhope, in rising to reply, spoke with such vehemence in vindication of himself and his colleagues, that he burst a blood-vessel, and died the next day. 'May it be eternally remembered,' says the *British Merchant*, 'to the honour of Earl Stanhope, that he died poorer in the king's service than when he came into it. Walsingham, the great Walsingham, died poor; but the great Stanhope lived in the time of the South Sea temptations.'

Philip, the second Earl Stanhope, died in 1786, aged seventy-two. His eldest son Charles (the third Earl) married Lord Chatham's eldest daughter, Hester Pitt, of which marriage was born the eccentric Lady Hester Stanhope. Both the above Earls were exceedingly liberal in their political opinions, and both were excellent mathematicians. The first was so in spite of his guardian, the celebrated Earl of Chesterfield, who prohibited him when a boy from the pursuit of his favourite study. He was also an accomplished linguist, a sound classical scholar, with so retentive a memory that he could repeat the whole of the *Iliad* and *Odyssey* by rote. Earl Philip was a munificent patron of learning and learned men. As a statesman, he was one of the most independent of his day. That day was one of splendid extravagance; but Earl Philip did not follow the mode. On one of his occasional visits to the House of Lords from Geneva, where he long resided, a new door-keeper seeing him about to pass into the House in a dress of extreme simplicity, impeded his entrance, with the remark, 'Now, then, honest man, go back! You can have no business in such a place as this, honest man!' The Earl was a determined republican, and made his son (Lord Mahon) offer himself to the citizens of Westminster in 1774, engaging to promote all popular causes, and to declare for all Wilkes's self-denying articles in their largest latitude. He was then only twenty-one years of age.

Earl Charles was a more advanced republican than his father; and when the French Revolution burst forth, he laid aside all the external ornaments of the peerage. But he is remembered for better things than this. When a young man, he gained a prize from the Society of Stockholm for a *Memoir on the Pendulum*. He was, perhaps, too universal a genius to be very useful to mankind; and among his projects, rather than his achievements, may be mentioned his arithmetical machine; his plan for securing buildings from fire; his new printing-press; his monochord for tuning musical instruments; and his designs for a vessel to sail against wind and tide (Dr. Doran's Notes to Walpole's *Last Journals*).

HORSE-SHOES AT OAKHAM CASTLE.

RUTLAND, the smallest county in England,—little more than half the size of Middlesex,—has its excellences thus sung by Drayton:

'Love not thyself the less, although the least thou art;
What thou in greatness wants, wise Nature doth impart
In goodness of thy soil; and more delicious mould,
Surveying all this isle, the sun did ne'er behold.
Bring forth that British vale, and be it ne'er so rare,
But Catmose with that vale for richness shall compare.
What forest nymph is found, how brave soe'er she be,
But Lyfield shows herself as brave a nymph as she?
What river ever rose from bank or swelling hill
Than Rutland's wandering Wash, a delicater rill?
Small shire that canst produce to thy proportion good,
One Vale of special name, one Forest, and one Flood.'

In our fine old author's Alexandrines we do not, however, find certain odd things for which this small shire is or has been noted—as Stilton cheese, trenchers, and Jeffrey Hudson, the dwarf of Oakham, served up at table in a cold pie; to which must be added the curious custom of nailing a horse-shoe on the castle-gate, which dates some seven centuries back.

Oakham, the county town, had anciently a Hall, which had been taken by the Conqueror into his own hands; since Edward the Confessor bequeathed the demesne in this county to his wife conditionally, that after her death it should descend to the Monastery of St. Peter at Westminster, which donation was confirmed by a charter dated 1064. A Hall was the usual appendage to a manor, and differed in its architectural character as well as in its nature from a castle. These Halls answer to the manor-houses of a later period; and in the Conqueror's record they are denominated *caput manerii*, thus marking the connection between the demesne and the residence and the feudal chief before he had received the king's licence to build an embattled dwelling. A Ferrers crossed the sea with the Conqueror, and upon his descendant Henry II. bestowed the manor of Oakham. Robert Ferrers was settled in Derbyshire, and in the 3d of Stephen (1137) created the first Earl. His son, Walkeline de Ferrers, held the barony of Oakham by the service of one knight's fee and a half in 12 Henry II.; and in 22 Henry II. he paid 100 marks for trespassing in the king's forests in these parts. His ancestors bore arms *semée* of horse-shoes, as designative of Master of the Horse to the Duke of Normandy. It is to him that the erection of the Hall, still existing, has been attributed; and upon evidence, says the Rev. C. H. Hartshorne, which there seems no reasonable ground for disputing. The style of architecture alone affords the strongest presumption that the building was erected towards the close of the twelfth century—from 1180 to 1190. Matthew Paris says that Walkeline de Ferrers was at the siege of Acre, in the Holy Land, with the English king, in the third year of his reign (1191). In 1201 he died, and was succeeded by his son Hugh, who dying in 1204 without issue, Isabella, his only sister, wife of Roger Lord Mortimer, became his heir; and this ended the connection of the Ferrers family with the town of Oakham.

The peculiar custom existing in this place, of compelling every Peer of Parliament, the first time he passes through the town, to give a horse-shoe, 'to be nailed upon the castle gate,' is of ancient standing, since it is mentioned by Camden as existing in his time. It is supposed to have come as a liberty from the Ferrers, who were early lords of the demesnes, though there seems no other warrant for this conjecture than the fanciful play upon the words *De Ferreriis*. By an inquisition found in the hundred rolls, made at Stamford before twelve jurors of the hundred of Martinsley, in the 3d Edward I. (1257), it seems that a custom analogous was then in existence. The jurors declare on their oath, that it appears to them that the manor and castle of Oakham were formerly in the hands of William the Conqueror, and were worth £100 a-year and upwards; that the king gave them to Hugh, who held that manor for him till Normandy was lost. The successors of Hugh at that time rebelled against King John, who thereupon granted the manor and castle to Isabella de Mortimer for her life by the same service; and after her death the manor came into the hands of Henry, father of King Edward, who conveyed it with the castle, in fee-dowry, to Senchia, wife of Richard Earl of Cornwall, to hold it for him in chief by the aforesaid service. The jurors at Stamford also found that every bailiff of Richard Earl of Cornwall took at Oakham, as well in the time of King Henry as now, toll of carriages bought or sold, and of all other things there, to the damage of £10 per annum, by what warrant they know not, and this unjustly. They also said that Peter de Nevil took ten marcs unjustly from the men of Oakham and Langham, by virtue of his office, that they should not have their dogs lawed. In the following year the jurors returned that the county of Rutland formerly belonged to the county of Northampton, until Henry III. granted it to the King of Germany (Richard Earl of Cornwall), whom they found had right of gallows, assize of bread and ale, pillory, and ducking-stool. And they said that the bailiffs of Oakham, in the reigns of Henry III. and Edward I., took toll of carriages, horses bought or sold, and all other merchandize at Oakham—they know not by what warrant. The transition to a commutation of a shoe for a money payment, or the reverse, is easily to be accounted for.

By these inquisitions is seen what was the origin of demanding a horse-shoe at Oakham; at least an insight is gathered into the practice, which has at various periods been countenanced by English monarchs and the highest judicial functionaries. In the second year of Richard II., Edward Plantagenet, second Duke of York, on being created Earl of Rutland, had granted to him the castle, town, and lordship of Oakham, and the whole forest of Rutland. This prince was trampled to death at the battle of Agincourt. By his will, made at Harfleur, 22d of August 1415, he directed the interment of his remains in the College of Fotheringhay, which he had founded. In 1399 the Duke of York was suspected of being concerned in an abortive conspiracy against his relative Henry IV., the Lincolnshire-born king, for which offence Sir John Holland, second son of the Earl of Kent, was beheaded. Another possessor of the castle, the Duke of Buckingham, in the reign of Richard III., was beheaded; as were a second Duke of Buckingham in the reign of Henry VIII., and Lord Thomas Cromwell in the year 1540.

The manor and castle repeatedly reverted to the Crown, and were again repeatedly granted. Among the possessors of them were Richard King of the Romans, brother of Henry III.; Edward Earl of Kent, brother of Edward II.; De Vere Earl of Oxford and Duke of Ireland, favourite of Richard II.; Thomas of Woodstock, uncle to the same king; the two Dukes of Buckingham already named; Thomas Cromwell Earl of Essex; and George Villiers Duke of Buckingham, the witty and profligate favourite of Charles II.

The architecture of the Hall is late Norman, or very early English. It is divided by three shafts on either side into four bays. It is smaller though earlier than the Hall at

Winchester, but in its sculpture and detail more beautiful. Nothing can exceed the spirit and gracefulness of the sculptured heads under the brackets. Those of Henry II. and his wife Margaret of Guienne are strikingly fine. The present position of the door is not the original one. When Buck published his view in 1720, the door was at the east end, like that in the refectory at Dover. The ancient roof was probably semicircular, like that existing still in the Bishop's palace at Hereford. The oldest portions of the present roof are two red beams put up by Villiers Duke of Buckingham, who also built the gateway. Altogether, this is one of the most perfect specimens of domestic architecture (twelfth century) in existence.[1]

With respect to the Horse-shoe custom, a contributor to a periodical work, writing at the latter end of the last century, says : 'The lord of this castle and manor claims by prescription a franchise of a very uncommon kind, viz. that the first time any peer of this kingdom shall happen to pass through the precincts of this lordship, he shall forfeit as a homage a shoe from the horse whereon he rideth, unless he redeems it with money; and according to the liberality of the nobleman who incurs the forfeit, a shoe is made in size, gilt, decorated, and inscribed with his title, and the date when compounded for, which is placed in the castle, or on

---

[1] Abridged in the main from a Lecture delivered in the Castle Hall, Oakham, by the Rev. Thomas James, M.A., Hon. Canon of Peterborough, and one of the Secretaries of the Architectural Society for the Archdeaconry of Northampton, which includes the county of Rutland.

the gate, in a conspicuous point of view. Five and sometimes ten guineas is the *douceur* on these occasions, which, the clerk of the market informed me, the Earl of Winchilsea (lord of the manor) permits him to have for a perquisite. When I was at Oakham, I copied such of the inscriptions of the shoes as were legible. Many are gone, for I find the late clerk of the market used to take down several old ones when a new one was fixed, which he gave in exchange to save himself expense. The gentleman who now holds the office rescued a number from the hands of a smith, which he caused to be fixed against the jury-box within the castle.' The ceremony of giving possession of lands or offices was, by the feudal law, accompanied with the delivery of certain symbols. In conformity to this practice, princes conferred bishoprics and abbeys by the delivery of a crozier and a ring, which was called their investiture. It seems to have been on this principle that the Lords de Ferrers were entitled to demand from every baron, on his passing through this lordship, a shoe from one of his horses, to be nailed upon the castle gate—the bailiff of the manor being empowered to stop the horses until service was performed. Although there are some very ancient shoes still on the walls of the castle, a great many have disappeared from time to time. The number of shoes now in the castle is 89, and there are two on the entrance-gates. The largest is 4 feet 8 inches by 4 feet 7 inches, and the smallest is $4\frac{3}{4}$ inches by $4\frac{1}{4}$ inches. The inscription on some of the shoes is effaced. In speaking of the horse-shoes, Mr. Wright, writing in 1684, says: 'The true original of this custom I have not been able, on my utmost endeavour, to discover; but that such is, and time out of mind hath been, the usage, appears by several monumental horse-shoes, some gilded and of curious workmanship, nail'd upon the castle-hall door.'

The following are the latest additions :—

Richard Henry Fitzroy Baron Raglan, 1859; James Lord Talbot de Malahide, July 25, 1861; Lord Camperdown, Nov. 28, 1861; The Earl of Ilchester, 1862; G. W. R. Fermor Earl of Pomfret, 1862; The Earl of Granville, 1864; The Earl of Carrick, 1866; Charles George Earl of Gainsborough, 1867; The Marquis of Exeter, Nov. 28, 1867.

THOMAS GARTON, *Governor of the Castle.*
THOMAS WAKELING, *Castle Keeper.*

July 1868.

The following is a list of those shoes on which inscriptions are now legible :—

Against the wall above the Judge's Bench on the east end of the Castle.—Henry Montague, May 12, 1607; Henry Lord Grey, 1614; William Earl Berners, 1704; Edward Earl of Lincoln, 1680; Edward Earl of Dudley; Elizabeth Baroness Percy, 1771; Heneage Earl of Aylesford, 1779; Charles Lord Barham, 1809; Heneage Earl of Aylesford, 1815; William Earl of Dartmouth, 1815; John Earl Brownlow, August 28, 1818; Brownlow Marquis of Exeter, K.G., Nov. 15, 1827; John Earl of Chesterfield, March 29, 1829; Robert Earl of Roden, Jan. 22, 1829; George Lord Calthorpe, 1831; Hugh Percy, Lord Bishop of Carlisle, June 1832; George Marquis of Cholmondeley, 1838; Arthur Duke of Wellington, K.G., 1838; Thomas Lord Denman, L.C.J.Q.B., March 8, 1839; Charles Lord Barham, Jan. 7, 1839; John Charles Earl Spencer, 1840.

Fixed to the wall on the side of the Castle.—Baptist Earl of Gainsborough, Dec. 17, 1604; Robert Earl of Cardigan, April

30, 1667; Edward Earl of Gainsborough, April 10, 1687; Edward Viscount Ipswich, 1687; Francis Lord Guilford, 1690; George Earl of Hertford, September 1703; Lewis Earl of Rockingham, May 30, 1733; Philip Lord Hardwick, August 6, 1736; Augustus Frederick Duke of Leinster, March 29, 1807; George Lord Bishop of Peterborough, 1810; Albemarle Earl of Lindsey, Nov. 11, 1811; R. W. P. Earl Howe, Jan. 9, 1832; Robert Earl of Cardigan, 1815; Marquis of Tweeddale, K. P. C. B., 1832; Charles Earl Fitzwilliam, 1841; Baron Methuen, Dec. 1, 1853; James Lord Wensleydale, 1856; Lord Vivian, 1856.

Inscriptions on the Shoes fixed on the south wall.—Henry Earl of Exeter, March 22, 1794; Gilbert John Lord Aveland, 1856.

Against the wall above the Judge's seat at the west end of the Castle.—His Royal Highness Frederick Duke of York and Albany, March 30, 1778 (a splendid shoe—coronet over it); His Royal Highness Ernest Augustus Duke of Cumberland, K.G., Sept. 1808; His Royal Highness the Prince Regent, Jan. 7, 1814 (an elegant shoe—coronet over it); Her Royal Highness Victoria, Duchess of Kent, Sept. 21, 1833; Her Royal Highness Princess Alexandrina Victoria (the Queen), Sept. 21, 1833; His Royal Highness Adolphus Frederick Duke of Cambridge, 1843; Bennet Earl of Harborough, 1753; Brownlow Earl of Exeter, 1759; William Lord Mansfield, L.C.J., 1763; Lewis Lord Sondes, 1766; Charles Lord Camden, 1766; John Frederick Duke of Dorset, 1782; Alexander Lord Loughborough, L.C.J., 1782; John Earl of Westmoreland, 1782; John George Earl Spencer, 1784; John Lord Clifton Earl of Darnley, of Ireland, 1791 (an elegant shoe—has his Lordship's crest over it); Thomas James Viscount Bulkeley, Oct. 10, 1793; Henry Earl of Exeter, March 27, 1794; William Earl of Lonsdale, K.G., 1807; G. C. Weld Lord Forester, 1829; John Singleton Lord Lyndhurst, March 4, 1830.

Against the wall above the Judge's Bench.—Elizabeth Baroness Percy, 1771; Heneage Earl of Aylesford, 1779.

HORSE-SHOES AT OAKHAM CASTLE. 267

Fixed on the outer gate.—Brownlow Earl of Exeter, April 10, 1733; John Earl of Exeter, 1774.

The following list of shoes appears in Wright's *History and Antiquities of Rutland*:—

Henry Lord Mordant, 1602; Edward Lord Dudley; William Earl of Pembroke; Philip Earl of Montgomery; Henry Lord Clifford, 1607; Lancelot Andrews, Lord Bishop of Ely, 1614; Lord Noel, 1617; Henry Earl of Huntington, 1620; Ferdinando Lord Hastings, 1621; John Lord Vaughan, 1621; Spencer Lord Compton, 1621; Thomas L. Cromwell Vic Le Cale, 1631; Nicholas Earl of Banbury, 1655; John L. Bellasis, Bar. of Worleby, 1667.

The following are from a list printed in 1796 :—

John Earl of Exeter, Aug. 7, 1714; Brownlow Earl of Exeter, April 10, 1755; Henry Earl of Gainsborough, 1764; Robert Earl of Harborough, 1772; Edward Earl Dudley; P. L. Wharton; George E. Cumberland; E. Wiloughby; Philip Earl of Mountnorris; 1602, * * Septein, Heri L. Mordant, 12th May 1607, Henri Montegle; Henry Lord Grey, 1614; Edward Earle of Lincoln, May 20, 1680; April 8, 1687, Thomas Earle of Stamford; Robert Earle of Cardigan, April 30, 1667; April 10, 1687, Edward of Gainsborough; Aug. 14, Edward Viscount Ipswich, 1687.

A curious story is told of 'the Golden Shoe,' presented by Lord Willoughby De Eresby, but stolen by some person who probably thought it was made of the precious metal. Still the shoe was much prized, it having been taken off his Lordship's favourite horse Clinker. The shoe was returned to Oakham in a parcel, by railway, on May 8, 1858, the day on which Lord Chief-Justice Campbell's shoe was placed in the Hall.

CHRISTMAS MUMMERS IN THE OLDEN TIME.

ONE of the most lasting things in the world is custom. To this day we celebrate Christmas with *mumming*, which our ancestors borrowed from the Roman Saturnalia; and its name from the Danish *mvmme*, or Dutch *momme*—disguise in a mask or the painting of faces. We can trace the Lord of Misrule, or master of merry disports, from the King's house to the house of every nobleman of honour or good worship—spiritual or temporal—down to the Mayors' and Sheriffs' feast, to the farmer's fireside, and the roystering in the highways and byways. Prince, peer, and peasant have for ages commemorated our great festival by the same merry means.

The ancient mumming, however, took this strange turn: It consisted in changing clothes between men and women, who were dressed in each other's habits; went from one neighbour's house to another, partaking of Christmas cheer, and making merry with them in disguise. Mr. Sandys, in his ingenious *Christmastide*, remarks that 'the mummeries or disguises were known here as early as the time of Henry II., if not sooner. They were not confined to the diversions of the king and his nobles; but a ruder class was in vogue among the inferior orders, where, no doubt, abuses were occasionally introduced in consequence. Even now, our country geese or guise dancers are a remnant of the same custom; and in some places a horse's head still accompanies these mummers.'

A more rational phase of mumming was the *ludi*, or plays, exhibited at court in the Christmas holidays, to be traced back as far as the reign of Edward III., though they are thought to be much older. The dresses appropriated in 1348 to one of these plays show that they were mummeries, and not theatrical *divertissements*. The king then kept his Christmas at his castle at Guildford, the picturesque keep of which remains to this day. The dresses consisted of 80 tunics of buckram of various colours; 42 vizors—14 faces of women, 14 of men, and 14 heads of angels, made with silver; 28 crests; 14 mantles, embroidered with heads of dragons; 14 white tunics wrought with the heads and wings of peacocks, 14 with the heads and wings of swans; 14 tunics painted with the eyes of peacocks; 14 tunics of English linen, painted; and 14 other tunics embroidered with stars of gold. The magnificent pageants and disguisings frequently exhibited at Court in the succeeding reigns, and especially in the reign of Henry VIII., were mummeries destitute of character and humour, their chief aim being to surprise the spectators 'by the ridiculous and exaggerated oddity of the vizors, and by the singularity and splendour of the dresses: everything was out of nature and propriety.' Such a strange scene will be remembered in Mr. Charles Kean's getting up of Shakspeare's 'Henry VIII.' at the Princess' Theatre, upon which much research was expended.

In a beautiful manuscript in the Bodleian Library, written and illuminated in the reign of Edward III., are some spirited figures of mummers wearing the heads of animals, among which the stag, with branching horns, is most prominent. Some of the heads are very grotesque, and remind one of the strange head-masks worn in the opening of pantomimes in the present day. The olden performance seems to have consisted chiefly in dancing, and the mummers were usually attended by the minstrels playing upon different kinds of musical instruments.

Stow describes a remarkable mummery in 1377, made by the citizens of London for the disport of the young Prince Richard, son to the Black Prince. They rode disguised and well horsed—130 in number—with minstrels and torchlights of wax to Kennington, beside Lambeth, where the young Prince remained with his mother. These maskers alighted, entered the palace-hall, and set to the Prince and his mother and lords cups and rings of gold, which they won at a cast, after which they feasted, and the Prince and lords danced with the mummers; 'which jollitie being ended, they were made to drink,' etc. Henry IV., in the second year of his reign, kept his Christmas at Eltham, whither 'twelve aldermen of London and their sonnes rode a-mumming, and had great thanks.'

The Cornish miracle-plays, which were not performed in churches, but in an earthen amphitheatre in some open field, continued to be exhibited long after the abolition of the miracles and moralities in other parts of the kingdom. Accordingly, we find them lingering in Cornwall to our time; and in Cornwall, Devon, and Staffordshire, the old spirit of Christmas is kept up more earnestly than in most other counties. In Cornwall they exhibit the old dance of St. George and the Dragon; and in the Staffordshire halls a band of bedizened actors perform the whole of the ancient drama. This famous mummery is imagined to refer to the time of the Crusades, and to have been invented by the warriors of the Cross on their return from Palestine. Mr. Sandys gives this Christmas play 'as represented in the West of England.' Hone, in his *Every-Day Book*, gives an extended version of 'St. George,' under the title of 'Alexander and the King of Egypt, a Mock Play, as it is acted by the Mummers every Christmas: Whitehaven.' In a scarce work, written in 1737, we find this record of 'St. George:'—

'*England's Heroe—Saint George for England.*—At Christmas are (or at least very lately were) fellows wont to go about from house to house, in Exeter, a-mumming; one of whom, in a (borrow'd) Holland shirt, more gorgeously beribboned over his waistcoat, etc., flourishing a faulchion very valiantly, entertains the admiring spectators thus:

> 'Oh! here comes I, Saint George, a man of courage bold,
> And with my spear I winn'd three crowns of gold.
> I slew the Dragon, and brought him to the slaughter,
> And by that very means I married Sabra, the beauteous King of Egypt's daughter.'

All the versions have evidently sprung from one original. The Worcestershire mumming is played by boys. The Valiant Soldier wore a real soldier's coat; Old Father Christmas carried holly; the Turkish Knight had a turban; and all of them were decked out with ribbons and scarves, and had their faces painted. Little Devil Doubt had a black face, and carried a money-box, a basin, and a bladder; with the bladder he thwacked the performer whose turn it was to speak. Beelzebub is identical with Old Father Christmas, who sings:

> 'In comes I, old Father Beelzebub;
> And on my shoulder I carry a club,
> And in my hand I carry a can,
> Don't you think I'm jolly old man?
> As jolly as I am, Christmas comes but once a-year;
> Now's the time for roast beef, plum-pudding, mince-pies, and strong beer.'

Miss Baker, in her *Glossary*, published in 1854, describes the mummers as young men, generally six or eight, who during the Christmas holidays, commencing on St. Thomas's Eve, go about in the rural districts of Northamptonshire, disguised, personating different characters, and performing a burlesque tragedy at such houses as they think will recompense them for their entertainment. Brackley is the only market-town where Miss Baker heard of the custom being observed. Some years since she witnessed the representation of a mock play by eight mummers, all masked, at the seat of Michael Woodhull, Esq., Thenford. The characters were Beelzebub, Activity, Age on the Stage, Doctor, Doctor's Horse, Jem Jacks, the Doctor's Man, Fool, and Treasurer, who carried a box for contributions. The fight is between Age and Activity; the Doctor is called in to assist Activity; the finale is the Fool playing the hurdy-gurdy, and knocking them all down; and the whole concludes with a general scuffle on the floor. The mummers are most frequently disguised with discolorations of red, white, and black on their faces, and any grotesque attire they can procure.

Mr. Joseph Nash, in his splendid work, *Mansions of England in the Olden Times*, has given us a splendid illustration of how Christmas was kept by our ancestors—when the lord of misrule was let loose—where morris-dancers, the hobby-horse, the dragon, the giant, the salvage-man, etc. are enjoying their Christmas festivities. He has chosen for his scene the banqueting-hall of Haddon, near Bakewell, in Derbyshire, so well known from its picturesque situation in a country celebrated for its enchanting scenery. This is probably the most perfect of the ancient mansions remaining, and is certainly better calculated than any other to convey an idea of the large establishment and extensive hospitality of the old English baron. It has been untenanted more than a century, but has escaped the fate which under such circumstances usually befalls the residences of the old nobility there, to suit the more moderate household and private style of living of their successors, being gradually pared down, until a very small portion of the once princely mansion can be traced in the dilapidated farm-house. This may be regarded the 'sixth age' of the decaying mansion previous to its ruined state, when the ivy-mantled walls afford shelter only to owls, forming the

> 'Last scene of all
> That ends this strange eventful history.'

Haddon Hall was erected at various periods, and affords excellent examples of the several styles of domestic architecture, from the Early Pointed to the Tudor and Elizabethan. Haddon was originally a 'barton,' or farm, appertaining to the lordship of Bakewell, which was given by William the Conqueror to his natural son William Peverell. It became forfeited to the Crown, and passed to the Avenell family; and in the reign of Richard I. it came into the possession of Sir Richard de Vernon by marriage, thenceforth becoming the chief residence of the Vernon family, until, by the marriage of Dorothy Vernon with Sir John Manners, second son of Thomas the first Earl of Rutland, which title he inherited, it came into the possession of the Manners family, through whom it has descended to the Duke of Rutland. His Grace, with good taste and laudable reverence for a noble relic, has preserved the Hall intact, for the gratification of the admirers of our national antiquities. The tapestry, panelings, and cornice in the drawing-room, and the shields in the dining-room, yet remain.

The long gallery retains its carved wainscoting and ornamented ceiling of the Elizabethan period. It was probably used as a ball-room, as well as for promenading; and from hence we may suppose Dorothy Vernon eloped with her lover on the day of her sister's nuptials. The chapel is a good specimen of the Early Pointed style, and is one of the most ancient portions of the building remaining.

It is impossible to visit this fine old place without echoing these sentiments:

> ' How many a Vernon thou hast seen,
> Kings of the Peak, thy walls within;
>   How many a maiden tender;
> How many a warrior stern and steel'd,
> In burganet, and lance, and shield,
>   Array'd with martial splendour!
>
> The grandeur of the olden time
> Mantled thy towers with pride sublime,
>   Enlivening all who near'd them;
> From Hippocras and Shevris sack
> Palmer or pilgrim turn'd not back,
>   Before thy altars cheer'd them.
>
> Since thine unbroken early day,
> How many a race hath pass'd away,
>   In charnel vault to moulder!
> Yet Nature round thee breathes an air
> Serenely bright, and softly fair,
>   To charm the awed beholder.'

LOVE PASSAGE FROM THE DIARY OF LADY COWPER.

LADY COWPER, whose charming *Diary* was published in the year 1864, was the wife of Lord Chancellor Cowper, and a Lady of the Bedcamber to Caroline Princess of Wales during a part of the reign of George I. She was originally a Miss Clavering, one of a Jacobite family in the north of England. She became acquainted with Lord Cowper by going to his chambers to consult him upon certain law business; whereupon, as she was pretty, clever, and accomplished, a toast of the Kitcat Club, and otherwise a highly attractive person, it is not surprising that Lord Cowper fell in love with her, and that they were forthwith married; though, for reasons with which we are not made acquainted, their marriage was for some time kept secret from their friends. The following story is told by Lady Cowper of a design upon her lord's affection, carried on by Lady Harriet Vere with much assiduity and craft, while his marriage with herself remained unknown. This amusing *embroglio* is thus told by her ladyship in her *Diary*:—

'My lord being a widower when the late queen gave him the seals, it was no wonder the young women laid out all their snares to catch him. None took so much pains as Lady Harriet Vere, whose poverty and ruined reputation made it impossible for her to run any risk in the pursuit, let it end as it would. She had made several advances to my lord by Mrs. Morley, her kinswoman, and finding nothing came of it, they immediately concluded my lord must be pre-engaged to somebody else; so they set a spy upon him, and found that he had country lodgings at Hammersmith, where he lay constantly; and upon inquiry they found I was the cause of this coldness to Lady H. Upon this they settled a correspondence under a feigned name with him, and in those letters (which were always sent by a fellow dressed up in woman's clothes, who could never be overtaken) they pretended to be some great person that threatened him, if he married me, to hinder the passing of his title. The first of these letters came the day before I was married. However, it did not hinder our marriage, though my lord thought it advisable to keep it a secret; and so he removed the next day to London. His correspondents seeing they had made him leave the place, thought it would be no hard matter to break the match; and from that time to the beginning of January, which was almost four months, my lord had a letter every day!—some of whole sheets of paper filled with lies about me, to say that I was a mean wretch, that I was coquette, and should be more so, that my playing so well was and would be a temptation to bring all the rakes in town about me, that it had been so thus far of my life, and that I was treated so familiarly by the rakish part of the town, that one night at a play, my Lord Wharton said to my Lord Dorchester, " Now that the opera is done, let's go and hear Molly Clavering play it over again " (which was all a plain lie, for I never did play in any public company, and only at home, when anybody that visited my Aunt Wood, with whom I lived, asked me; and for those two lords, I had never been in a room with either of them in my whole life).

'These,' continues the Diarist, 'are only specimens of what lies they invented to hurt me. At last, when they thought they had routed me by the ill impressions they had falsely given of me, upon a day when my lord was at the House of Lords, one Mr. Mason, of the House of Commons, came to him and told him that Mrs. Weedon (a client of my brother's that had a foul cause in the Court of Delegates) desired to speak with him. My lord at first refused, but at length she teased him so much, that he consented to see her; and by her appointment, and saying she had a very fine lady to recommend to him (which gave him a thought he should find out his correspondent), he waited upon her at Mrs. Kirk's, which was the place appointed. He had some little jealousy before he went that the fine lady was Lady Harriet Vere, for she and Mrs. Kirk had always been in a hackney-coach every Sunday for at least a month to ogle him, and pass and repass his coach when he went and came from the chapel. He found he was right; for there she was, set out in all her airs, with her elbow upon a table that had two wax-candles on it, and holding her head, which she said ached. There she displayed herself, and so did her two artificers, and not a word said of the cause. This interview brought on several others, and those visits from my lord to Mrs. K. and Mrs. W., to try to make this match. They told him that the queen had promised Lady H. £100,000 when she married. He said upon that score he durst not presume to marry her, for he had not an estate to make a settlement answerable to so great a fortune; and at last they pressed him so much, that he owned he was engaged to me, and that it would be barbarous to ruin an innocent young woman, who had no fault but receiving his visits so long. They could not agree with him that it was barbarous, for it was only serving me in my own kind, for I was contracted to Mr. Floyd, whom I had left for him. My lord said they were mistaken in that affair (which he knew full well). However, this did not discourage them; and once, when he seemed to yield, he brought Mrs. Kirk to confess the pains they had been at to bring this about; and she mentioned particularly the letters, which were contrived and writ at her house, and copied afterwards by Lady H. V. herself. As soon as my lord had got this confession, he wrote to Lady H., in answer to a love-letter from her (for she pretended to be terribly in love with him), to excuse himself, and say that he resolved to marry me, for now he was assured that he had met with a wife whose conduct was unblemished; for that the greatest enemy I had in the world had been writing every day an invective against me, which was duly sent to him; and that, now all the letters were laid out before him, he did not find anything I was accused of but of playing the best upon the harpsichord of any woman in England, which was so far from being a fault, that it was an argument to him that I had been used to employ many of my hours alone, and not in the company of rakes, as they would suggest. But they thought there was hope, since they did not believe that we were actually married; and my lord could never get quit of their importunity till he owned our marriage to them, though it was before he owned it publicly; and even after that both Mrs. K. and Lady H. V. wrote frequently to him. This I had not inserted but as a justification for my endeavouring to hinder her coming into the princess's bedchamber.'

The history of the *Diary* is singular. It was commenced by Lady Cowper, in her own capacity of Lady of the Bedchamber, and she undertook to write down all the events worth remembering while she was at court, as a corrective to 'the perpetual lies that one hears' there. Had this *Diary* remained complete as written, and still more if revised and digested as she intended, it would have been a still more valuable contribution to history, and still more important as a record of the social aspects of the time. If Lady Cowper does not fill up this blank completely, it is simply because the greater portion of her *Diary* was destroyed by herself, under a misplaced apprehension, at the time when Lord Cowper was falsely accused of complicity in Layer's plot. What remains, however, which is somewhat more than Lord Campbell had before him when he was writing the life of the Lord Chancellor himself, nevertheless covers the two principal passages in the reign of the first George, and the most critical perils of the Hanoverian dynasty. The rebellion of 1715 on the one hand, and on the other the quarrel between the king and the prince, which jeopardized the 'interests' of the Revolution by shaking the stability of the throne, are both included and illustrated in this *Diary*. Moreover, Lord Campbell, who saw the major part of it in MS., justly describes it as a charming production, and adds that it well deserves to be printed, for it gives a more lively picture of the Court ot England at the commencement of the Brunswick dynasty than he had ever met with; in which sense we ourselves regard it, though unhappily, for the reasons we have mentioned, it is so brief and fragmentary.

THE SIEGE OF LATHOM HOUSE.

THIS ancient manor-house, which became the scene of one of the most memorable sieges recorded in our history, was situated in the township of Chapelrig of Lathom, which, at the Domesday survey, belonged to Orm, a Saxon, from whom the parish of Ormskirk, in the county of Lancaster, derives its name. His descendant, Robert Fitzhenry of Lathom, founded the Priory of Burscough in the reign of Richard I., and may be regarded as the Rodolph of the race of Lathom. His grandson, Sir Robert de Lathom, greatly augmented his inheritance by his marriage with Arnicia, sister and co-heir of Thomas Lord of Alfreton and Norton; and his son and successor, a knight like his father, still further added to his patrimony by winning the rich heiress of Sir Thomas de Knowsley, who brought him the fair lordship which to this day continues to be the princely residence of her descendants, the Earls of Derby. The eventual heiress of the Lathoms, Isabella, daughter of Sir Thomas de Lathom, married Sir John Stanley; and henceforward, for several

THE SIEGE OF LATHOM HOUSE. 283

hundred years, and during the period of its chief historic distinction, Lathom House was held by the Stanleys.

Sir John Stanley, who thus acquired the hand and inheritance of the heiress of Lathom, became Lord-Deputy of Ireland, and received a grant of the manor of Blake Castle, in that kingdom. In 1405 he had a commission in conjunction with Roger Leke, to serve on the city of York and its liberties; and also upon the Isle of Man, on the forfeiture of Henry Percy Earl of Northumberland; and in the 7th of Henry IV., being then treasurer of the household to the king, he obtained licence to fortify a house at Liverpool (which he had newly built) with embattled walls. In the same year, having taken possession of the Isle of Man, he obtained a grant in fee of the said isle, castle, and pile—anciently called Holm Town—and of all the isles adjacent, as also all the regalities, franchises, etc., to be holden of the said kings, his heirs and successors, by homage, and the service of two falcons, payable on the days of their coronation. On the accession of Henry V. he was made a Knight of the Garter, and constituted Lord-Lieutenant of Ireland for six years, in which government he died 6th January 1414. The grandson of this famous knight, Sir Thomas Stanley, also Chief Governor of Ireland, and Chamberlain to Henry VI., was summoned to Parliament as Lord Stanley in 1456. He married Joan de Gonshill, a lineal descendant of King Edward I., and had four sons: the eldest, Thomas, second Lord Stanley and first Earl of Derby, celebrated for his participation in the victory of Bosworth Field; and the second, Sir William Stanley of Holt, the richest subject of his time: he was beheaded for his adherence to Perkin Warbeck.

The Earls of Derby continued to possess Lathom House, and to reside there in such magnificence, that Camden says, 'With them the glory of hospitality seemed to fall asleep.' And the Stanleys were regarded with such veneration and esteem, that 'God save the Earl of Derby and the King' was a familiar, harmless inversion.

On the death of William Richard George, ninth Earl, his daughter and co-heiress, Henrietta Lady Ashburnham, sold the estate to Henry Furness, Esq., from whom it was purchased, in 1724, by Thomas Bootle of Melling, Chancellor to Frederick Prince of Wales. He died without issue, having bequeathed his property to his niece Mary, only daughter and heir of his brother Robert Bootle, Esq., and wife of Richard Wilbraham, Esq. of Rode, M.P. for Chester.

By this devise, the ancient and historic seat of Lathom vested in the Wilbrahams, and is now possessed by Edward Bootle Wilbraham Lord Skelmersdale, the son and successor of the heiress of Bootle. His Lordship's daughter is married to Edward Geoffrey Stanley, present Earl of Derby; and thus the name of its former possessors has become again associated with the ancient manor-house.

At the period of its memorable siege in 1644, Lathom was under the government of the famous Charlotte de la Tremouille Countess of Derby. This heroic lady was

The Siege of Lathom House.

daughter of Claude Duke de Tremouille; and, by her mother, Charlotte Brabanton de Nassau, was granddaughter of William Prince of Orange, and of Charlotte de Bourbon of the royal house of France. Thus highly born, and allied besides to the kings of Spain and Naples and the Dukes of Anjou, Charlotte de la Tremouille did not sully the renown of her illustrious descent. After the battle of Nantwich, the united forces of the Parliament, under Sir Thomas Fairfax, accompanied by the regiments of Colonels Rigby, Egerton, Ashton, and Holcroft, marched to Lathom House, where they arrived on the 28th of February. The house was well calculated for defence, standing in a boggy flat, and being defended by a wall six feet thick, strengthened by nine towers, on each of which were mounted six pieces of ordnance, and surrounded by a moat twenty feet broad. In the defence, the Countess of Derby had the assistance of Major Farmer, and the Captains Ffarington, Charnock, Chisenhall, Rawstorne, Ogle, and Molyneux.

> 'Twas there they raised, 'mid sap and siege,
> The banner of their righted liege
>   At their she-captain's call,
> Who, miracle of womankind,
> Lent mettle to the meanest hind
>   That mann'd her castle wall.'

On his arrival before Lathom, Sir Thomas Fairfax obtained an audience of the Countess, who had disposed her soldiers in such an array as to impress the Parliamentary General with a favourable opinion of their numbers and discipline. The offer made by Sir Thomas was, that on condition of her surrendering the house to the troops under his command, herself, her children, and servants, with their property, should be safely conducted to Knowsley, there to remain, without molestation, in the enjoyment of one-half of the Earl's estates. To this alluring proposal the Countess mildly but resolutely replied, that a double trust had been confided to her,—faith to her lord, and allegiance to her sovereign; and that, without permission, she could not order the required surrender in less than a month, nor then, without their approbation. The impetuous temper of the Parliamentary army could not brook this delay; and after a short consultation, it was determined to besiege the fortress rather than attempt to carry it by storm. At the end of fourteen days, while the works were being constructed, Sir Thomas Fairfax sent a renewed summons to the Countess, but with no better success; the reply of the Countess being, that she had not forgotten her duty to the Church of England, to her prince, and to her lord, and that she would defend her trust with her honour and with her life.

Being ordered into Yorkshire, Sir Thomas Fairfax confided the siege to Colonel Peter Egerton and Major Morgan, who, despairing of success by negotiation, proceeded to form their lines of circumvallation with all the formality of German tactics. The progress of the besiegers was continually interrupted by sallies from the garrison, which drove the soldiers from their trenches, and destroyed their works. At the end of three months a deep breach was cut near the moat, on which was raised a strong battery, where a mortar was planted for casting grenades. In one of these discharges the ball fell close to the table where the Countess and her children were sitting, and broke part of the furniture to atoms. A gallant sally destroyed the enemy's works, killed a number of the besieging army, and captured the mortar. The Countess not only superintended the works and commanded the operations, but frequently accompanied her gallant troops to the margin of the enemy's trenches. The Parliament, dissatisfied with all this delay, superseded Colonel Egerton, and confided the command to Colonel Rigby. Fresh works were now erected, but they shared the same fate as the former; and Colonel Rigby, on the approach of Prince Rupert into Lancashire, was obliged to raise the siege at the end of four months, and to seek shelter for himself and his army in Bolton.

The capture of that town, which followed soon after, under the combined operations of Prince Rupert and the Earl of Derby, yielded numerous trophies to the victorious army; and all these were presented to the heroic defender of Lathom House, in testimony of the memorable triumph achieved under her command, by a gallant band of three hundred soldiers, assailed as they had been by ten times their own number.

After the siege was raised, the Countess accompanied her lord to the Isle of Man, leaving Lathom House to the care of Colonel Rawstorne. In July in the following year, the siege was renewed by Colonel Egerton at the head of four thousand men, who took up their quarters at Ormskirk. The garrison made a gallant and successful stand for some time; but being at length reduced to extremities for want of the munitions of war, and disappointed in the expectation of a reinforcement from the king, who was in the month of September in that year at Chester, the commander was obliged to surrender his charge into the hands of the Parliamentary forces upon bare terms of mercy, on the 2d of December. The besiegers soon converted the most valuable effects of the house into booty. The towers, from whence so many fatal shots had been fired, were thrown down, the military works were destroyed, and the sun of Lathom seemed for ever to have set.

In the fruitless enterprise of 1651 the Earl of Derby again raised the royal standard; but being defeated by Lilburne at Wigan Lane, and subsequently taken, he was executed at Bolton. The Countess and her children were for a time rigorously imprisoned, and actually subsisting on the alms of their impoverished friends. Thus she languished till the Restoration, when the family estates returned into the possession of her eldest son. She passed the short remainder of her days at Knowsley Hall, and, dying there on 21st March 1663, was buried at Ormskirk. Lord Derby has the famous Vandyke portrait of the Countess, and another of her painted when she was advanced in life, both of which were sent to the National Portrait Exhibition at South Kensington. James Stanley, the seventh Earl of

Derby, met with the lady at the Hague, upon his return from his travels; and though she was very young, they were married June 25, 1626. After their marriage they appear to have participated in the gaieties of the Court of Charles I. Bassompierre mentions his house being the resort of foreigners of distinction; and the name of the Countess is found frequently with those who, with the Queen Henrietta Maria, took part in the masques and other diversions of the palace. At Shrovetide 1630 was presented at Court Ben Jonson's masque *Chloridia;* and Charlotte de la Tremouille was one of the fourteen nymphs who sat round the goddess Choris (the Queen) in the bower: 'their apparel white, embroidered with silver, trimmed at the shoulders with great leaves of green, embroidered with gold, falling one under the other.'

Of the ancient house at Lathom, that stood such stout sieges, not a vestige now remains. 'The ramparts,' says Mr. Heywood, 'along whose banks knights and ladies have a thousand times made resort, hearkening to stories as varied as those of Boccaccio; the Maudlin Well, where the pilgrim and the lazar devoutly cooled their parched lips; the mewing-house; the training-ground; every appendage to antique baronial state,—all now are changed, and a modern mansion and a new possessor fill the place.'

The siege of Lathom House is so full of chivalrous and dramatic effect, from the intrepid valour and heroic spirit displayed by the Countess, that it has been fully chronicled. In Seacombe's *History of the House of Stanley*, is an account attributed to Samuel Butler, Bishop of Sodor and Man. The MS. of Captain Edward Halsall's account of the siege is among the A. Wood MSS. in the Ashmolean Museum, and has been twice printed in accessible books. Sir Walter Scott has set his own impress upon the great subject in his popular novel of *Peveril of the Peak*.

There are some traditional stories of Lathom which are interesting. Sir Bernard Burke mentions a tradition little known: that when Henry VIII., subsequently to the execution of Sir William Stanley, visited Lathom, the Earl, after his royal guest had viewed the whole house, conducted him up to the leads for a prospect of the country. The Earl's fool, who was among the company, observing the king draw near to the edge, not guarded by a balustrade, stepped up to the Earl, and pointing down to the precipice, said, 'Tom, remember Will.' The king understood the meaning, and made all haste down-stairs out of the house; and the fool long after seemed mightily concerned that his lord had not courage to take the opportunity of avenging himself for the death of his brother (*Seats of Great Britain*, vol. i.).

A curious instance of the retention of a proverbial saying, long after the occasion of it has passed away, is, that it is a very common expression in Lancashire to say of a person having two houses, even if temporarily, that he has 'Lathom and Knowsley.' Formerly, the Earl of Derby had two splendid residences in Lancashire, both which passed as already described. Though separate pos-

THE SIEGE OF LATHOM HOUSE.

sessions for above 150 years, the expression 'Lathom and Knowsley' still survives.

Another Lancashire proverb is, 'There's been worse stirs than that at Lathom,' alluding, no doubt, to the havoc made there when the Parliamentary forces took it in 1645. This saying comes in when a 'flitting' or whitewashing, or any other occurrence of an unpleasant nature makes an apology needful on the score of untidiness and confusion.

The legend of a Child being borne away by an Eagle, and thus having greatness thrust upon it, is common to many lands. It is associated with the De Lathom family; but Baines, in his *History of Lancaster*, gives the following passage respecting King Alfred the Great, quoting from a Saxon chronicle:

'Of the many humane traits in his character, one is mentioned which serves to show that our popular Lancashire tradition of the *Eagle and Child* is of the date of several centuries earlier than the time of the De Lathoms: "One day, as Alfred was hunting in a wood, he heard the cry of a little infant in a tree, and ordered his huntsmen to examine the place. They ascended the branches, and found at the top, in an eagle's nest, a beautiful child dressed in purple, with golden bracelets, the marks of nobility, on his arms. The king had him brought down, and baptized and well educated; from the accident he named the foundling Nestingum."'

In a poem written by Bishop Thomas Stanley 200 years

after the supposed event, this marvellous tale, in its episcopal form, may be condensed thus: Once upon a time there was a certain Lord Lathom dwelling at Lathom House, who had attained the patriarchal age of fourscore years without having had children. All hope had long been past, for his wife was as old as himself. Without Providence interposed by a miracle, he was destined to go down to the grave childless, and be buried by the unloving hands of strangers in blood and affection. With his mind filled with these bitter reflections, the spring months of his eightieth year passed slowly onward,—the last spring, as he thought, that Lathom House and its fair domain should belong to one of his name. He was, however, destined to a happy surprise; for one day an eagle which had built its nest in Terleslowe wood—a portion of the Lathom domain—was seen to have something uncommon in its nest. An examination was made; and the wonder of the simple-minded serfs may be imagined when, as well as the ordinary inmates of an eagle's nest, they found a male infant clad in a red mantle. The Lord of Lathom was at once informed of this strange discovery, and he concluded without hesitation that his prayers had been answered, and that to him, as to the patriarch of old, an infant heir had been sent for the solace of his declining years. The child, men thought, was unbaptized, for salt was found bound around its neck in a linen cloth; so a solemn christening was had, and no doubt the good old man feasted his neighbours as joyously as if the 'little stranger' had indeed been of his own lineage.

THE SIEGE OF LATHOM HOUSE. 293

This boy, in process of time, became the father of Isabella Lathom, who was in after days the wife of Sir John Stanley. From this time the crest of 'the Eagle and Child' was assumed. It is in the vernacular 'the Bird and Bairn,' and is a common sign in Lancashire.

The close of the career of 'the Great Stanley,' as the seventh Earl was styled, is a narrative of touching interest, and should be told in fuller detail. In 1651, Charles II. being at Worcester, and hoping to be joined by the English Royalists, issued invitations to his friends to support him with all the force they could raise. To the Earl of Derby, who was in the Isle of Man, Charles sent the Order of the Garter. The Earl hastily arranged his affairs, and set off to join the king, committing his noble Countess and three of his children to the care of the Receiver-General. He took with him from the Isle of Man 300 Royalists. Before he arrived in Lancashire Charles had quitted the county, but left Major-General Massey to confer with the Earl. They met at Warrington, where, not agreeing as to the dismissal of the Papists, Derby, with only his 300 followers from the Isle of Man, and 300 more who joined him out of Lancashire and Cheshire, gathered together at Preston. Advancing to Wigan (on 25th August), they were set upon in a narrow lane by 1800 dragoons under Colonel Lilburne, and the foot militia, whom Cromwell had detached to hang upon the king's rear. Derby performed prodigies of valour. He received seven shots in his breastplate, thirteen cuts in his beaver, five or six wounds in his arms and shoulders, and had two horses killed under him. Twice he made his way through the whole body of the enemy; but being overwhelmed with numbers, mounting a third horse, he, with Governor Greenhalgh and five others, fought his way through, and, with his wounds green and sore, he was enabled to join his Majesty in the fatal field of Worcester, September 3d. From this battle Derby conducted the king to the Whiteladies and Boscobel; thence making his way into Cheshire with about forty others, he fell in the way of a regiment of foot and a troop of horse, to whom he surrendered on quarter for life and conditions for honourable usage. These terms of surrender were most disgracefully violated; the Earl was tried by court-martial on a charge of high treason, and sentence of death was passed upon him, directing his execution to take place in four days at his own town of Bolton. Meanwhile, he wrote a long and affectionate letter to his wife. Derby had nearly escaped from the leads of the castle at Chester by means of a long rope thrown up to him from the outside of the fortress: he fastened this securely, slid down, and got down to the banks of the river Dee, where a boat was waiting to convey him away. He was here discovered, seized, conveyed back to the castle, and more securely guarded, until his removal to Leigh, and thence to Bolton for execution. The Earl, after his attempt to escape, wrote another sorrowful letter to his wife, and one to his children in the Isle of Man. His two daughters, Lady Catherine and Lady Amelia, who were in

THE SIEGE OF LATHOM HOUSE.

Chester, had their last interview with him on the 14th of October, as he set out on his way to Leigh.

The execution of the Earl took place at Bolton on the 15th of October, amidst the tears, groans, and prayers of the townspeople. Just before he suffered, Derby requested that the block might be so placed that he could face the church; and this having been done, he said, 'I will look to thy sanctuary while here, as I hope to live in thy heavenly sanctuary hereafter.' Then laying himself with his neck on the block, and his arms stretched out, he said, 'Blessed be God's glorious name for ever and ever. Amen. Let the whole earth be filled with His glory.' He then gave the signal to the executioner by lifting up his hands; but the executioner blundering, the Earl gently upbraided him with not at once discharging his office when he was so ready to depart. Repeating the same words of Scripture, the Earl a second time lifted up his hands, 'the executioner did his work, and Derby passed away.' When the body was put into the coffin to be carried to Ormskirk for burial, the following lines, by an unknown hand, were thrown into it:

> 'Wit, Beauty, Courage, all in one lie dead,
> A Stanley's hand, Vere's heart, and Cecil's head.'

Within eight days after his execution, his Manx subjects rose in rebellion against the authority of his Countess and her family.

We have selected and abridged these details of the closing scene from a work of remarkable interest and value for its authenticity, entitled *The Great Stanley; or, James Seventh*

Earl of Derby, and his Noble Countess Charlotte de la Tremouille, in their Land of Man. A Narrative of the Seventeenth Century. By the Rev. J. C. Cumming, M.A., F.G.S. 1867. The work is cleverly illustrated from Manx scenery and antiquities, and is dedicated, by permission, to the present Earl of Derby.

The narrative is modestly acknowledged to be compiled from documents existing in the Rolls Office at Castletown and in the registers of the Isle of Man, from the Manx Statute-book and State papers, and from private family records. 'At the same time,' continues the preface, 'an endeavour is made to elucidate the Manx popular feeling existing at that period of history in connection with their ancient and dearly-cherished "Tenure of the Straw,"[1] their struggles for the maintenance of which against the great Stanley led to disaffection towards the Government, the betrayal of his Countess to the Parliament, the execution as a traitor of the celebrated William Christian, and ultimately to the Act of Settlement of 1703—the Manx Magna Charta, procured from James the tenth Earl of Derby, through the exertions of the Apostolic Bishop Thomas Wilson.'

[1] By stipulation, or delivery of the *stipula*, or straw, the Manx held their estates, which they were consequently said to hold by 'the tenure of the straw.'

THE MANOR OF WAKEFIELD AND SANDAL CASTLE.

THE Manor of Wakefield, we learn from Domesday Book, is very extensive, including that of Halifax, and stretching from Normanton to the boundaries of Lancashire and Cheshire. It is more than thirty miles in length from east to west, and comprises more than one hundred and eighteen towns, villages, and hamlets: of these Wakefield and Halifax are the chief; and the two churches mentioned in Domesday are Wakefield and Sandal churches.

It is probable that the manor of Wakefield was granted, in the reign of William Rufus, between the years 1091 and 1097, to William de Warren, second Earl of Surrey, who by charter granted to God and St. Pancras of Lewes, besides other churches, the church of Wakefield, with its appurtenances. William, the first Earl of Warren, standing nearly allied to the Conqueror, viz. nephew to the Countess his great-grandmother, accompanied the Conqueror to England; and having distinguished himself at the battle of Hastings, obtained an immense portion of the spoil.

He had large grants of land in several counties: so extensive, indeed, were those grants, that his possessions more resembled the dominions of a sovereign prince than the estates of a subject. He was married to Gundred, the daughter of the Conqueror. This potent noble founded the priory of Lewes in Sussex, and endowed it with the church of Wakefield and Sandal Magna, besides lands. He died in 1089, and was buried in the chapter-house of his priory at Lewes. His wife Gundred died in 1085, about three years before him, and was also buried in the chapter-house at Lewes.[1]

The great Earl was succeeded by his son William between 1091 and 1097; and he gave the churches of Conisboro

---

[1] In October 1845, in the formation of the Brighton and Hastings Railway, the workmen had to cut through the site of Lewes Priory, the principal Cluniac monastery in England. At about two feet from the surface they met with an oblong leaden coffer, or chest, surrounded with Caen stones, upon removing which appeared legibly inscribed upon the upper end of the coffer-lid the name Gundrada. Next the workmen brought to light a second coffer, inscribed Willelm, which was at once assigned to William de Warrene. The lids of the coffers were not fastened, but merely *flanged* over the edges. Both were ornamented externally with a sort of lozenge or network pattern in relievo, such as our plumbers to this day ornament coffins with. The bones of both skeletons, and the teeth, were in fine preservation. The height of the Earl must have been from six feet one inch to six feet two inches, and that of the Countess from five feet seven inches to five feet eight inches. Mr. Lower, F.S.A., suggests that the letters are not of later date than the earlier part of the thirteenth century. Now the characters in the name of Gundrada tally exactly with those in the same word on her marble tomb extant in Southover church; thus establishing two facts: viz. first, that, after a separation of two cen-

and Wakefield to his father's monastery. The Earl was slain in the Holy Land in 1147, and left only one daughter, his heiress; and this great lady could be given to no husband but one of royal extraction. She was first married to William of Blois, one of the sons of King Stephen, who died without issue in 1159. She was afterwards given by Henry II. to his half-brother Hameline, an illegitimate son of Geoffrey Earl of Anjou.

In charters of this date, we find a grant of pannage or liberty of hogs feeding in all the Earl's woods there, reserving only the rent of 2d. for every hog, and 1d. for every pig. That there was an immense wood upon Wakefield Heath in ancient times, is evident from these deeds; so

turies, the bones of the noble Gundreda and her tomb were again brought into juxtaposition; and secondly, the coffers, or cists, and the tomb are unquestionably coeval.

An interesting inquiry (says Mr. Lower) arises out of this discovery. The remains had certainly been removed from their original resting-place, and re-interred in the coffers, in conformity with a practice not unusual in early times. Gundrada died at Castle Acre, in Norfolk—*vi partûs cruciata*—on the 27th of May 1085, and was buried at Lewes Priory, as proved by the charter of De Warrene, made shortly prior to his own decease, in which he expresses his desire to be interred by her side. The church is believed to have been the place of interment. As the convent increased in affluence, a new church was commenced building in 1243, but not finished until 1268; and Mr. Lower assumes, therefore, that the bodies of the founders were in this interval exhumed from the old church (which would then be dismantled) and deposited in the coffers for re-interment in the chapter-house, upon the site of which, there is reason to believe, the bones were found. The two coffers were subsequently placed in a tomb erected for their reception in Southover church. (See *Curiosities of History*, 1857, pp. 116–7.)

thick a wood, that a person was employed in directing travellers over that very place where now is the full road between Leeds and Wakefield.

We now pass over the manorial history, to Edward the eldest son of Edmund Langley Duke of York, who succeeded to the manor after his father's death, and was slain at Agincourt in 1415. Dying without issue, his estates came to his nephew, Richard Duke of York. Sandal Castle appears to have been a favourite residence of his. We find from William of Worcester, that the lords of the party of Lancaster were laying waste his lands in Yorkshire, when he hastened to Sandal Castle, and arrived there the 21st of December 1460. The battle of Wakefield ensued, in which he lost his life.[1]

This battle was fought on the 30th of December, and was indeed a fight of brother against brother; for on the side of the Yorkists there fell Sir John Harrington, who had married the sister of the Lord Clifford, who made himself but too conspicuous on the side of the Lancastrians. Sir Thomas (Sir John's father) also died of his wounds on the following day. As to the site of the battle of Wake-

[1] Although Shakspeare assigns a prominent part in the battle of Wakefield to Richard, where his father, the Duke of York, was taken and put to death, after exclaiming :

'Three times did Richard make a lane to me,
And thrice cried, Courage, father, fight it out!'

Richard (born 2d October 1452) was only in his ninth year when that battle was fought.

field, it has been supposed by some writers to have been fought on the flat meadows called the *Pugneys*, which stretch from the castle to the banks of the Calder; but, unluckily for those who have imagined the name to have been derived from the Latin *pugna* (a battle), and therefore indicative of the exact site of the bloody engagement, Mr. Lumb, the keeper of the Rolls Office at Wakefield, has discovered that the fields in that direction bore the name of *Pukenall* at least forty-seven years prior to the battle of Wakefield.

It is much more probable that the battle took place in front of the castle, and on the open space of ground which is even at the present day called Sandal Common. The spot where the Duke of York was killed upon the green is about four hundred yards from the castle, close to the old road from Barnsley, now called, from the sign of a public-house, Cock and Bottle Lane. It is a triangular piece of ground, in size about a rood or ten feet, with a fence about it, which the tenant of the place is bound by his lease to maintain; and it has been ever since the Duke's death free from taxes. Camden says that there was a cross erected on it to the memory of the Duke, which was destroyed in the Civil Wars. There have been two rings found on the site of the battle. The first, on the inside, bore an inscription, '*Pur bon amour;*' and outside were delineated the figures of three saints. Camden gives a print of it. The other ring had on it inscribed the letter R, and very probably belonged to the Duke of York.

Between the Calder and a place called Bellevue, there have been found a quantity of old horse-shoes, which very probably belonged to some of the horses of the men slain in the battle of Wakefield. The spot where the Duke of Rutland was slain still goes by the name of the Fall Ings, and lies on the left-hand side of the bridge going to Heath. There was an old house standing a few years ago close to the chapel on the bridge; and there was a tradition that the Duke of Rutland died in it.

By the death of Richard Duke of York, the manor of Wakefield again came to the Crown in the person of Edward IV., who by the battle of Towton[1] had become firmly seated on the throne. It is a remarkable circumstance, that two of the possessors of Wakefield, Thomas Earl of Lancaster and Henry Earl of Holland, were beheaded,—the latter by sentence of the High Court of

---

[1] Proclamations forbidding quarter were issued before the battle of Towton. Like Leipsic, it reached over the night; but, unlike Leipsic, even the hour of darkness brought no rest. They fought from four o'clock in the afternoon throughout the whole night—on to noon next day. Like Waterloo, it was fought on a Sunday; and the accounts of contemporary writers state, in words very like those letters from Mont St. Jean, that for weeks afterwards the blood stood in puddles and stagnated in gutters, and that the water of the wells was red. No inaccuracy is more frequent in ancient authors than that of numbers, and generally on the side of exaggeration. But on this occasion we can form a more correct estimate of the carnage by the concurrence of unusually respectable testimonies; and perhaps, in these times, it will give the best idea of it to say, that the number of Englishmen slain exceeded the sum of those who fell at Vimeira, Talavera, Albuera, Salamanca, Vittoria, and Waterloo.—*English Review*, No. 2.

Justice for attempting to restore Charles I. to the throne; whilst three others were slain in the battle-field. Such is the eventful history of the possessors of this extensive manor.

Leland describes Wakefield as 'a very quik market towne, so that al vitail is very good and chepe there: a right honest man shal fare wel for two pens a meale.' The bridge over the Calder was built about 6 Edward III. On the east side is 'a chapel of our lady:' a few years ago the pointed Gothic arch was widened. An extraordinary legend is related by Roger de Hoveden, which shows the antiquity of the Wakefield mills: 'In the year 1201, Eustace, abbot of Flaye, came over into England, preaching the duty of extending the Sabbath from three o'clock P.M. on Saturday to sunrising on Monday morning, pleading the authority of an epistle written by Christ Himself, and found on the altar of St. Simon at Golgotha. The shrewd people of Yorkshire treated the fanatic with contempt, and the miller of Wakefield persisted in grinding his corn after the hour of cessation; for which disobedience,' says the historian gravely, 'his corn was turned into blood, while the mill-wheel stood immoveable against all the water of the Calder. Again, in 1452, we find the miller fined for taking too much mulcture.'

Pindar Fields, which by tradition are said to have been the site of Robin Hood's exploit with the valiant Pindar George of the Green, lie at the east end of the town. In the court-rolls of the manor of Wakefield of the reign of Edward II., there appears a Robertus Hode living in the town, and having business in that court. In a parcel of deeds of Edward III.'s reign, relating to Coldhindley, which is about eight miles from Wakefield, we find a Robert, William, and Adam Hode mentioned.[1] It will be remembered that Barnsdale Forest, where Robin Hood is said to have lived, lies at no great distance from Coldhindley.

We now pass on to Sandal Castle, which is probably of earlier date than the Conquest. In 1317, John the eighth and last Earl of Warren, who was a man of licentious character, while residing at Sandal Castle, was involved in a scandalous intrigue with Alice de Lacey, wife of his neighbour Thomas Earl of Lancaster; she, on the Monday before Ascension Day, was carried off by violence, and conveyed to a castle of the Earl of Warren at Reigate, in Surrey. The Earl of Lancaster proceeded to avenge himself by laying siege to the Earl's castle, and Sandal was demolished by him in revenge for this; but it was rebuilt by the Earl of Warren in 1321. In the year 1318 the Earl of Lancaster obtained a grant from the Earl of Warren of his manor of Wakefield, probably as a make-peace for the offences committed against him by the Earl; but he only enjoyed it for three years, being attainted for high treason, and beheaded at his Castle of Pontefract.

There is an inquisition of Sandal Castle taken in the

[1] The name of Robin Hood was common in the thirteenth and fourteenth centuries.

time of the last Earl, in which are some curious particulars. First, there was a fish-pond, valued at nothing, because all the fish died, probably on account of some mineral impregnations; second, the meadow-ground lay in open field, and was worth five shillings per acre—the pasture-ground was inclosed, and only worth one-tenth of that sum; lastly, the fishery, a mill-pond of four acres, was worth one-third more than the best meadow-ground.

Richard Duke of York lay at the castle before the battle of Wakefield; and the fortress seems to have been of some note in the reign of Richard III. John Wodrove, receiver of Wakefield for Edward IV., had a warrant by privy seal, dated 3d of June, 2d Richard III., for an allowance of such sums of money as he should employ in making a tower in the castle in Someshall or Sandal; also, a warrant granting him a tun of wine yearly for the use of the said castle; and on the 20th of June following, the king being then at York, assigned the manors of Ulverston and Thornham in support of the expenses of his household appointed. In October following, orders were given for building a bakehouse and brewhouse within Sandal Castle by the advice of John de la Pole, Earl of Lincoln, and others of the king's council lying therein. The portrait of John Wodrove and his wife, with his arms and his crest, were formerly in the window of Wakefield old church. In the reign of Queen Elizabeth we find that the fees in the castle were, per day: captain, 16d.; porter, 8d.; guns, 6, fee, 6d.; footmen's fee, 6d.

Sandal Castle was garrisoned for the king in the time of the Civil Wars under Colonel Bonivant, and surrendered after a siege of three weeks, a few days after Pontefract Castle. Boothroyd, the historian of Pontefract, informs us that the governors of Sandal and Pontefract Castles were accustomed to light fires on their towers as a signal to each party that good news had been received; and on April 30, 1646, it was resolved by the House of Commons that, being an inland castle, it should be made untenable, and no garrison kept or maintained in it; it was then completely demolished. The moat of the castle may yet be traced, and the masonry of the central keep, or round tower, is visible. There are several hewn stones, quite fresh and square, lodged at the foot of a tree at the bottom of a broad walk which appears to have crossed the drawbridge. There seems to have been a park at Wakefield and Sandal Castle from very early times.

In the 5th Edward IV., Sir John Saville had a grant from the king of the herbage of Wakefield Park. Sir Thomas Wentworth had a grant from Henry VIII. of the keepership. In the 1st of Queen Elizabeth, Henry Saville is mentioned as the queen's keeper of it; there being some dispute between him (the plaintiff) and Anthony Wilson for hunting and destruction of deer there. In the 2d of Elizabeth we also find Sir John Tempest, steward of the lordship of Wakefield, and constable of Sandal Castle, disputing with Henry Saville, in the court of Lancaster, for the office of keepership of the game in the New Park of Wakefield and Sandal Castle Park, the paling and the office of bow-bearer there. A farm-house, standing on the left bank of the Calder, and looking up the stream, is still called Lodge-gate, and was undoubtedly an entrance to the park which extended over the neighbouring hills. Another entrance also bears the name of the Deer-gate.[1]

[1] The substance of this narrative is condensed from an excellent paper by George Wentworth, Esq., in the *Journal of the British Archæological Association*, 1864; with considerable additions.

The chapel on Wakefield Bridge was rebuilt in 1847, save one small piece at the east end. The ancient beautiful west façade is now built up as the front of a boat-house or summer-house, on the margin of a lake in the grounds of Kettlethorpe Hall, two miles distant. A brass-plate inscription tells: 'This structure is built with the remains of the original west front and other fragments of St. Marie's, Chantry, which stood on Wakefield Bridge.' It was built in the reign of Edward III., about 1357; and restored by Edward IV. after the battle of Wakefield, 1400, who dedicated the chapel to the memory of his father the Duke of York. It was defaced by unseemly repairs in 1794. In 1847 the ancient portion was purchased by the Hon. George Chapple Norton, and re-erected by him at Kettlethorpe. The so-called restoration on Wakefield Bridge is reclaimed to an ecclesiastical purpose, a weekly service being performed in it every Thursday evening.—See a paper in the above-quoted *Journal* by F. R. Wilson, Esq.

MIDDLEHAM CASTLE AND RICHARD III.

N a rocky eminence near the small market town of Middleham, in the North Riding of Yorkshire, are the ruins of the ancient castle, built about 1190 by Robert Fitz-Ranulph. In the reign of Henry VI. it belonged to the Earl of Salisbury, who marched hence with 4000 men towards London to demand redress for his son's grievances. Here, also, according to Stow, the bastard Falconbridge was beheaded in 1471. Edward IV. was confined for a time in Middleham Castle by Richard Nevill, Earl of Warwick, after he had been taken prisoner at Wolvey, but he subsequently escaped while hunting in the park.

After defeating the Earl of Warwick at Barnet, Edward IV. gave Middleham Castle to his brother, the Duke of Gloucester, afterwards Richard III., who took a great liking to the place, and who was preparing to found a college in Frodingham Field when he died. The church of St. Mary and St. Alkeld, at Middleham, had been made collegiate by Richard when Duke of Gloucester.

His only son Edward was born here; but since that time

hardly anything is known of the history of the castle, except that it was inhabited in 1609 by Sir Henry Linley. Tradition says that it was reduced to ruins by Cromwell; but there is no historical evidence to prove it.

The character of Richard the Third has been so vilified by party historians, that only of late years has the general reader given the short-lived monarch credit for any qualities likely to render him popular. In seeking to clear him of great crimes, however, he is proved to have possessed patriotism and integrity. After the victory of Towton, the title of Duke of Gloucester, with an ample appanage in the shape of lordships and manors, were at once conferred on Richard, who, at an unusually early age, was also appointed to three or four offices of the highest trust and dignity; and he amply justified the confidence reposed in him. That he was brave we are assured. The chief glory of the well-fought field of Barnet belonged to Richard; but unluckily it was the scene of a tragedy in which the part of the first villain has been popularly assigned to him.

Richard's superiority to all sordid considerations was strikingly displayed during the invasion of France in 1475, when Edward, at the head of one of the finest armies that ever left the English coast, was cajoled and out-manœuvred by Louis XI. into doing worse than nothing. The expedition ended in a disgraceful treaty, by which Edward was to receive certain sums of money which he wanted for his personal pleasures. Richard alone refused to barter English honour for French gold. 'Only the Duke of Gloucester, who stood aloof on the other side for honour, frowned at this accord, and expressed much sorrow, as compassionating the glory of his nation blemished in it.' Habington, from whom we quote, suggests that the Duke had a further and more dangerous aim: 'As who, by the dishonour of his brothers, thought his credit received increase; and by how much the king sank in opinion, he should rise.' Bacon adopts the same method of depreciation: 'And that out of this deep root of ambition it sprang that, as well as the treaty of peace, *as upon all other occasions*, Richard, then Duke of Gloucester, stood ever upon the side of honour, raising his own reputation to the disadvantage of the king his brother, and drawing the eyes of all (especially of the nobles and soldiers) upon himself.' We have here, from his worst calumniators, the admitted fact that, down to 1475, his means were noble, be his end and motives what they may.

Richard was for several years Lord Warden, or Keeper of the Northern Marches; and while residing in a sort of royal capacity at York, he so ingratiated himself with the people of that city and neighbourhood, that they stood by him to the last. On the death of his brother he was in the fulness of his fame as a soldier and statesman. He was also the first prince of the blood; and he must have been endowed with an amount of stoical indifference and self-denial, seldom found in high places at any time, if no ambitious hopes dawned upon him.

The received accounts of Richard's mode of ascending the throne are contradictory; and it is difficult to believe that he laid much stress on the voices of the rabble in Guildhall, although here again Shakspeare is supported by More. Richard must have been sure of a powerful party, or he never would have ventured to present himself as king before the very Parliament which he had summoned in the name of the nephew he deposed. This important fact is made clear by Mr. Gairdner, who, admitting that this Parliament was not formally called together, asserts that it did meet, and that the petition to Richard to assume the crown was presented by a deputation of the lords and commons of England, accompanied by another from the city of London, on the very day that had been originally appointed for its meeting.

From this mock election in June, says More, Richard commenced his reign, and was crowned in July with the same provision that was made for the coronation of his nephew. The day before the ceremony, he and his queen rode from the Tower through the city to Westminster, with a train comprising three dukes, nine earls, and twenty-two barons. There was a large attendance of peers, lay and spiritual, and great dignitaries at the ensuing ceremony in Westminster Hall; and More records as most observable, that the Countess of Richmond, mother to King Henry VII., bore up the queen's train in the procession. Richard soon afterwards left London on a royal progress towards York, where he was crowned a second time.

Richard laid himself out from the commencement of his reign to found a reputation for moderation, equity, and forgiveness of private injuries. 'The day after his acceptance of the crown,' says More, 'he went to Westminster, sat himself down in the court of King's Bench, made a very gracious speech to the assembly there present, and promised them halcyon days. He ordered one Hog, whom he hated, and who was fled to sanctuary for fear of him, to be brought before him, took him by the hand, and spoke favourably to him, which the multitude thought was a token of his clemency, and the wise men of his vanity.' He formally enjoined the great barons to see to the equal administration of justice in their provinces; and a contemporary sketch of his progresses speaks of 'his lords and judges in every place sitting determining the complaints of poor folks, with due punition of offenders against the laws.' In a circular letter to the bishops, he expresses his fervent desire for the suppression of vice. His legislative measures are admitted to have been valuable additions to the statute-book.

Edward IV. was always in want of money, and was in the habit of personally appealing to his wealthiest subjects for contributions. Richard went on an opposite tack. When the citizens and others offered him a benevolence, he refused it, saying, 'I would rather have your hearts than your money.'

He disafforested a large tract of country at Witchwood, which his brother had cleared for deer; and showed at the same time his wish to promote all manly and popular amusements by liberal grants and allowances to the masters of his hounds and hawks. There is, moreover, extant a mandate to all mayors and sheriffs, not to vex or molest John Brown, 'our mater-guider, and ruler of all our bears and apes to us appertaining.' Richard is commended by contemporaries for his encouragement of architecture; and the commendation is justified by a list of the structures which he completed or improved.

His love of music is inferred from the extreme measures he adopted for its gratification. Turner quotes a warrant 'empowering one of the gentlemen of his chapel to take and seize, for the king's use, all such singing men and children expert in the science of music, as he could find and think able to do the king service, in all places in the kingdom, whether cathedrals, colleges, chapels, monasteries, or any other franchised places, except Windsor.' He was visited by minstrels from foreign countries, and gave annuities to several professors of the gentle science, 'and also,' adds Turner, 'perhaps for his fondness for their sonorous state music, to several trumpeters.' Mr. Jesse, in his *Memoirs*, will have it that Richard's nature was originally a compassionate one; and he appeals to the pensions considerately bestowed by him on the widows of his enemies, Lady Hastings, Lady Rivers, Lady Oxford, and the Duchess of Buckingham.

The shortness of Richard's reign favours the idea that the nation, exasperated beyond endurance by his villanies, rose and threw him off like an incubus. But nothing of the kind occurred. The people at large were too much inured to scenes of blood and acts of cruelty to be shocked by them. They cared little or nothing whether a few princes or lords more or less were put to death, so long as they were not fleeced by a tax-gatherer, or oppressed by a local tyrant; and Richard, like Cromwell at a later period, took good care that there should be no usurped or abused authority besides his own. He was not weighed in the balance, and found wanting, till two discontented nobles, the Stanleys, threw their whole weight into the opposing scale. The numerical inferiority of Richard's army is a conclusive proof that his cause was not a pre-eminently popular one.

The pair who contended on Bosworth Field for a kingdom are thus portrayed: 'Richard was better versed in arms; Henry was better served. Richard was brave; Henry a coward. Richard was about five feet four, rather runted, but only made crooked by his enemies, and wanted six weeks of thirty-three; Henry was twenty-seven, slender, and near five feet nine, with a saturnine countenance, yellow hair, and grey eyes.'

As to the person of Richard: 'the truth,' says Walpole, 'I take to have been this: Richard, who was slender, and not tall, had one shoulder a little higher than the other, a defect, by the magnifying-glasses of party, by distance of time, and by the amplification of tradition, easily swelled to a shocking deformity.' The impression left by a marked personal peculiarity may be unconsciously heightened and transmitted till it becomes inextricably woven into the web of history.

The strongest argument in favour of Richard's personal appearance is that drawn from Dr. Shaw's address to the citizens of London preparatory to the usurpation: 'My Lord Protector, that very noble prince, the pattern of all heroic deeds, represents the very face and mind of the great Duke his father. His features are the same, and the very express likeness of that noble Duke.' At these words the Protector was to enter as if by chance; and although the point was missed by his non-appearance till a few minutes later, such a *coup de theatre* would hardly have been hazarded if Richard either presented no resemblance, or a miniature and caricature one, of his father.

Richard lost nothing of his vigilance or unrelenting sternness in his last hours. Going the rounds at Bosworth, he found a sentinel asleep, and stabbed him, with the remark: 'I found him asleep, and have left him as I found him.'[1]

---

[1] This narrative of the personal history of Richard III. is in the main condensed from a very able paper in the *Edinburgh Review*, No. cxv. 1862, with additions.

THE VALE OF WHITE HORSE.

AS the railway traveller passes through the middle district of the Great Western line, he will, doubtless, remark that the sky-line of the chalk-down, as seen from the valley, is continually broken by the elevation of some earthwork, carrying the mind's eye back to times of war and bloodshed, spoliation and conquest. This earthwork is known as Uffington Castle, and occupies the summit of White Horse Hill, 700 feet in diameter from east to west, and 500 feet from north to south. It is surrounded by a double vallum or embankment, the inner one high, and commanding an extensive view in every direction, the outer one slighter. On the steep escarpment of the hill, just below the entrenchment, our traveller will see the rude outline figure of a horse at full gallop, formed by removing the thin layer of turf and exposing the white surface beneath of the chalk. Hence the figure is called the *White Horse.* This is believed to have been cut as a memorial of the battle of Æscesdun, or Ash-tree Hill, in which the West Saxons, under Ethelred and Alfred in 871, defeated the Danes

The Vale of White Horse.

with great slaughter on this spot. Be this as it may, the Horse is either of Saxon origin or of higher antiquity. Asser minutely describes how 'the Pagans (Danes) had got the higher ground, and how the battle was begun upon a spot where grew a single thorn-tree, which he himself had afterwards seen, the whole account having been given him by a faithful eye-witness. After a bloody and obstinate dispute, one king and five counts were killed on the Pagan side, with many thousands of common men; and the rest were dispersed all over the wide plain of Ashdown, and pursued all that night and the next day as far as to their castle at Reading.'

The White Horse is a rude figure about 374 feet in length, and is said to cover an acre of ground. The face of the chalk-down is 893 feet above the sea-level; and when the afternoon sun shines upon the figure, it may be seen ten, twelve, and even fifteen miles distant; and from its immense size it forms a remarkable object. Wise, the antiquary, is in raptures with the skill displayed in the Horse, and in the admirable choice of a situation where it is little exposed to injury or decay. The inhabitants of the neighbourhood had an ancient custom of assembling to *scour the Horse*, i. e. to clear away the turf where it has encroached upon the outline of the Horse. On such occasions a rural festival was formerly held, and the people were regaled by the lord of the manor; but they do not appear to have observed that custom since 1780; it may possibly have dwindled to a common, purposeless fair. We remember to have been at Englefield Green in the summer of 1833, and there to have heard of a custom, then common in Berkshire, of boys '*going up to chalk-pits*' annually: may not this be a relic of the *White Horse scouring?* We need hardly remind the reader of Mr. T. Hughes's very popular story of 'The Scouring of the White Horse,' published a few years since.

The site of Æscesdun, or Ashdown, has, however, been much disputed. Wise, in a letter to Dr. Mead, contends for the ridge of the chalk-hills extending from Wantage into Wiltshire, and thinks that the White Horse cut on the hill is a memorial of the victory. Aston, a village near Wallingford, and Ashampstead, a village about equally distant from Wallingford, Newbury, and Reading, have each their partisans. Mr. Sharon Turner, in his *History of the Anglo-Saxons*, inclines to the opinion that Merantune, (where shortly afterwards the Saxons sustained a severe defeat, in which Ethelred was mortally wounded,) was Moreton, near Wallingford.

Leland, Camden, and Aubrey take but passing notice of the White Horse, as does the author of *A Tour through England*, published in 1738; and 'they,' Wise observes, 'leave us much in the dark about the antiquity and design of it, with the curiosity, but at the same time with the haste, of travellers.' Wise expected better things of Camden, who might surely have inquired into the origin of the ceremony of *scouring the horse*, 'which, from time immemorial, has been solemnized by a numerous concourse of people from all the villages round about.' This writer is not, however, surprised at 'the custom being lost in the mazes of antiquity, though the festival was of a more general nature than wakes, or feasts of the dedication of churches, which are traced to the origin of fairs; now the latter are confined to single parishes, whereas, though the Horse stands in the parish of Uffington, yet other towns claimed, by ancient custom, a share of the duty upon this occasion, which distinction should render the White Horse Festival more important and memorable.'

The White Horse was the standard of the Saxons before and after their coming into England; it was a proper emblem of victory and triumph, as we read in Ovid and elsewhere. The position of the Horse is not rampant or prancing, as represented in the arms of Savoy, whose princes are descended from those of Saxony; but the Horse is current, or galloping, as described in the arms of the House of Brunswick to this day. Wise, in his pamphlet upon this point, 1738-42, says: 'If any disputes should arise among heralds about these different bearings of the horse, as likewise whether he ought to be current for the dexter part or sinister, which, I believe, is a point not entirely settled, I think, till some other more ancient record shall be produced, they may be fairly denominated from this authentic one of 867 years' standing.'

The White Horse is to this day the ensign of the county of Kent, where it is a favourite inn-sign. The White Horse of Hanover dates from the House of Hanover succeeding to the throne of these realms—the White Horse being the badge of that house.

Just under the White Horse Hill is a knoll of chalk called the Dragon Hill, described as a mound or barrow, intended to cover the dead, the horse being supposed to commemorate the victory. This would be a plausible link in the chain of the antiquary's theory, were it certain that the mound is artificial; but this is supposititious. At all events, the neighbouring downs are thickly strewn with tumuli and other marks of an early population.

The entrenchments, too, are very interesting; and the advantage which has been taken of the natural ravines to aid in forming camps, is very striking to the student of military antiquities. On the chalk hills north of Lambourn many barrows are found, especially one covered irregularly with large stones. Three of the stones have a fourth laid on them, in the manner of the British cromlechs. By the country people this is called *Wayland Smith;* and they have a tradition of an invisible smith residing here, who would shoe a traveller's horse, if it was left here for a short time, with a piece of money by way of payment. How pleasantly this strange tradition is introduced in the romance of *Kenilworth*, by Sir Walter Scott, must be remembered.

Wise leaves the entire story to lovers of the fancies of fiction, and concludes with these matter-of-fact remarks: ' These stones are, according to the best Danish antiquaries, a burial-altar. Their being raised in the midst of a plain field near the great road, seems to indicate some person there slain and buried; and such person was probably a chief or king, there being no monument of this sort near that place, perhaps not in England beside. If it be allowed me likewise that King Ethelred lay encamped at Hardwell, this will afford another argument for its being raised for the king slain, whose troops were opposed to King Ethelred's division, as those of the Count's were to Alfred's, for the stones are about half a mile from Hardwell Camp.' About a mile from Wayland Smith, a succession of barrows have been traced, which Wise concluded to denote the burial-places of certain of the Danish counts.

Wayland Smith has been lucidly described in the large *History of the Great Western Railway*, published in 1846: 'Wayland Smith's Cave is a combination of a cromlech with a regular Druidical circle. The circle is composed of between thirty and forty stones, some of which are overthrown and partially buried, while all are more or less displaced. Within the circle, three stones are set on edge, so as to form a chamber, which is roofed by a fourth. This is the cave. In front of the cave is a sort of cruciform alley of stones, two areas of which are closed at the ends, while the third is open, and forms the entrance to the cromlech. This curious relic stands by the side of the old Ridge Way. The stones are all grey-wethers, and similar to those of Abury and the Trilithons of Stonehenge. The modern proprietor of this curious Druidical remain has had the good taste to plant a small wood of fir-trees around it, throwing the whole into a deep gloom, well suited to its ancient character.'

We are induced to extend our antiquarian ramble to another relic of kindred interest, namely, the noted Blowing Stone, which is situated at Kingston Lisle, five miles due north of Lambourn, and the same distance from Wantage. At the back of the stone grows an old elm-tree. The stone itself is a species of red sandstone. It is about three feet high, three feet six inches broad, and two feet thick; but it is of rough and rather irregular surface. It has several holes in it of various sizes. There are seven holes in the front, three at the top, a large irregular broken hollow at the north end (as it stands north and south), and one if not more holes at the back. If a person blows in at any one of three of the holes, an extremely loud noise is produced—something between a note upon a French horn and the bellowing of a calf; this can be heard in a favourable state of weather at Farringdon Clump, a distance of about six miles; and a person standing at about a yard distant from either end of the stone while it is blown into, will distinctly feel the ground shake. The holes in the stone are of various sizes; but those which, if blown into, produce the sound, easily admit a person's finger. The hole most commonly used to produce the sound is at the top of the stone; and if a small stick, eighteen inches long, be pushed in at this hole, it will come out at a hole at the back of the stone, about a foot below the top, and almost immediately below the hole blown into. It is evident that this is the place at which the air finds its exit, as, after the stone has been blown into at the top for a considerable time, this hole becomes wet. There seems, however, no doubt that there are chambers in the stone, as the irregular broken hollow at the north end of it has evidently formed a part of another place, at which a similar sound might have been produced. In the neighbourhood there exists a tradition that this stone was used for the purpose of giving an alarm on the approach of an enemy. In the *Penny Cyclopædia*, whence the above description has been abridged, the belief is stated that there is no account of the Blowing Stone in any other publication. Its position is marked in the Ordnance map.

The Vale of White Horse to this day presents to the curious observer the earthworks and other relics of warlike times—the means of our early civilisation. Here may be traced the camp and the castle, the rude trophy of triumph cut upon the face of the lofty hill, and the grave of the victor—' the desolator desolate'—in the peaceful valley. There are the works of centuries since—of the early Briton, the Roman, the Saxon, and the Dane, whose ancient roads, in their directions, afford abundant studies for the patient antiquary and topographer. Through this long lapse of ages, defaced by the struggles for the mastery among war-tribes, the Vale of White Horse has maintained its fame for containing some of the most fertile lands in England; including rich pastures and corn-lands, and a belt of rich lands along the Thames, whose pent-up waters and tributary streams must have fed considerable lakes in past ages.

On the hills which border the Thames may be enjoyed extensive views over the Vale of White Horse into Oxfordshire; and in general the aspect of the country from any considerable hill is that of great richness and variety. The contrast is suggestive. Here 'Decay's effacing fingers' have spared us studies of the past, which luxuriant Nature, in her reproductiveness, invests with picturesque beauty; the Roman road of centuries ago is almost obliterated by the railway of to-day; and the green turf was once the site of the tower'd city, with its 'busy hum of men.'

THE DUKE OF MONMOUTH'S LAST DAYS.

MANY are the memorials which exist to this day of 'the unfortunate Duke of Monmouth,' the natural son of Charles II.; and whose popularity with the nation, still more than the presumed partiality of his father, made him a somewhat formidable competitor for the succession in the actual circumstances of the legitimate heir.

Somerset and Dorset were the closing scenes of Monmouth's career. In 1680 he made a memorable progress, accepting the hospitality of his distinguished friends, and visiting the estates of the country party; but the gentlemen of the court shrank from contact with one whose connection with the opposition and democratic members of Parliament was so notorious. In August, when Monmouth started on his progress, incredible numbers flocked to see this great champion of the English nation who had been so successful against the Dutch, French, and Scots. He first went into Wiltshire and honoured the worthy Squire Thynne, of Longleate House, with his company for some days. From Longleate, Monmouth journeyed into Somerset, caressed with the joyful acclamations of the country people, who cried, 'God bless King Charles and the Protestant Duke!' In some towns and parishes through which he passed they strewed the streets and highways with herbs and flowers, especially at Ilchester and South Petherton; others presenting him with bottles of wine. When the Duke came within ten miles of White Lackington House, the seat of George Speke, Esq., one mile distant from Ilminster, he was met by two thousand persons on horseback, whose number increased to twenty thousand. To admit so large a multitude, several perches of the park paling were taken down. His Grace, his party, and attendants, took refreshment under the famed sweet Spanish chestnut-tree, now standing, which measures at three feet from the ground upwards of twenty-six feet in circumference. The old branches have been mostly removed by the ravages of time; but there are others attached to the stock which produce large timber, as well as a quantity of fruit every year. White Lackington House is now a farm: a great part of the edifice has been pulled down.

It was in the village of Norton St. Philip's, between Bath and Frome, that the ill-fated Duke was attacked on June 27, 1685, by the Royalists, whose advanced guard had marched from Bath under the Duke of Grafton, Monmouth's half-brother. Colonel Holmes, who was at the head of Monmouth's army, had an arm nearly shot off in the engagement; and it is related that the brave soldier, unassisted, completed the amputation with the cook's knife in the kitchen of the George Inn at the village. This large old mansion was formerly a granary belonging to Hinton Abbey: its capacious porch, the designs of some of its windows, its overhanging upper storeys (upon rude corbels), and its inner gallery leading to what once were bed-chambers, all denote the pile to have been erected in the early portion of the fifteenth century.

Macaulay has thus vividly described the capture of Monmouth: 'On Cranbourne Chase the strength of the horses failed. They were, therefore, turned loose. Monmouth and his friends disguised themselves as countrymen, and proceeded on foot towards the New Forest. They passed the night in the open air; but before morning they were surrounded on every side. At five in the morning Grey was seized by two of Lumley's scouts. It could hardly be doubted that the chief rebel was not far off. The pursuers redoubled their vigilance and activity. The cottages scattered over the heathy country on the boundaries of Dorsetshire and Hampshire, were strictly examined by Lumley, and the clown with whom Monmouth had changed clothes was discovered. Portman came with a strong body of horse and foot to assist in the search. Attention was soon drawn to a place well fitted to shelter fugitives. It was an extensive tract of land separated by an inclosure from the open country, and divided by numerous hedges into small fields. In some of these fields the rye, the peas, and the oats were high enough to conceal a man; others were overgrown by fern and brambles. A poor woman reported that she had seen two strangers lurking in this covert. The near prospect of reward animated the zeal of the troops. . . . The outer fence was strictly guarded, the space within was examined with indefatigable diligence, and several dogs of quick scent were turned out among the bushes. The day closed before the search could be completed; but careful watch was kept all night. Thirty times the fugitives ventured to look through the outer hedge, but everywhere they found a sentinel on the alert: once they were seen and fired at. They then separated, and concealed themselves in different hiding-places.

'At sunrise the next morning the search was recommenced, and Buyse was found. He owned that he had parted from the Duke only a few hours before. The corn and copsewood were now beaten with more care than ever. At length a gaunt figure was discovered hiding in a ditch. The pursuers sprang on their prey. Some of them were about to fire, but Portman forbade all violence. The prisoner's dress was that of a shepherd. His beard, prematurely grey, was of several days' growth. He trembled greatly, and was unable to speak. Even those who had often seen him were in doubt whether this were the brilliant and graceful Monmouth. His pockets were searched by Portman, and in them were found, among some raw peas gathered in the rage of hunger, a watch, a purse of gold, a small treatise on fortification, an album filled with songs, receipts, prayers, and charms, and the George with which, many years before, King Charles II. had decorated his favourite son.'

The incidents and circumstances of the capture have been described with more particularity as to the names of the places. The decisive battle of Sedgemoor was fought on the 5th of July, after which Monmouth and his friends fled across the boundaries of Wiltshire; at Woodyates' Inn, near Salisbury, on the road to Blandford, they turned their horses adrift; and thence crossed the country, nearly due south, to 'the Island' in the parish of Horton, in Dorsetshire, where, in a field called to this day 'Monmouth Close,' was found the would-be king. An ash-tree, at the foot of which he was found crouched in a ditch, and half-hid under the fern, is standing, and bears the carved initials of persons who had visited it: it was propped up for preservation.

In one of the fields of peas, tradition tells that the Duke dropped a gold snuff-box. It was picked up some time afterwards by a labourer, who carried it to Mrs. Wedale of Horton—probably the proprietor of the field —and received in reward fifteen pounds, which was said to be half its value.

On his capture, the Duke was first taken to the house of Anthony Etterick, Esq., a magistrate, who resided at Holt, which adjoins Horton. Tradition, which records the popular feeling rather than the fact, reports that the poor woman who informed the pursuers that she had seen two strangers lurking in the Island—her name was Amy

Farrant—never prospered afterwards; and that Henry Parkin, the soldier who, spying the skirt of the smock-frock which the Duke had assumed as a disguise, recalled the searching party just as they were leaving the Island, burst into tears, and reproached himself bitterly for his fatal discovery (*Notes and Queries*).

The late Earl of Shaftesbury, many years ago, took some pains to identify the localities of the capture, and the Close, which latter is on his lordship's estate, St. Giles's. What he learned upon the spot convinced him that the Duke was not going to Christchurch, but to Bournemouth, where he expected to find a vessel. Monmouth Close, as the inclosure has been called since the capture in July 1685, is in the direct line from Woodyates to Bournemouth. Lord Shaftesbury had printed, for the information of persons visiting the spot, an account of the Close and the capture, in which it is stated that when the Duke's pursuers came up, an old woman gave information of his being in the Island, and of her having seen him filling his pockets with peas. The Island was immediately surrounded by soldiers, who passed the night there, and threatened to fire the neighbouring cots. The Duke, when taken, was quite exhausted with fatigue and hunger, having had no food since the battle but the peas which he had gathered in the field. The family of the woman who betrayed him were ever after holden in the greatest detestation, and are said to have fallen into decay, and to have never thriven afterwards. The house where she lived, which overlooked the spot, has fallen down: it was with the greatest difficulty that any one could be got to inhabit it. The Duke being asked what he would do if set at liberty, answered, that if his horse and arms were restored, he only desired to ride through the army, and he defied them all to take him again.

Monmouth was brought to London on July 15th, and had on the same day an interview with the king, who obdurately refused to grant him his life, or even the briefest respite. 'Though,' says Hume, 'he might have known, from the unrelenting severity of James's temper, that no mercy could be expected, he wrote him the most submissive letters, and conjured him to spare the issue of a brother who had ever been so strongly attached to his interests. James finding such symptoms of depression and despondency in his prisoner, admitted him to his presence, in hopes of extorting a discovery of his accomplices; but Monmouth would not purchase life, however loved, at the price of so much infamy. Finding all efforts vain, he assumed courage from despair, and prepared himself for death with a spirit better suited to his rank and character.' Having been attainted shortly after his landing, he was delivered to the executioner, and beheaded on Tower-hill the same day. The Duke is stated, in the folio dictionary of Pierre Richelet, to have given six guineas to the executioner to do his work well.

The statute of Monmouth's attainder is one of the briefest on record. It runs thus: 'Whereas James Duke of Monmouth has, in a hostile manner, invaded this kingdom, and is now in open rebellion, levying war against the king, contrary to the duty of his allegiance, Be it enacted by the King's most excellent Majesty, by and with the advice and consent of the Lords Spiritual and Temporal, and Commons, in this Parliament assembled, and by the authority of the same, That the said James Duke of Monmouth stand and be convicted and attainted of high treason, and that he suffer pains of death, and incur all forfeitures, as a traitor convicted and attainted of high treason.' This was passed and received the royal assent in a single day, on the strength of a letter from Gregory Alford, the Mayor of Lyme, announcing the landing of Monmouth at that port.

The Duke landed on the 17th of June with only 150 men; but the whole kingdom was alarmed, fearing that the disaffected would join them, many of the train-bands flocking to him. At his landing he published a declaration, charging his Majesty with usurpation, and several horrid crimes, on pretence of his own title, and offering to call a free Parliament. The declaration was ordered to be burned by the hangman, the Duke proclaimed a traitor, and a reward of £5000 to any one who should kill him.

Monmouth's followers exhibited more courage than their leader, and seemed determined to adhere to him in every fortune. The negligent disposition made by Feversham invited Monmouth to attack the king's army at Sedgemoor, near Bridgewater; and his men in this action showed what a native courage and a principle of duty, even when unassisted by discipline, is able to perform. They threw the veteran forces into disorder, drove them from their ground, continued the fight till their ammunition failed them, and would at last have obtained a victory, had not the misconduct of Monmouth and the cowardice of Grey prevented it. After a combat of three hours the rebels gave way, and were followed with great slaughter. About 1500 men fell in the battle and pursuit.

It is traditionally related that on the 8th of July Monmouth was brought a prisoner to Ringwood, and halted at an inn there. The narrator, who was a native of Ringwood, used to tell that her grandmother was one of the spectators when the royal prisoner came out to take horse; and she never failed to recount how he rejected any assistance in mounting, though his arms were pinioned; but placing his foot in the stirrup, sprang lightly into his saddle, to the admiration of all observers.

Hume's account of the execution is thus minute:—

'This favourite of the people was attended to the scaffold with a plentiful effusion of tears. When he saw the axe, he touched it, and said it was not sharp enough. He gave the hangman only half the usual fee, and told him that if he cut off his head cleverly, and not so butcherly as he did the unfortunate Russell's, his man would give him the rest.' [This differs from the anecdote already quoted from the French dictionary.] 'This precaution served only to dismay the executioner; he struck a feeble blow on Monmouth, who, raising his head from the block, looked him in the face, as if reproaching him for his failure. He gently laid down his head a second time, and the executioner struck him again and again to no purpose. He then threw aside the axe, and said he was incapable of finishing the bloody office. The sheriff obliged him to renew the attempt, and at two blows more the head was severed from his body.

'He was executed, in the thirty-sixth year of his age, on the 26th July 1685. He possessed many good qualities, and some that were bad. Had he lived in less turbulent times, he might have been an ornament to the court, and of service to his country. But the indulgence of Charles, the caresses of faction, and the allurements of popularity, seduced him into an enterprise which exceeded his capacity. The goodwill of the people followed him even after his death; and such was their fond attachment, that many believed he was still alive, and that some person resembling him had suffered in his stead.'

Soon after his execution Monmouth was buried in the Tower, beneath the communion-table, in the chapel of St. Peter's, from whence it is believed to have been removed. In the year 1852, in taking down the old chapel at Nuneham Regis, in Warwickshire, was found a decapitated body, which was surmised to be that of Monmouth. The chapel was the property of the Buccleuch family. Monmouth married Ann, the daughter and heir of Francis Scott, Earl of Buccleuch, who was in some measure estranged from him by his improper connection with Lady Ann Wentworth. Yet the tender interview that is recorded between Monmouth and his wife previous to his execution, gives countenance to the idea that she may have procured his remains for deposit privately within her own family receptacle; and under such circumstances it may readily be conceived that such secrecy would be used as not to leave any memento along with the corpse, as to whom it might belong, the very circumstance of decapitation being thought probably quite sufficient now as then for designation. Such is the conjecture of a Correspondent to *Notes and Queries*. Another Correspondent shows that Nuneham Regis did not belong to the Duke and Duchess of Monmouth at all, but descended to the family of Buccleuch from the Dukes of Montague. Then the peaked beard, which this corpse is described to have had, could not have belonged to Monmouth, for at the time of the capture his beard was of several days' growth; and within the week between his capture and execution, it could hardly have become a peaked beard.

Again, says this Correspondent, it may be doubted whether Monmouth's widow would have cared to show much respect to his remains, when it is remembered that after his last interview and parting with her, which some have spoken of as very tender, even on the scaffold, 'he went on to speak of his Henrietta,' and maintained that she, with whom he had been living illicitly, was 'a young lady of virtue and honour.' The Duchess certainly showed much feeling during her interview; but she must soon have recovered her composure, if it be true, as stated by Dalrymple, that she breakfasted with the king the morning after the execution. Though Nuneham Regis did not belong to the Duke of Monmouth, it is worthy of remark that it was the property of another illustrious man, who lost his life on the scaffold for an attempt precisely similar to that of Monmouth, viz. John Dudley, Duke of Northumberland. There can be no doubt that Monmouth was buried in the Tower. Holinshed accurately describes the position of his grave as being between the two queens, Catherine Howard and Anne Boleyn, and next to the Duke of Somerset. Do they still repose there?

The Duke of Monmouth lived in a magnificent mansion built by Wren, and which formed the south side of Soho Square. After the Duke's death the house was purchased by Lord Bateman. In 1717 a principal saloon was used as an auction-room.

J. T. Smith, in *Nollekens and his Times*, describes the pulling down of *Monmouth House*, which he witnessed. The gate entrance was of massive iron-work, supported by stone piers, surmounted by the crest of the Duke of Monmouth; and within the gates was a court-yard for carriages. The hall was ascended by steps. There were eight rooms on the ground-floor. The principal one was a dining-room towards the south, the carved and gilt panels of which had contained whole-length pictures. At corners of the ornamented ceiling, which was of plaster, and over the chimney-piece, Monmouth's arms were proudly displayed. The staircase was of oak, the steps very low, and the landing-places were tessellated with woods of light and dark colours. Upon ornamented brackets were busts of Seneca, Caracalla, Trajan, Adrian, etc. The principal room on the first floor was lined with blue satin, superbly decorated with pheasants and other birds in gold. The chimney-piece was richly ornamented with fruit and foliage; in the centre, within a wreath of oak-leaves, was a circular recess for a bust. The beads of the panels of the brown window-shutters, which were very lofty, were gilt; and the piers between the windows had been filled with looking-glasses. The paved yard was surrounded by a red brick wall, with heavy stone copings, twenty-five feet in height.

Among the memorials left by the unfortunate Duke are some MSS., which are interesting in establishing several points referred to by historians. After Monmouth was beheaded, the articles found on his person were given to the king. At James's deposition, three years afterwards, all his manuscripts, including those that had belonged to Monmouth, were carried into France, and they remained till the Revolution in that country, a century afterwards. Among them was the manuscript volume of 157 pages, 'filled with songs, recipes, prayers, and charms,' already mentioned. It was purchased at a book-stall in Paris in 1827, afterwards brought to England, and is now in the British Museum. This book shows the remains of silver clasps that have been destroyed, and part of the leather cover at each side torn away, seemingly for receiving some name or a coat of arms; it being dangerous to possess at that period of the French Revolution books with royal arms on them. The several books were sent to St. Omer's; the larger ones were burned, and some small ones were saved; but all trace of them was lost. The Abbé Waters—a collateral descendant of Lucy Waters, the Duke of Monmouth's mother—was the person with whom George IV. negotiated for the Stuart Papers, and from whom the volumes which have since appeared as Clarke's *Life of James the Second* were obtained; and it is from the Abbé Waters we have the account of the destruction of King James's autograph papers.

The book just named has on the inner cover the words 'Baron Watiers,' or 'Watrers,' and is believed to be that referred to in the following note, by Lord Dartmouth, to the modern editions of Burnet's *Own Time:* 'My uncle, Colonel William Legge, who went in the coach with him [Monmouth] to London as a guard, with orders to stab him when he was taken, and his table-book, which was full of astrological figures that nobody could understand; but he told my uncle that they had been given to him some years before in Scotland, and he now found they were but foolish conceits.' The most curious passages in this book are the Duke's memorandums of his journeys on two visits to the Prince of Orange in the year previous to his last rash adventure. There is an entry naming Toddington, a place remarkable in the history of the Duke. Near it was the residence of Lady Henrietta Maria

Wentworth, Baroness (in her own right) of Nettlestead. Five years before the execution, her mother observed that, despite the Duke being a married man, her daughter had, while at court, attracted his admiration, and she was hurried away to Toddington. In 1683, after the failure of the Rye House Plot, Monmouth was banished from the royal presence; and it was to Toddington that he retired. When, on retracting the confession which he had made on the occasion, he was banished the kingdom, the companion of his exile was Lady Henrietta Wentworth.

In Macaulay's History we find that the latest act of the Duke on the scaffold, before submitting to the stroke of the executioner, was to call his servant, and put into the man's hand a toothpick-case, the last token of ill-starred love. 'Give it,' he said, '*to that person!*' After the description of Monmouth's burial occurs this affecting passage: 'Yet a few months, and the quiet village of Toddington, in Bedfordshire, witnessed a yet sadder funeral. Near that village stood an ancient and stately hall, the seat of the Wentworths. The transept of the parish church had long been their burial-place. To that burial-place, in the spring which followed the death of Monmouth, was borne the coffin of the young Baroness Wentworth, of Nettlestead. Her family reared a sumptuous mausoleum over her remains; but a less costly memorial of her was long contemplated with far deeper interest: her name, carved by the hand of him she loved too well, was, a few years ago, still discernible on a tree in the adjoining park.'

340 THE DUKE OF MONMOUTH'S LAST DAYS.

The charms and recipes, conjurations and incantations in the pocket-book, are very curious; extracts from old recipe-books are mixed in the oddest way with abridgments of English history, and memorandums, chiefly of a private and personal kind. 'Altogether, this commonplace work is highly indicative of the weakness, vanity, and superstition which stood forward so prominently in the character of the rash but unfortunate Duke of Monmouth.' Sir Frederick Madden has ascertained, by a careful comparison of the above manuscript and pocket-book 'with several undoubted letters of the Duke of Monmouth,' that the whole of the volume (or nearly so) is certainly in the Duke's handwriting. Some lines written on the fly-leaf of the volume confirm the fact beyond all cavil. They are the autograph of King James himself, and are as follows: 'This book was found in the Duke of Monmouth's pocket when he was taken, and is most of his owne handwriting.' Among the verses are the following, conjectured to be composed by Monmouth:

> 'O how blest and how innocent
> And happy is a country life!
> Free from tumult and discontent;
> Heer is no flattery, nor strife,
> For 'twas the first and happiest life,
> When first man did injoie him selfe.
> This is a better fate than king's.
> Hence jentle peace and love doth flow,
> For fancy is the rate of things.
> I am pleased because I think it so;
> For a hart that is nobly true,
> All the world's arts can ne'er subdue.'

The prayers breathe a spirit of the most humble and ardent piety, and if composed by the Duke himself, exhibit the weakness of his character in a more favourable light than the remainder of the volume. One paragraph is striking: 'Mercy, mercy, good Lord! I ask not of Thee any longer the things of this world; neither power, nor honour, nor riches, nor pleasures. No, my God, dispose of them to whom Thou pleasest, so that Thou givest me mercy.'

Of greater historical value is the Diary of the Duke, mentioned by Wellwood in the sixth edition of his *Memoirs*, printed in 1718, and of which he says: 'A great many dark passages there are in it, and some clear enough, that shall be eternally buried for me; and perhaps it had been for King James's honour to have committed them to the flames.'

'It is curious to remark the complete subjugation in which Charles at this period stood towards his brother; occasioned, perhaps, by the foreign supplies which he scrupled not to receive, being dependent on his adhesion to the policy of which the Duke of York was the avowed representative. Shortly before his death, Charles appears to have meditated emancipation from this state of thraldom; and Hume says: "He was determined, it is thought, to send the Duke to Scotland, to recall Monmouth, to summon a Parliament, to dismiss all his unpopular ministers, and to throw himself entirely upon the goodwill and affections of his subjects." This passage accords with the entries in Monmouth's pocket-book, dated Jan. 5, and Feb. 3.'

There has also been preserved a curious and richly ornamented sword, left, as it is believed, by the Duke of Monmouth among the villagers of Dorsetshire on his flight from the field of Sedgemoor. It was found in 1844 in the hands of a knot of rustic mummers at Woodyates Inn, and was purchased from them for the sum of eighteenpence. The guard and pommel of the sword are chased with royal emblems, portraits, and military subjects, and the whole has been richly plated. Among these ornaments we have the Rose and Crown, the Prince of Wales's Feathers, and Charles I. and his queen. In this view it is clear that the sword could not have been *made* for Monmouth. He never claimed to be Prince of Wales. Mr. Hewitt is inclined to believe that the sword belonged originally to Monmouth's father, Charles II., when Prince of Wales; this would be during his residence at the Hague; and the weapon is thought to be Dutch.

¹[Among our national documents are preserved the following: —'An order under the royal sign manual, signed with a trembling hand, for the commitment of the Duke of Monmouth's children, July 9, 1685; warrant for the delivery of the body of James Duke of Monmouth to the Sheriff of London on the 15th of July, between the hours of 9 and 11 in the forenoon, for execution on Tower Hill, July 13, 1685; the king's order to allow the Duke of Monmouth and Lord Grey to have each a servant; that the Bishop of Ely is to acquaint the Duke of Monmouth "that he is to dy to-morrow," and that he may see his children, 14th July 1685; the king's order for the Duchess of Monmouth to have access to the Duke, either this day, "or to-morrow morning," 14th July 1685; the king's order to permit the Duchess of Monmouth "to dispose of the body of her daughter, that is now dead in the Tower, as shee shall think fitt," 12th of August 1685.']

THE LADY ALICE LISLE.

IT will be remembered that, after the overthrow of the unfortunate Duke of Monmouth at Sedgemoor, near Bridgewater, his scattered partisans sought protection and relief; some in the hovels of the poor and naked like themselves, and others at the mansions of the gentry in the neighbourhood, whose principles were not unfavourable to Monmouth, or whose humane feelings led them to offer still more readily an asylum to the fugitives. Of the latter class was the venerable hostess of Miles Court, whose husband had distinguished himself among those who sat in judgment on Charles I. Her own better feelings had always attached her to the House of Stuart; and her son had displayed his courage in favour of James II. at that very battle which had just blasted the hopes of his antagonist. The only rebel of her kindred, the Colonel himself, had long ago retired an outlaw from his country, and was 'shot dead at Lausanne, in Switzerland, by three ruffians engaged for that purpose by some of the royal family.' Nevertheless, the widow of the regicide had been marked out by the Government for destruction.

THE LADY ALICE LISLE.

It was at that notorious tribunal, in horrible mockery nicknamed 'The Merciful Assize' of Winchester, and before Chief-Justice Jeffreys, that the infirm yet stately Lady Alice Lisle, now past her seventieth year, stood arraigned for high treason, in having concealed and supported two of Monmouth's followers in a cell or vault at Moyles Court, originally constructed to secure the persecuted priesthood of either party from the malice of their pursuers. The aspect of the judge and prisoner presented a remarkable contrast. The countenance of the former betrayed nothing of that pride or ferocity which might be imagined from the character of the man. From continued habits of intoxication and sensuality, his face and demeanour were indicative rather of sottish indolence and brutal doggedness than of active cruelty or revenge.

Few witnesses were called in the present case, yet their hasty evidence seemed too dilatory for the judge's petulance; he declared the charge to be established, and directed the jury to find their verdict accordingly. But the spirit of the indignant matron was not so tamely to be extinguished. She rose majestically from the seat which her infirmities had demanded, rather than her wishes entreated. She raised her lofty form to its full proportions, and cast around, for a moment, her wan yet impressive features, maintaining in wrinkles and fatigue the serenity if not the fire of youth. Then, with an air which awed even the heartless judge upon the bench, she warned the jury of their duty, reminding them that 'the services her son had just performed should

The Lady Alice Lisle.

now exonerate her from regal animosity, had any accrued to her name from the disloyalties of her husband; that her crime amounted to no more than this: that in ignorance both of the condition of the fugitives and of the law, which now pretended to condemn her, she had opened her doors to the hungry, the naked, and the forlorn; that even this offence, if offence it were, must rest upon her own confession alone, as no evidence had proved the fact upon her trial; that she had been allowed neither notice of the accusation, nor counsel, nor defences; and that the safety of his Majesty's subjects was far more endangered by one unjust trial and condemnation than by conspiracies or treason of his people; and that their own bodies had better be given over to the anger of a bigoted taskmaster than their minds to the fangs of conscious iniquity, and their souls to that place of torment whither the curses of a murdered woman would irrevocably consign them.'

The effect of this appeal was visible even on the judge: he leaned forward, with his eyes half raised from the ground, and without suppressing a malicious smile, he motioned the jury to withdraw. They remained absent an unusual time, during which intense anxiety pervaded all except the judge himself, who rolled about from side to side with manifest uneasiness and displeasure. At length the foreman appeared, and pronounced 'Not guilty.' An indistinct murmur of approbation followed, whilst the mortified judge, lifting his unwieldy limbs from the chair, his eyes swollen with rage, his mouth foaming, his hands clenched, and stamping with rage, yet with the impotence of a child, gave vent to a loud, rapid, and unconnected volley of oaths; whilst, shaking his fist with frightful vehemence, he drove back the terrified jurymen by the menace of his gesture.

Again he sat down; wrath and disappointment gave way at length to a smile of contempt, which indicated that some scheme was at hand to prevent the recurrence of a like rebuff. Again the door opened; the same messenger of justice returned, and commenced an apologetic preface, which was speedily interrupted by a demand of their decision. The same verdict was delivered as before; and every one expected from the judge a still more terrible burst of fury. But their expectations were baulked: he merely nodded in sarcasm, and beckoning to a sergeant, who attended with some score of that barbarous troupe distinguished by the title of 'Kirke's Lambs,'[1] whispered him to keep guard at the door of the jury-room till the verdict was a third time brought in. The very mention of this merciless brigade, the recollection of the horrid cruelties practised by the Colonel and themselves, was sufficient to

[1] After the death of Monmouth, and the suppression of the revolt, the Earl of Feversham hanged twenty-two men at Bridgewater, on the evening of the battle of Sedgemoor, without any form of trial; and on the Earl leaving the command to Colonel Kirke, the severity and violence of the soldiery were increased, so that Kirke's name was long the object of popular execration in the west of England. Between Kirke and Jeffreys, in their 'campaign,' as the king jocularly called it, the south-western counties were strewed with the carcases and the dismembered limbs of human beings, women as well as men, butchered by the sword or the axe.

subdue a stouter heart than that of a juryman in the days of Jeffreys. He alone could feast his eyes upon them; and as he sat in delightful anticipation of success, he reached down the *black cap* which hung above his head, and handled it and examined it with evident satisfaction. A third time the door opened; and the verdict having been first communicated to the sergeant, and by him, with a smile of approbation, to the judge, 'Guilty; death,' was recorded. Four judges sat the silent witnesses of these proceedings; and the jury, finding themselves rudely shut out from all means of saving the prisoner, at length consented, rather than have a further collision with the court, to deliver the prey to the destroyer. The strange scene in court has been painted by Mr. E. M. Ward, R.A., and is one of his finest historical works. A slight tumult succeeded; but a few brandished swords restored silence. The Lady Alice remained totally unmoved. She listened to her doom with firmness and composure, and seemed, in one glance towards the bench, to bid farewell to her enemies for ever.

On the following morning she was placed at the bar, when Jeffreys, having pronounced sentence, issued his orders that the prisoner should be burnt alive in the afternoon of the same day. Lady Lisle suffered death on the 2d of September in the market-place at Winchester, her sentence being changed by the king, at her own request, from burning to decapitation. She appeared at the place of execution with great composure, and delivered a paper to the sheriff, in which she observed: 'My defence was such as might be expected from a weak woman; but such as it was, I did not hear it repeated again to the jury. But I forgive all persons who have done me wrong, and I desire that God will do likewise.' A plain slab inscribed to her memory is in Ellingham Churchyard.

By the above special commission, having Chief-Justice Jeffreys at its head, a great number of persons were condemned and executed at Dorchester, Exeter, and especially Taunton and Wells. The prisoners for trial in Somersetshire alone were above 1000; and of these at least 239 were executed, and probably more. The sentences were carried into effect in thirty-six different towns and villages, among which they were distributed. At Dorchester, in the Town Hall, they have still the chair in which Jeffreys sat at the Assizes.

Jeffreys, who is scarcely over-coloured in the above narrative, is thus described by Burnet: 'All people,' he says, 'were apprehensive of very black designs when they saw Jeffreys made Lord Chief-Justice, who was scandalously vicious, and was *drunk every day*, besides a drunkenness of fury in his temper, that looked like enthusiasm. He did not consider the decencies of his post, nor did he so much as affect to seem impartial, as became a judge, but ran out upon all occasions into declamations that did not become the bar, much less the bench. He was not learned in his profession; and his eloquence, though viciously copious, yet was neither correct nor agreeable.'

Long after the judge had gone to his grave, his infamous

memory outlived him; and persons sixty years of age can remember his name in frequent mention, coupled with epithets of truculent notoriety, and of even traditionary influence. In Devonshire and the neighbouring counties, the children playing at the game called 'Tom Tiddler's Ground' (and which consists in making forays into the ground of Tom Tiddler for the purpose of 'picking up gold and silver,' until Tom can catch one of the marauders, who then takes his place), instead of calling the territory 'Tom Tiddler's Ground,' style it 'Judge Jeffreys's Ground;' and as the holder is supposed to be an ogre of vindictive and sanguinary habits, is it supposing too much that the memory of the terrible judge of 'The Merciful Assize' is still retained in the very sports of the children in the districts over which he exercised his fearful sway? (See *Notes and Queries*, No. 158.)

WEST HORSLEY PLACE AND THE WESTONS.

NEARLY in the centre of the county of Surrey lies one of its oldest historic estates—West Horsley Place—where the very ancient family of Weston of Weston have been seated from the time of the Norman Conquest. The present mansion is partly of the time of James I.; but the memories of the old place, and its noble possessors, extend long beyond that period.

From Domesday Book it appears that Walter Fitz-Otho de Windsor held this manor, then called *Orselei*. He was then Governor of Windsor Castle, whence his descendants took their name. William de Windsor, and his son Walter, accompanied King Richard on an expedition to Normandy in 1194; and William probably died there. Hugh de Windsor, who lived in the reign of Henry III., dying without male heirs, the estate passed to Christiana—called in some pedigrees his sister, but in others his daughter and heiress. Whichever degree of kinship should be assigned to her, she conveyed the estate in marriage to Sir Ralph Berners; but upon his death, in 1297, it reverted to Christiana as his widow. Among the curious memorial entries, we find, in the reign of Edward III., Sir John Berners paid to the heirs of Hugh de Windsor 'half a pound of cumin-seed at Easter.'

James, the son and heir of Sir John Berners, was one of the obnoxious favourites of Richard II.; and he was involved in the ruin that befel Richard himself in 1388, when his folly and tyranny had incited the principal nobility (headed by his uncle the Duke of Gloucester) to an insurrection against his government. Sir James Berners was arrested, and committed a prisoner to the castle at Bristol; and having been attainted by the Parliament, he was beheaded, and his estates were forfeited to the crown. Stow, after mentioning the decollation of Lord Beauchamp of Holt, on Tower Hill, says: 'Sir James Berners, Knight of the King's Court, a lustie young man, was in the same place beheaded.'

Juliana Barnes, or Berners, Abbess of Sopewell, near St. Albans, in 1460, and authoress of the celebrated work generally called *The Boke of Seynt Albans*, containing tracts on hawking, hunting, fishing, etc., is said to have been the daughter of Sir James Berners; but the statement is doubtful.

King Richard, in 1393, granted the manor of West Horsley, with the park and warrens, to the widow of Sir James Berners. Henry IV., in the first year of his reign, made a grant in fee of the estate to her son Sir Richard Berners; and three years afterwards he obtained a licence from the king to put this manor in feoffment, that he might be enabled to make a settlement on his wife Philippa, the daughter and heiress of Edmund Dalyngruge. This lady survived her husband, and was married to Sir Thomas Lewknor; but Margery, the only daughter of Sir Richard Berners, on his death in 1421, succeeded to the possession of his estates, including the manor, park, warrens, and advowson of West Horsley. She married Sir John Feriby; and he dying without issue, she was married a second time to Sir John Bourchier, a knight of the garter, and Constable of Windsor Castle. He died in 1474; and, agreeably to his own directions, was interred in the Chapel of the Holy Rood within the Abbey of Chertsey, to whose monks he gave a silver cross, and other articles, valued at forty pounds.

Sir Humphrey Bourchier, K.B., the eldest son of Sir John, lost his life in the service of King Edward IV. at the battle of Barnet in 1471; and the succession to the family estates devolved on John Bourchier, the eldest son of Humphrey, who, on the death of his grandfather, became Lord Berners, and sat in several Parliaments in the reigns of Henry VII. and Henry VIII. He distinguished himself at the battle of Blackheath in 1497, where the Cornish insurgents were defeated; and he served as captain of the pioneers at the siege of Terouanne in 1535, when the king, Henry VIII., commanded in person.

But Lord Berners is most advantageously known as the translator of the Chronicles of Froissart, by command of the king. This work was published in folio in 1525; and in 1528 he had a grant of the manors of Ockham, Effingham, Woldingham, and Titsey (part of the forfeited estates of Edward Duke of Buckingham), which may have been designed by his royal master as the reward of his learned labour.[1]

Lord Berners had previously received many especial marks of the monarch's favour. He held the office of Chancellor of the Exchequer for life; was Lieutenant-General of the town and marches of Calais; and was appointed, with other persons of rank, to attend the Princess Mary on her voyage to France, to become the queen of Louis XII. in 1514. Lord Berners died at Calais in 1532-3,

---

[1] Froissart has been happily styled the Herodotus of the Middle Ages. 'More important than the poems of Dante and Chaucer, or the prose of Boccaccio, was the introduction of the new literature represented by Froissart. Hitherto chronicles had for the most part consisted of the record of such wandering rumours as reached a monastery, or were gathered in the religious pilgrimages of holy men. But at this time there came into notice the most inquiring, enterprising, picturesque and entertaining chronicler that had ever appeared since Herodotus. John Froissart, called by the courtesy of the time Sir John, in honour of his being priest and chaplain, devoted a long life to the collection of the fullest and most trustworthy accounts of all the events and personages characteristic of his time. From 1326, when his labours commenced, to 1400, when his active pen stood still, nothing happened in any part of Europe that Froissart did not rush off to verify on the spot. If he heard of an assemblage of knights going on at the extremities of France, or in the centre of Germany; of a tournament at Bordeaux, a court gala in Scotland, or a marriage festival at Milan, his travels began—whether in the humble guise of a solitary horseman, with his portmanteau behind his saddle and a single greyhound at his heels, as he jogged wearily across the Border till he finally arrived in Edinburgh; or in his grander style of equipment, gallant steed, with hackney led beside him, and four dogs of high race gambolling round his horse, as he made his dignified

leaving by his wife Catherine, daughter of John Duke of Norfolk, two daughters, one of whom—Joan, the wife of John Knyvet, Esq.—became the sole heiress of his estates, but held them for only two years. She died in 1561; but long before that period West Horsley Manor, and other estates in Surrey which had been granted to Lord Berners, were transferred to other proprietors, though in what manner is uncertain. In 1536 we find the manor in the hands of Henry Courtenay, Marquis of Exeter, who in 1538, with his lady, was attainted of high treason for an alleged conspiracy to dethrone the king, and raise to the throne Reginald Pole, afterwards Cardinal, and in the reign of Queen Mary, Archbishop of Canterbury. Their estates escheated to the Crown. The Marquis, with some other conspirators, were beheaded on the 9th of January following on Tower Hill, and the Marchioness was punished by imprisonment.

journey from Ferrara to Rome. Wherever life was to be seen and painted, the indefatigable Froissart was to be found. From palace to palace, from castle to castle, the unwearied pursued his happy way, certain of a friendly reception when he arrived, and certain of not losing his time by negligence or blindness on the road. If he overtakes a stately cavalier, attended by squires and men-at-arms, he enters into conversation, drawing out the experiences of the venerable warrior by relating to him all he knew of things and persons in which he took an interest. And when they put up at some hostelry on the road, and while the gallant knight was sound asleep on his straw-stuffed couch, and his followers were wallowing amid the rushes on the parlour floor, Froissart was busy with pen and note-book, scoring down all the old gentleman had told him, all the fights he had been present at, and the secret history (if any) of the councils of priests and kings.'—Abridged from *Eighteen Christian Centuries* by the Rev. J. White.

The manor of West Horsley was granted to Sir Anthony Browne, his Master of the Horse. Upon his death the estate of Horsley devolved for life to his widow, the Fair Geraldine. She was twice married; but upon her demise West Horsley descended to Sir Anthony Browne, the son of her first husband. He dying in 1592, left this estate to his grandson; after his decease, in 1629, it was sold to one of the Carews of Beddington, in Surrey, by which sale was discharged the mortgage made on the estate to John Evelyn. The purchaser must have been Sir Nicholas Throckmorton, Knt., the adopted heir of his uncle, Sir Francis Carew, son of Sir Nicholas Carew, K.G., beheaded in 1539. He was Master of the Horse to King Henry VIII. From Sir Nicholas it would seem that, either by gift or devise, West Horsley passed to his nephew Carew Raleigh, the son of his sister Elizabeth, by the ill-fated Sir Walter Raleigh. Carew was born in the Tower during his father's imprisonment there, about 1604–5. Soon after his father's decapitation he was introduced at Court by his kinsman the Earl of Pembroke; but the conscience-smitten King James not liking his presence, and saying that 'he appeared to him like his father's ghost' (so like he was in face and figure), the Earl advised him to travel, which he did until the death of the king, when he returned to England.[1] He soon

---

[1] See 'Sir Anthony Browne and his Descendants,' *ante*, p. 66 *et seq*. The story of Geraldine, though promulgated by the grave Anthony Wood, and, as he affirms, upon the authority of Drayton, has been stoutly contested as a mere fiction borrowed by the antiquary from a

afterwards petitioned Parliament to be restored in blood, with a view to obtain restitution of the estate and castle of Sherborne in Dorsetshire,[1] which had belonged to Sir Walter, and had been granted by the Crown to Digby Earl of Bristol; but the new king, Charles I., having (when Prince of Wales) received a bribe of ten thousand pounds to secure that property to the Earl, although he received him with civility, plainly told him that unless 'he would quit all his right and title to Sherborne, he neither could nor would pass the bill of restoration.' At first Mr. Raleigh refused to forego his claims, yet he was eventually prevailed on to do so, on receiving promises of courtly advancement, which were never fulfilled; but an Act to restore him in blood was passed in the king's third year. He was afterwards made one of the gentlemen of the Privy Chamber. He

little romance written by Nash, and published in 1593, containing the adventures of an imaginary hero, whom he calls Jack Wilton.

[1] Sherborne Castle, frequently called Sherborne Lodge, was built by Sir Walter Raleigh, and was his favourite residence. Notwithstanding the restorations and additions which have been made, Raleigh's house has been preserved in the centre. In the house are many portraits, and the famous picture of the procession of Queen Elizabeth to Lord Hunsdon's, which has been engraved by Virtue, and lithographed for Nicholi's *Progresses of Elizabeth*. In the fine pleasure-grounds which surround the Lodge is a grove planted by Raleigh, which still bears his name. Here also is 'Raleigh's Bower,' in which, tradition says, he smoked the first pipe of tobacco in England. A Roman tessellated pavement has been discovered in the grounds. Here, too, are the remains of an early Norman castle, built by Roger, Bishop of Sarum, in the reign of King Stephen, and which changed hands once or twice in the civil war of Stephen and the Empress Maude. In the castle is a little chapel, with just room for the priests to officiate; but it was so

married the Lady Philippa, relict of Sir Anthony Achley, a young and rich widow. By her he had several children, three of whom were born at West Horsley, which he had made his principal residence; and he continued to reside there many years. During Cromwell's supremacy, Raleigh was twice returned to Parliament. He was appointed Governor of Jersey by the favour, as reported, of General Monk. After the Restoration, Charles II. would have conferred on him some personal honour; but this was declined, on which the king knighted his eldest son, Walter, who died soon after at West Horsley, and was interred in the parish church, where also two others of his family—Carew and Henrietta—were buried.

In 1665 Mr. Raleigh sold this estate to Sir Edward Nicholas for £9750. According to Oldys, Mr. Raleigh

arranged that those in the adjoining apartment could see the elevation of the host. It is a valuable example of similar arrangements in the houses and castles of the middle ages. In the great civil war the castle was held for the king by the Marquis of Hertford. It was taken by the Parliamentarians in 1642. In 1645 the Royalists held it again, until it was stormed by Cromwell and Fairfax with their forces, notwithstanding the gallant defence of Sir Louis Dives, the governor. After this the castle was demolished. The whole area comprehends four acres, and is surrounded by a deep ditch, on the inner bank of which the foundations and fragments of the walls (six or seven feet thick), enclosing the greater ballium or court, may be traced. The gatetower, and some parts of the buildings in the centre of the ballium, also remain.

At Bingham Melcombe is the ancestral house of Colonel Bingham, a specimen of the small country squire's residence of the sixteenth century, with its handsome apartments, rich paintings, heraldic-stained windows, and bowling-green, enclosed by a stupendous yew-hedge.

died in 1666; and although he says it was thought by Anthony Wood that he was buried at (St. Margaret's) Westminster, in the same grave with his father, 'it is asserted at West Horsley, in Surrey, which was his seat, that the son was buried there; and they have a tradition that when he was interred, the head of Sir Walter Raleigh, which had been kept by him, was put into the grave with his corpse.'[1]

With reference to this tradition, Oldys quotes a letter he had seen, written by William Nicholas, Esq. (the last possessor of West Horsley of his family), in which he writes, he 'verily believes' the head he saw dug up there in 1703 (most probably on the occasion of his mother's funeral) from the side of a grave where a Carew Raleigh had been buried, was that of *Sir Walter Raleigh*, there being no bones of a body to it, nor room for any, the rest of that side of the grave being firm chalk. Notwithstanding the current opinion that the body of Sir Walter was interred in St. Margaret's Church, Westminster, the following short note, recorded by Manning from the Carew papers at Beddington, gives cause to believe that he was interred at Beddington, though privately, and at night:—

---

[1] Cayley says: 'The head (of Sir Walter Raleigh), after being shown on either side of the scaffold, was put into a leather bag, over which Sir Walter's gown was thrown, and the whole conveyed away in a mourning-coach by Lady Raleigh. It was preserved by her in a case during the twenty-nine years which she survived her husband, and afterwards, with no less piety, by their affectionate son Carew, with whom it is supposed to have been buried at West Horsley, in Surrey.'

'To my best b[rother]
   Sur Nicholas
      Carew, at
         beddington.

'I DESIAR, good brother, that you will be pleased to let me berri the worthi boddi of my nobell husban, Sur Walter Ralegh, in your chorche at beddington, wher I desiar to be berred. The lordes have give me this ded boddi, though they denied me his life. This nit hee shall be brought you, with two or three of my men. Let me her presently,

'E. R.'

'God hold me in my wites.'

Unfortunately there is no date to this note, yet no reasonable cause can be assigned for any refusal by Sir Nicholas of his sister's request.

Sir Edmond Nicholas, who settled at West Horsley soon after the above purchase, was secretary to Villiers Duke of Buckingham when Lord High Admiral. He also filled other appointments, adhered to the party of the king during the Civil War, and followed Charles II. into exile. After the Restoration, Sir Edmond Nicholas was reinstated as Secretary of State. He resigned in 1663, having declined a peerage offered him by the king, as a cheap reward for his long and faithful services. He then retired from public life, and passed his few remaining years at West Horsley. He died in 1669, aged 77. He was succeeded by his eldest son John, who, like his father, attended Charles II. in exile. He died in 1704, at the age of 81. He married the Lady Penelope, daughter of Spencer Compton, Earl of Northampton, who was slain during the Civil Wars at Hopton Heath, near Stafford. Lady Nicholas also met with a violent death, being killed at Horsley by the falling of a chimney during the great storm of 1703. Sir John, who entered all his expenses and memoranda in small almanacks, thus records the accident: '*Nov. 26th.*—This night was the dreadful storm and tempest, wherein my deare wife was killed in our bed by the fall of the chimney, and I was wonderfully preserved by God's providence. Væ! væ! væ! A little after three on Saturday morning this sad affliction befel me.'

In *An Exact Relation of the late Dreadful Tempest*, quarto, 1704, are the following particulars: 'My Lady Penelope Nicholas, living at Horsley with Sir John Nicholas, a learned and antient gentleman, was, as it was conceived, killed by the fall of a stack of chimneys; and her husband, Sir John, was taken out of the rubbish very dangerously hurt. But the chirurgeons, who viewed the body, gave in their opinion, "That her ladyship, being between 80 and 90, was killed by the fright of that most terrible storm; and though her leg was broke, yet no blood, nor matter flowing from it, [that] she was dead before the fall of the chimney."'

The last of Sir John Nicholas's three sons, coming into the possession of West Horsley, and dying a bachelor, bequeathed the estate, by will, to Henry Weston, Esq. He formed a design of rebuilding the mansion of West Horsley; and he one day showed the plan for a new house to the Duke of Marlborough, who looked at him, and said, ' Pray,

Mr. Weston, how old are you?' 'I was so struck,' said he, 'at the question, that I laid aside all thoughts of building, and only made some alterations.' He died in 1759.

In the pedigree of the Weston family, its origin is traced to Radulphus de Wistaneston, who held certain lands under the Lord de Braose, in the twentieth year of William the Conqueror. The pedigree is entered on a roll of vellum. It enumerates all the lands and estates that have belonged to different branches of the family, down to 1624, and has the arms blazoned of all the families which the Westons have intermarried with. The pedigree fills eight pages in Brayley's *History of Surrey*.

West Horsley Place, the family mansion of the Westons, is a gabled brick edifice of the time of James I., but with alterations in the reigns of George I. and II. The house is thought to have been originally erected by Sir Anthony Browne, after his marriage with the Fair Geraldine; and a plan of the old drawing-room ceiling bears the crest of the Earl of Kildare, the father of the Fair Geraldine; also the initials A. B., and various crests, all known to have belonged to the Browne family.

Here is preserved a collection of portraits (many of the Westons) originally formed by Sir Edward Nicholas, including Sir Walter Raleigh, apparently an original; Jerome Weston, Earl of Portland, by Vandyke; Sir Richard Fanshawe, ambassador to Spain; Sir William Perkins of Chertsey; and his brother, Captain Matthew Perkins. Among the papers of Sir William Perkins, at West Horsley, are documents relating to his having sold to the Crown a precious stone, which he calls 'a carbuncle, more valuable than a diamond,' for which he received the sum of £12,000. At Horsley, too, is a collection of papers of curious things, ' as well during the troubles, as since,'—the Restoration, the Popish Plot, and the Revolution, and its Parliaments and journals,—all which, if digested into a method, ' would form an authentic record of transactions for near one hundred years past.'

SUTTON PLACE AND THE WESTONS.

The Westons of Sutton (*Sudtone*, in Domesday), are also a family of considerable antiquity. The manor descended to Margaret Countess of Richmond, the mother of Henry the Seventh; and on her decease, in 1509, it came into the possession of her grandson, Henry the Eighth. This prince granted the manor of Sutton, with its appurtenances, to Sir Richard Weston, Knt., with licence to impark land and pasture, wood, heath, and furze, with free warren within the limits of the forest. The grantee, Sir Richard Weston, was the founder of Sutton Place, and the elder brother of William Weston, the last Prior of the house of the Knights Hospitallers of St. John of Jerusalem, at Clerkenwell. Sir Richard was a gentleman of the Privy Chamber to Henry VIII., Master of the Court of Wards and Liveries, Treasurer of Calais, and Under-Treasurer of England. He had an only son, named Francis, who was made a Knight of the Bath at the coronation of Anne Boleyn. He was one of the five unfortunate persons involved in the fate of that queen; for, being accused of high treason, in holding an alleged criminal intercourse with her, he was convicted on trial, and beheaded on Tower Hill, on the 17th of May 1536, whilst his father was still living.

Among his descendants was Sir Richard Weston, remembered for his valuable improvements in agriculture and commerce. In 1782, Mrs. Melior Mary Weston dying unmarried, devised the estate and manor of Sutton to John Webb, Esq., of Sarsfield Court, when he assumed the name and arms of Weston; this gentleman being a maternal descendant of Robert Weston of Prested, in Essex, who lived in the reign of Henry VI., and was the brother of John Weston of Bolton, the ancestor of the Westons of Sutton.[1]

Sutton Place was so named to distinguish it from the more ancient manor-house called Sutton House, the re-

[1] Humphrey Weston, who resided at Prested, in Richard the Second's reign, was, by different wives, the founder of two different families. The *Westons of Sutton* descended from his son John, by his first wife, Catherine; whilst the ancestor of those who continued at *Prested* was Robert, his son by Joan, his second wife; and from a younger branch of which sprang Richard Weston, created Earl of Portland by Charles I. *John Weston*, who was Prior of St. John's, Clerkenwell, in the years 1477 and 1485, and *William*, his nephew, who was also Prior of the same house on the eve of its dissolution, were both of this family. The latter is represented to have died of grief on the very day when the Act was passed for dissolving his monastery, viz. on the 7th of May 1540, 32d of Henry VIII.

mains of which were wholly removed in the last century. The present mansion was erected by Sir Richard Weston in the reign of Henry VIII., probably in 1529 or 1530, and is situated about three miles north-east of Guildford. Originally the buildings formed an entire quadrangle, enclosing an open court. It consisted of three storeys, surrounding a Tudor-arched gateway, and lit by square-headed windows; at each angle was a projecting tower, which rose to a considerable height. The entrance gateway was taken down in 1786. The interior of the south-east side was rebuilt about 1721, it having previously lain in ruins from the time of Queen Elizabeth, who was entertained here in a gallery upwards of 140 feet in length, when on her way to Chichester, in September 1591. Shortly after her departure the gallery took fire, either from the extraordinary quantity of fuel used on that occasion, or the neglect of the servants to see it properly extinguished, when a great part was reduced to ashes. The structure is mostly of red brick, with finishings of brick of light, warm ochre colour, resembling Caen stone. Most of the larger bricks are marked, or charged, alternately with the initials R. W., and a *tun* and bunches of grapes, within Gothic borderings; they are thus evidently intended as a rebus on the name of the founder, Richard Weston.

The present interior of the mansion is in plain modern style. The great hall, forming the entire centre, measures nearly 51 feet in length, 25 feet in breadth, and 31 feet in height. Its windows contain many curious specimens of ancient stained glass; shields of arms and other armorial cognizances and devices of former ages, brought from the older manor-house.

'Among them is the White Hart, collared with a branch of oak, fructed, and on the body a crescent, sable; the Red Rose for Lancaster; the arms of England, with the Rose *en soleil*, Edward the Fourth's cognizance; the Red and White Roses conjoined, denoting the union of the rival houses of York and Lancaster; the Crown in a Hawthorn Bush, with initials H. and E. on either side, for Henry the Seventh and Elizabeth his queen; the Falcon and Tower for Anne Boleyn; a Saracen's Head, the crest of Weston, boldly executed; a Daisy springing from a Tun; the letters H. E. P. and a Tun (possibly for Septon); the initials $\frac{N}{I\,A}$, with the date 1567 entwined by a double knot; a *Fleur-de-lis* under a Crown, with the initials E. R. at the sides for Queen Elizabeth; a Wolf; a Grasshopper; a Shield (several times repeated) containing quarterly, 1st and 4th, Erm. on a Chief, Az. five Bezants, *Weston;* 2d and 3d, Arg. three Camels, Sab., *Dister;* a small portrait of King Charles the First; and a Book charged with a hart, stars, and key; over the book a crown, and below, the motto *Respice Suspice*, 1630.'

Among the devices of a different character are,—a negro playing on a lute; a village festival at sheep-shearing time; a goose playing on the bagpipes; a woman holding an infant swathed in cross bandages; and a clown crossing a brook. The latter is arrayed as a fool in a yellow coat, and wears a cap and hood, with apes' ears, a cock's comb, and bells; under his belt are thrust five goslings, confined by their necks, and he grasps two others tightly in his hand. Mr. A. J. Kempe states this design to be evidently copied from the rare old book, George Withers' *Emblems*, 1635.

The fact is, that the clown being sent by his mistress to fetch home some goslings, a river being in the way, he took up the birds under his girdle (by which means they were strangled) lest they should be drowned. The tale is thus moralized by Withers:

> 'The best good turn that fools can do us,
> Prove disadvantages unto us.'

The verses annexed to the picture in the book are:

> 'A fool sent forth to fetch the goslings home,
> When they unto a river's brink were come,
> (Through which their passage lay,) conceived a fear
> His dame's best brood might have been drowned there;
> Which to avoyd, he thus did show his wit,
> And his good nature in preventing it :
> He underneath his girdle thrusts their heads,
> And then the coxcomb through the water wades.
>
> Here learn that when a foole his helpe intends,
> He rather does a mischief than befriends!'

The upper walls of the apartment are nearly covered with large pictures, chiefly landscapes; and at the lower end is a rude picture of *the Deluge*, with this explanatory inscription on the frame:

'In the Deluge, the most powerful of the Human race, and the strongest of the Animal creation, may be supposed to Perish last, and the most likely thing to be rescued from the wreck of the Universe is a beautiful little Female. In this picture, therefore, while the Solitary summit of the last Mountain remains uncovered by the Waters, one of the Gigantic Antediluvian Princes gains his last refuge with His little Daughter; and a hungry Lion, who had swam thither for shelter, Springing on the Maiden, the Father, conscious of his own Strength and superiority, expresses Indignation rather than Terror.'

At the sides of the staircase are old portraits and landscapes, and some of the rooms are lined with embossed leather, richly gilt.

The Westons of Sutton have been uniformly distinguished by their stedfast adherence to the principles of the Romish Church; and there is now a Catholic chapel in the southeast gallery of the mansion, but much dilapidated; its mullioned windows are ivy-mantled. Over the marble altar is a small gilt crucifix, and in the lumber-room is a small bell, dated 1530. Such are a few of the decaying glories of Sutton Place.

Sutton Park and its attached grounds are about three miles in circuit. On the Wey, near the southern extremity of the demesne, is one of the 'Tumbling Bays,' of which Aubrey speaks. This is a strong dam formed of loose stones, aggregated on each other, across the bed of the river, and continued obliquely down the stream for some distance. When the river is full, the scene here is very picturesque; the rushing and foaming of the stream over its irregular bed forming an animated waterfall.

THE CLIFFORDS OF CRAVEN.

THERE is no district in England which abounds in more beautiful and romantic scenery than the remote and rarely-visited district of Craven, in Yorkshire. Its long ridge of low and irregular hills, terminating in the enormous masses of Pennigent and Ingleborough; its deep and secluded valleys, containing within their hoary ramparts of grey limestone fertile fields and pleasant pasturages; its wide-spreading moors, covered with the different species of moss and ling, and fern and bent grass, which variegate the brown livery of the heath, and break its sombre uniformity; its crystal stream of unwearied rapidity; its indigenous woods of yew and beech, and ash and alder, which have waved in the winds of centuries; its projecting crags, which fling additional gloom over the melancholy tarns that repose in dismal grandeur at their feet; its hamlets and towns, and ivy-mantled churches, which remind the visitor of their antiquity by the rudeness, and convince him of their durability by the massiveness, of their construction,—these are all features which require to be seen only once to be impressed upon the recollection for ever.

But it is not merely for the lovers of the wild and beautiful and picturesque that the localities of Craven possess a powerful charm. The antiquary, the novelist, and the poet, may all find rich store of employment in the traditions which are handed down from father to son respecting the ancient lords and inhabitants of the district. In Dr. Whitaker's *History of Craven* there is a groundwork laid out for at least a dozen ordinary novels. To say nothing of the legendary tales which the peasantry relate of the minor families of the district—of the Bracewells, the Tempests, the Lysters, the Romilys, and the Nortons, whose White Doe, however, has been immortalized by the poetry of Wordsworth—can anything be more pregnant with romantic adventure than the fortunes of the successive chieftains of the lordly line of Clifford?—their first introduction to the North, owing to a love-match made by a poor knight of Herefordshire with the wealthy heiress of the Viponts and the Veseys!—their rising greatness, to the merited disgrace and death of Piers de Gaveston and his profligate minions! and their final exaltation to the highest honours of the British peerage, which they have now enjoyed for five hundred years, by the strong hand and unblenching heart with which they have always welcomed the assaults of their most powerful enemies!

Of the first ten lords of Skipton Castle, four died on the field and one upon the scaffold. 'The black-faced Clifford' —who sullied the glory which he acquired by his gallantry at the battle of Sandal, by murdering his youthful prisoner the Earl of Rutland in cold blood at the termination of it—has gained a passport to an odious immortality from the soaring genius of the Bard of Avon. But his real fate is far more striking, both in a moral and in a poetical point of view, than that assigned to him by our great dramatist. On the evening before the battle of Towton Field, and after the termination of the skirmish which preceded it, an unknown archer shot him in the throat as he was putting off his gorget, and so avenged the wretched victims whose blood he had shed like water upon Wakefield Bridge. The vengeance of the Yorkists was not, however, satiated by the death of 'the Butcher,' as Leland informs us that they called him; for they attainted him in the first year of the reign of Edward IV., and granted his estates a few years afterwards to the Duke of Gloucester, who retained them in his iron grasp till he lost them, with his crown and life, at the battle of Bosworth.

The history of his son is a romance ready made. His relations, fearing lest the partisans of the House of York should avenge the death of the young Earl of Rutland on the young Lord Clifford, then a mere infant, concealed him for the next twenty-five years of his life in the Fells of Cumberland, where he grew up as hardy as the heath on which he vegetated, and as ignorant as the rude herds which bounded over it. One of the first acts of Henry VII., after his accession to the throne, was to reverse the attainder which had been passed against Clifford's father; and immediately afterwards the young lord emerged from the hiding-place where he had been brought up in ignorance of his rank, and with the manners and education of a mere shepherd! Finding himself more illiterate than was usual even in an illiterate age, he retired to a tower which he built in the beautiful forest of Barden; and there, under the direction of the monks of Bolton Abbey, gave himself up to the forbidden studies of alchemy and astrology.

His son, who was the first Earl of Cumberland, embittered the conclusion of his life by embarking in a series of adventures which, in spite of their profligacy, possess a very strong romantic interest. Finding that his father was either unwilling or unable to furnish him with funds to maintain his inordinate riot and luxury, he became the head of a band of outlaws, and, by their agency, levied aids and benevolences upon the different travellers on the king's highway. A letter of the old lord, his father, is extant, in which he complains in very moving terms of his son's degeneracy and misconduct. The young scapegrace, wishing to make his father know from experience the inconvenience of being scantily supplied with money, enjoined his tenantry in Craven not to pay their rents, and beat one of them, Henry Popely —who ventured to disobey him—so severely with his own hand, that he lay for a long while in peril of death. He spoiled his father's houses, etc., 'feloniously took away his proper goods,' as the old lord quaintly observes, 'apparelling himself and his horse all the time in cloth-of-gold and goldsmith's work, more like a duke than a poor baron's son.' He likewise took a particular aversion to the religious orders, 'shamefully beating their tenants and servants, in such wise as some whole towns were fain to keep the churches both night and day, and durst not come at their own houses.'

Whilst engaged in these ignoble practices—less dissonant, however, to the manners of his age than to those of ours—he wooed and won and married a daughter of the Percy of Northumberland; and it is conjectured, upon very plausible grounds, that his courtship and marriage with a lady of the highest rank, under such disadvantages on his part, gave rise to the beautiful old ballad of 'The Nut-Brown Mayde.'

The poem opens with a declaration of the author, that the faith of woman is stronger than is generally alleged; in proof of which he proposes to relate the trial to which the 'Nut-Brown Mayde' was exposed by her lover. What follows consists of a dialogue between the pair, and ends thus:—

> '*He.*—Ye shall not need further to dread;
>   I will not disparage
> You (God defend!) sith ye descend
>   Of so great a lineage.
> Now, understand; to Westmoreland,
>   Which is mine heritage,
> I will you bring; and with a ring,
>   By way of marriage,
> I will you take, and lady make,
>   As shortly as I can:
> Thus have you won an earl's son,
>   And not a banished man.'

The lady becoming very unexpectedly the heiress of her family, added to the inheritance of the Cliffords the extensive fen which the Percys held in Yorkshire; and by that transfer of property, and by the grant of Bolton Abbey, which he obtained from Henry VIII. on the dissolution of the monasteries, her husband became possessed of nearly all the district which stretches between the castles of Skipton on the south, and of Brougham (or, as the Cliffords, to whom it belonged, always wrote it, Bromeham) on the north.

The second Earl of Cumberland, who was as fond of alchemy and astrology as his grandfather, was succeeded by his son George, who distinguished himself abroad by his buccaneering expeditions in the West Indies against the Spaniards. Among the numerous children of whom he was the father, the most celebrated was the Countess of Pembroke and Montgomery, whose long life of virtuous exertion renders her well qualified to figure as the heroine of a tale of chivalry. The anecdotes which are told of this high-spirited lady in the three counties of York, Westmoreland, and Cumberland, are full of heroic interest and adventure. Her defence of Bromeham Castle against the intrusion of her uncle of Cumberland; her riding cross-legged to meet the judges of assize, when she acted in person at Appleby as high-sheriff by inheritance of the county of Westmoreland; her hairbreadth escapes and dangers during the Great Rebellion,—are the romantic characteristics of the woman. Her courage and liberality in public life were only to be equalled by her order, economy, and devotion in private. 'She was,' says Dr. Whitaker, 'the oldest and most independent courtier in the kingdom' at the time of her death. 'She had known and admired Queen Elizabeth; she had refused what she deemed an iniquitous award of King James,' though urged to submit to it by her first husband, the Earl of Dorset; 'she rebuilt her dismantled castles in defiance of Cromwell, and repelled with disdain the interposition of a profligate minister under Charles the Second.' A journal of her life, in her own handwriting, is still in existence at Appleby Castle. She was a girl in the reign of James I.; and she says, what will no doubt shock modern notions, that when she went with her mother to Theobalds, in Hertfordshire, on the occasion of that king's coming from Scotland, their clothes were covered with vermin, simply because they had sat for a while in Sir Thomas Erskine's chamber.

The family mansion of the Cliffords was situated on Clerkenwell Green at that period. Anne Clifford lived also in the days of the Commonwealth; and to her is attributed the spirited reply to Cromwell's secretary, Williamson: 'I have been neglected in a court, and baulked by an usurper; but I shall not be dictated to by a subject: your man shan't stand.' The reply, however, must be classed with popular errors. It was in all probability never uttered or written, but was invented as the subject of a paper in *The World*, not far short of a century subsequent to her death.[1]

[1] Blackwood's *Edinburgh Magazine*, 1829.

SCRIVELSBY AND THE QUEEN'S CHAMPIONSHIP.

THE family of Dymoke ranks, in point of antiquity, male and female, with the most ancient in the kingdom. It derives the celebrated office of Champion from the baronial house of Marmyun, or Marmyon, with the feudal manor of Scrivelsby, to which the championship is attached. The village of Scrivelsby lies about two miles south of Horncastle, on the road towards Boston, Lincolnshire. Inherited successively by the Marmyons, the Ludlows, and the Dymokes, this famed estate is rich in historic associations. It appears in Domesday-book to have been then holden by Robert de Spencer, but by what service is not stated. Shortly after, the Conqueror conferred the manor of Scrivelsby, together with the castle of Tamworth, on Robert de Marmyon, lord of Fonteney, whose ancestors were, it is said, hereditary champions to the Dukes of Normandy previously to the invasion of England. Scrivelsby was, by the terms of the grant, to be held by grand serjeantry, to perform the office of champion at the king's coronation. The lord of Fonteney, thus invested with these extensive possessions in the conquered country, fixed his residence therein, and became a magnificent benefactor to the church, bestowing on the nuns of Oldbury the lordship of Polesworth, with a request that the donor and his friend Sir Walter de Somerville might be reputed their patrons, and have burial for themselves and their heirs in the abbey—the Marmyons in the chapter-house, and the Somervilles in the cloister.

The direct male line of the grantee expired with his great-grandson Philip de Marmyon, a gallant soldier, who, in requital of his fidelity to Henry III. during the baronial war, was rewarded, after the victory of Evesham, with the governorship of Kenilworth Castle. His death occurred 20 Edward I. (1292), and he was then found to have been seised of the manor of Scrivelsby and the castle of Tamworth. He left daughters only; and between them his estates were divided, Scrivelsby falling to the share of Joan, the youngest co-heir, and it was by her conveyed in marriage to Sir Thomas de Ludlow. The offspring of the alliance consisted of one son, John de Ludlow, who died issueless; and one daughter, Margaret, the lady of Scrivelsby, who inherited from her brother that feudal manor; and wedding Sir John Dymoke, a knight of ancient Gloucestershire ancestry, invested him with the championship, which office he executed at the coronation of Richard II. From that period to the present—a space of nearly five hundred years—the Dymokes have uninterruptedly enjoyed this important estate of Scrivelsby, and continuously performed the duties its tenure enjoins.

The second champion was Sir Thomas, the son of Sir John Dymoke, who at the coronations of Henry IV. and Henry V. executed the duties for his mother. His son, Sir Philip Dymoke, officiated as champion of Henry VI., who made a mandate to the keeper of his wardrobe to deliver to the champion such furniture, etc., as his ancestors have been accustomed to have on these occasions. His son, Sir Thomas Dymoke, by his connection with the Lords Wells and the Lancastrian interest, was brought to the scaffold in the reign of Edward IV. His son, Sir Robert Dymoke, who was of very tender years at the time of his father's unhappy death, officiated as champion at the coronation of Richard III., Henry VII., and Henry VIII. He was one of the principal commanders at the siege of Tournay, and was a knight banneret. His son, Sir Edward Dymoke, officiated at the coronations of Edward VI., Queen Mary, and Queen Elizabeth. The last male representative, Sir Henry Dymoke, Bart., succeeded to the estates and the hereditary championship at the decease of his father, the Rev. John Dymoke, in 1828, he having previously performed the duties as deputy for that reverend gentleman at the coronation of King George IV.

Sir Walter Scott tells us: 'The champion was performed (as of right) by young Dymoke, a fine-looking youth, but bearing perhaps a little too much the appearance of a maiden knight to be the challenger of the world in a king's behalf. He threw down his gauntlet, however, with becoming manhood, and showed as much horsemanship as the crowd of knights and squires around him would permit to be exhibited. On the whole, this striking part of the exhibition somewhat disappointed me, for I would have had the champion less embarrassed by his assistants, and at liberty to put his horse on the *grand pas;* and yet the young lord of Scrivelsby looked and behaved extremely well.' Haydon the painter describes Wellington, Howard, and the champion standing in full view as the finest sight of the day: 'The herald read the challenge; the glove was thrown down; they then all proceeded to the throne.' Sir Henry Dymoke was the seventeenth of his family who inherited the ancient office of champion. Sir Henry also officiated as champion at the coronation of William IV. and our present Most Gracious Sovereign; but the ceremonial was then shorn of its ancient chivalric state.

Sir Henry Dymoke was created a baronet in 1841. He died 28th April 1865, when the baronetcy became extinct; and the estate of Scrivelsby and the office of champion passed to his only brother, the Rev. John Dymoke, rector of Scrivelsby and Roughton, Lincolnshire, now the Honourable the Queen's Champion.

One gentleman, a scion of the house of Dymoke in the female line, Edmund Lionel Welles, Esq. of Grebby Hall, county Lincoln, has, since the death of the baronet, assumed, by royal licence, the additional surname and arms of Dymoke; no doubt in the contemplation of the championship, in failure of male issue, being one day granted to him or his descendants.

The greater part of Scrivelsby Court, the ancient baronial seat, was destroyed by fire towards the close of the last century. In the portion consumed was a very large hall, ornamented with panels, exhibiting in heraldic emblazonment the various arms and alliances of the family through all its numerous and far-traced descents. The loss, says Sir Bernard Burke, has been in some degree compensated by the addition made to the remnant which escaped the flames; but the grandeur of the original edifice can no longer be traced.

The annexed version of an old Anglo-Norman ballad describes with perspicuity and truth the transmission of the lands of Scrivelsby :—

> 'The Norman Barons Marmyon
>   At Norman Court held high degree;
> Knights and champions every one,
>   To him who won broad Scrivelsby.
>
> Those Lincoln lands the Conqueror gave,
>   That England's glove they should convey,
> To knight renowned amongst the brave,
>   The Baron bold of Fonteney.
>
> The royal grants, through sire to son,
>   Devolved direct *in capite*
> Until deceased Phil Marmyon,
>   When rose fair Joan of Scrivelsby.
>
> From London City on the Thames,
>   To Berwick Town upon the Tweed,
> Came gallants all of courtly names,
>   At feet of Joan their suit to plead.

Yet, maugre, all this goodly band,
  The maiden's smiles young Ludlow won,
Her heart and hand, her grant and land,
  The sword and shield of Marmyon.

Out upon Time, the scurvy knave,
  Spoiler of youth, hard-hearted churl;
Hurrying to one common grave,
  Good wife and ladie—hind and earl.

Out on Time—since the world began,
  No Sabbath hath his greyhound limb,
In coursing man—devoted man,
  To age and death—out, out on him.

In Lincoln's chancel, side by side,
  Their effigies from marble hewn:
The *anni* written when they died,
  Repose De Ludlow and Dame Joan.

One daughter fair, survived alone,
  One son deceased in infancy;
De Ludlow and De Marmyon,
  United thus in Margery.

And she was woo'd as maids have been,
  And won as maids are sure to be,
When gallant youths in Lincoln green,
  Do suit, like Dymoke, fervently.

Sir John de Dymoke claim'd of right
  The Championship through Margery,
And 'gainst Sir Baldwin Freville, knight,
  Prevail'd as Lord of Scrivelsby.

And ever since, when England's kings
  Are diadem'd—no matter where,
The Champion Dymoke boldly flings
  His glove, should treason venture there.

On gallant steed, in armour bright,
   His visor closed, and couched his lance,
Proclaimeth he the monarch's right
   To England, Ireland, Wales, and France.

Then bravely cry, with Dymoke bold,
   Long may the king triumphant reign!
And when fair hands the sceptre hold,
   More bravely still—Long live the Queen!'[1]

---

[1] Burke's *Visitations of Seats and Arms*, vol. i. pp. 188, 189.

BRADGATE AND LADY JANE GREY.

'This was thy home, then, gentle Jane!
　This thy green solitude; and here,
At evening, from thy gleaming pane,
　Thine eye oft watch'd the dappled deer,
While the soft sun was in its wane,
　Browsing beneath the brooklet clear.
The brook runs still, the sun sets now,
The deer yet browseth; where art thou?'

IN the most sequestered part of the county of Leicester, deserted and solitary, backed by rude eminences, and skirted by romantic and lowly valleys, are the remains of Bradgate, the birthplace and abode of the beauteous Lady Jane Grey, the accomplished but unfortunate daughter of the House of Suffolk. The approach to this spot from the little village of Cropston is strikingly suggestive. On the left is a group of venerable trees, at the extremity of which are the remains of the magnificent mansion of the Greys of Groby. A winding troutstream washes the walls of the edifice, until it reaches the fertile meadow of Swithland. The beautiful vale of Newtown adds to the romantic loveliness of the scene; and in the distance, upon a hill, is a tower called 'Old John,' commanding a magnificent view of the adjacent country, including the far-off Castle of Belvoir, and the remains of Nottingham Castle.

Leland thus describes Bradgate as it appeared in his time: 'From Leicester to Bradgate, by ground welle wooded, 3 miles. At Brodegate is a fair parke and a lodge, lately builded there by the Lord Thomas Gray, Marquise of Dorsete, father to Henry that is now Marquise. There is a fair and plentiful spring of water, brought by Master Brok, as a man would juge, agayne the hille, thoroug the lodge, and thereby it dryvitt a mylle. This park was part of the old Erles of Leicester's landes, and sins by heirs generales it cam to the Lord Ferreres of Groby, and so to the Grayes. The park of Brodegate is a vj. mile's cumpace.'

Bradgate lies on the border of the ancient forest of Charnwood in the hundred of West-goscote, about two miles from Groby, and four from Leicester. A park was enclosed here as early as 1247, as appears from an agreement made between Roger de Quincy, Earl of Leicester, and Roger de Someroy, Baron of Dudley, respecting their mutual hunting in Leicester Forest and Bradgate Park. As a parcel of the manor of Groby, Bradgate formerly belonged to Hugh Grandmeisnell, a Norman, to whom it was given, with other lands in the county, by William the Conqueror; and who was created Baron of Hinckley and High Steward of England by William Rufus. By the marriage of Hugh

Grandmeisnell's daughter and co-heir Petronella, Bradgate passed to Robert Blanchmaines, Earl of Leicester; and afterwards, by marriage also, to Saker de Quincy, Earl of Winton. In the reign of Edward I. it came into the family of the Ferrers by the marriage of Margaret, daughter and co-heir of Roger de Quincy with William de Ferrers, second son of William de Ferrers, Earl of Derby, whose son and heir, William, was in 1293 created Baron Ferrers of Groby.

In 1444, on the death of William Lord Ferrers of Groby, without any surviving male issue, Bradgate descended to Sir Edward Grey, Knight, in right of his wife Elizabeth, sole daughter and heir of Henry, the son of the last-mentioned William (who had died during his father's lifetime); and he was accordingly, in 1446, summoned to Parliament, under the title of Sir Edward Grey, Knight, Lord Ferrers of Groby. Sir John Grey, his son, who succeeded as Lord Ferrers of Groby, was slain at the battle of St. Albans in 1460. He married Elizabeth, daughter and co-heir of Richard Widville, Earl of Rivers, who, after his death, became the queen of Edward IV. He left two sons—Sir Thomas and Sir Richard Grey. Sir Thomas was, in 1471, created Earl of Huntingdon and a Knight of the Garter, and in 1475 was advanced to the dignity of Marquis of Dorset. Henry, his grandson, the third Marquis of Dorset, succeeded to the title in 1530, and married the Lady Ferrers, eldest daughter and co-heir of Charles Brandon, Duke of Suffolk; and of his illustrious consort Mary, Queen Dowager of France, and youngest sister of Henry VIII., by whom he had issue three daughters—the Lady Jane Grey, Katherine, and Mary.[1]

The male heir of the family was continued by his younger brother John, ancestor of the present Earl of Stamford and Warrington. The Lady Katherine married Lord Herbert, eldest son of the Earl of Pembroke; and the Lady Mary, Martin Keyes, Esq., of Kent, sergeant-porter to Queen Elizabeth.

The family of Grey, we may here mention, was of Norman origin. Rollo, or Fulhert, the chamberlain of Rollo Duke of Normandy, was possessed, by gift from Robert, of the castle and lands of Croy in Picardy, from whence he took the name of *De Croy*, afterwards *De Grey*. The first notice we find of this family in England is shortly after the Conquest, when Arnold de Grey, grandson of the above-mentioned Rollo, became lord of Water Eaton, Stoke, and Rotherfield, in right of his wife Joan, daughter and heiress of the Baron de Ponte de l'Arche. The above descent is deduced by a French genealogist and antiquary of great repute, Francis de Belleforest of Cominges.

Having arrived at that period in the history of Bradgate when it became celebrated as the birthplace of the greatest

---

[1] Her two brothers dying without issue, the Marquis of Dorset was, in favour to her, though otherwise, for his harmless simplicity, neither misliked nor much regarded, created Duke of Suffolk, fifth Edward VI. On the death of the Duke of Suffolk (who was executed shortly after Lady Jane Grey), the Lady Frances married Adrian Stokes, Esq. She lies buried in St. Edmund's chapel, Westminster Abbey, where an alabaster monument was erected to her memory.

ornament of the age, it behoves us to describe the mansion itself, which became the scene of the childhood and early studies of the incomparable Lady Jane Grey, who was born here in the year 1537. Old Fuller describes the mansion as 'fair, large, and beautiful.' It was erected in the early part of the reign of Henry VIII. by Thomas Grey, the second Marquis of Dorset. It was square in plan, with a turret at either corner. It was principally of red brick, and the materials were mostly brought from the manor-house of the Earl of Warwick at Sutton-Coldfield.

Bradgate became the favourite residence of the Dorset family, more especially that of Henry, the father of Lady Jane. Of him it has been said, that he loved to live in his own way, and was rather desirous to keep up that magnificence for which our ancient nobility were so much distinguished in the place of his residence in the country, than to involve himself in the intrigues of a court (Howard's *Lady Jane Grey*).

Of this once princely mansion, which has for many years, with the exception of the chapel and kitchen, been in ruins, scarcely enough of the walls remains to assist the careful observer in designating the several apartments. But a tower yet stands which tradition assigns as that occupied by the Lady Jane. Traces of a bowling-green, which Nichols imagines to have been the tilt-yard, are visible; and the garden-walls, with a broad terrace, less than thirty years ago were nearly entire. The ruins of the water-mill mentioned by Leland might then be seen, and also the little stream near which is a group of noble chestnut-trees. The spot occupied by the pleasure-grounds could also be traced; 'and though,' observes Nichols, 'they have now somewhat the appearance of a wilderness, yet they strongly indicate that once, where the nettle and the thistle now reign in peace, the rose and the lily sprang luxuriantly.'

The chapel—a small building adjoining the Lady Jane's tower, and the only part of the mansion on which any care for its preservation has been bestowed—contains a handsome monument in alabaster, in memory of Henry Lord Grey of Groby (cousin to the Lady Jane Grey) and his wife. Their effigies lie recumbent beneath an arched canopy, supported by composed Ionic columns. The Lord Grey is encased in armour, and robed. The head rests on a helmet, and the gauntlets are placed at the feet. The lady is clothed in a gown and short jacket; and suspended from her waist-belt is a chain with tassels at the ends; a long ruff covers the neck. The whole is surmounted by the family arms and supporters. In a vault in the middle of the chapel, made to contain three coffins, repose the remains of Lady Diana Grey, daughter of Thomas Earl of Stamford; Thomas Earl of Stamford, and Mary Countess Dowager of Stamford. The chapel has been repaired and paved; the key is in the charge of the keeper at the lodge.[1]

[1] Bradgate is the most famous of the picturesque ruins with which the neighbourhood of Leicester abounds, and which, nearly in the middle of England, has been the scene of many stirring events in its history. In the *Illustrated London News* of July 18, 1868, appeared a set of views in Leicester, full of Rembrantish effect, from the pencil of Samuel Read,

The melancholy associations connected with the history of Lady Jane Grey have invested Bradgate with an interest which, notwithstanding its picturesque beauty, the locality would not otherwise have possessed. The story of her 'almost infancy' would be incredible were it not well authenticated.

Burton calls her 'that most noble and admired princess, Lady Jane Grey, who, being but young, at the age of seventeen years, as John Bale writeth, attained to such excellent learning in the Hebrew, Greek, and Latin tongues, and also in the study of divinity, by the instruction of Mr. Aylmer, as appeareth by her many writings, letters, etc., that, as Mr. Fox saith of her, had her fortune been answerable to her bringing up, undoubtedly she might have been compared to the house of Vespasian, Sempronius, and Cornelia, mother of the Gracchi, in Rome, and in these days the chiefest men of the universities.'

Old Fuller says, 'She had the innocencie of childhood, the beautie of youth, the soliditie of middle, the gravity of old age, and all at eighteen; the birth of a princesse, the learning of a clerk, the life of a saint, yet the death of a malefactor for her parents' offences.'

the well-known painter, of the Old Water-Colour Society. In the accompanying letterpress the writer mentions the ruins of 'Bradgate, the scene of the early life of one whose untimely fate is perhaps the most pathetic episode in English history—Lady Jane Grey. At Whitwick, near Charnwood Forest, is the Abbey of St. Bernard, where the old monastic system is still carried out in its integrity; and the stranger and the destitute may, as in the olden time, present themselves at the monastery gate for the daily dole.'

Aylmer was a clergyman of the Reformed religion, and domestic chaplain to Lady Jane's father. An account of his residence at Bradgate is given in the *Jewel of Joy*, written by Thomas Becon in the reign of Edward VI. Aylmer was afterwards promoted to the see of London by Queen Elizabeth.

It was at Bradgate that Roger Ascham, the tutor of the Lady Elizabeth, paid that memorable visit to Lady Jane Grey, the particulars of which interview he has thus affectingly described in his *Schoolmaster:*—

'Before I went into Germanie, I came to Brodegate, in Leicestershire, to take leave of that noble Lady Jane Grey, to whom I was exceeding much beholding. Her parentes, the Duke and the Dutchesse, with all the householde, Gentlemen and Gentleweemen, were hunting in the Parke. I found her in her chamber reading Phædon Platonis in Greeke, and that with as much delite as some gentlemen would read a merry tale in Bocase. After salutation and dutie done, with some other talke, I asked her why shee should leese such pastime in the Parke. Smiling, she answered me: I wisse, all their sport in the Parke is but a shadow to that pleasure that I finde in Plato. Alas, good folke, they never felt what true pleasure ment. And how came you, Madame, quoth I, to this deepe knowledge of pleasure; and what did chiefly allure you vnto it, seeing not many women, but very fewe men, have attained thereunto? I will tell you, quoth shee, and will tell you a troth which perchance ye will marvel at. One of the greatest benefits that ever God gauve me is, that hee sente so sharpe and seuere parentes, and so gentle a schoolmaster. For when I am in presence of either father or mother, whether I speake, keepe silence, sit, stand, or go, eat, drinke, be mery, or sad, bee swoing, playing, dancing, or anything els, I must doe it, as it were, in such weight, measure, and number, euen so perfectly as God made the world, or ells I am so sharply taunted, so cruelly threatened, yea, presently sometimes with pinches, nippes, and bobbes, and other wayes which I will not name, for the honor I beare them, so without measure misordered, that I think myself in hell till time come that I must go to Mr. Elmer, who teaches me so gently, so pleasantly, with such faire allurements to learning, that I thinke all the time nothing while I am with him. And when I am called from him, I fall on weeping; because whatever I do els but learning is full of greefe, trouble, feare, and whole misliking vnto mee; and thus my booke hath been so much my pleasure and more, that in respect of it, all other pleasure in very deede bee but trifles and troubles vnto mee.—I remember this talke gladly, both because it is so worthy of memory, and because also it was the last talke that ever I had, and the last time that ever I saw that noble and worthy lady.'

Lady Jane's scholarship was sound. Mildred, the wife of Lord Burghley, is described by Ascham as the best Greek scholar among the young women of England, *Lady Jane Grey always excepted.* Lord Macaulay, however, considers the highly educated ladies of this period to have been unfairly extolled at the expense of the women of our time, through one very obvious and very important circumstance being overlooked. 'A person who did not read Greek and Latin could read nothing, or next to nothing; and all the valuable books extant in the vernacular dialects of Europe would hardly have filled a single shelf. In looking round a well-furnished library, how many English or French books can we find which were extant when Lady Jane Grey and Queen Elizabeth received their education? Chaucer, Gower, Froissart, Rabelais, nearly completed the list. It was therefore absolutely necessary that a woman should be uneducated or classically educated. Latin was then the language of courts as well as of the schools; of diplomacy, and of theological and political controversy. This is no longer the case; the ancient tongues are supplanted by the modern languages of Europe, with which English women are at least as well acquainted as English men. When, therefore, we compare the acquirements of Lady Jane Grey with those of an accomplished young woman of our own time, we have no hesitation in awarding the superiority to the latter.'

To return to Bradgate. On the attainder of the Duke of Suffolk, the family lost all claim to the titles and estates, until James I., by letters patent, bearing date 21st July 1603, bestowed the barony of Groby on Sir Henry Grey of Pergo, nephew of the last-mentioned nobleman. Sir Henry was the son of the Lord John Grey (youngest brother of the last Duke of Suffolk) by his wife Mary, daughter of Viscount Montacute, to whom, through the interest of his wife, had been granted, in 1559, the site of a capital messuage in Essex, called Pergo, a part of the ancient and royal manor of Havering-at-Bower (Morant's *Essex*).

On returning to the home of his ancestors, Sir Henry Grey immediately disposed of his property in Essex, and settled at the family mansion at Bradgate. Here he lies buried. He was succeeded by his eldest grandson Henry, who married Anne, daughter and co-heir of William Cecil, Earl of Exeter, in whose right he became possessed of the manor, borough, and castle of Stamford, whence he took the title of the earldom on being created a peer, March 6th, 1628, by Charles I.; and from him is lineally descended the present Earl of Stamford and Warrington.

In 1645 an order was made that the Countess of Stamford (being then at Bradgate) should have the protection of the House of Lords, that no soldiers or commanders should be quartered in the house or park. In 1694 the mansion had a narrow escape from destruction by fire, caused, it is said, by the then Countess of Stamford; and, according to tradition, it was fired in three several places. The cause of this rash attempt has been variously accounted for, but all agree in stating that the Countess had an intrigue with her husband's chaplain. Thoresby says, she set it on fire, or caused it to be set on fire, at the instigation of her sister, who then lived in London. The story is thus told: Some time after the Earl had married, he brought his lady to his seat at Bradgate. Her sister wrote to her desiring to know 'how she liked her habitation, and the country she was in.' The Countess wrote for answer that 'the house was tolerable, but that the country was a forest, and the inhabitants all brutes.' The sister, in consequence, by letter desired her to 'set fire to the house and run away by the light of it.' The former part of the request, it is said, she put immediately into practice. The burning is now visible.

A separation immediately afterwards took place, and the Earl married, secondly, Mary, daughter and co-heir of Joseph Maynard, Esq. In the following year, Bradgate was honoured by a visit from King William, when, it is related, that a large room with a bow-window was fitted up for his reception. An old man, who was living in 1804 at Anstey, aged 81, remembered the principal part of Bradgate quite entire. He had been in all the rooms, and said there was a door out of the dining-room into the chapel. The same person recollected being told by his father (who was only thirty years older than himself), that he was carried, when a child, to the end of Anstey town, to see King William pass across the fields on his way to Bradgate.

Shortly after the death of the Countess Dowager of Stamford, in 1722, Bradgate appears to have been deserted by the family as a residence, and to have gradually fallen into a state of dilapidation. Towards the close of the last century, the then Earl disposed of the materials of the building, on condition that the purchaser should remove them from the ground within a given period. Luckily, however, for the admirers of history and antiquities, the contract was not fulfilled. Some parts were left standing; and, with the exception of natural decay, remained in nearly the same state.

The youthful Lady Jane Grey, who was of the blood-royal of England, being the great-granddaughter of Henry VII., was the delight of all except her parents, whose severity would in modern times be termed brutal, yet did not alienate her willing obedience. Filial obedience proved her ruin. Her father, then created Duke of Suffolk, presuming on his own power and favour, and the declining health of Edward VI., undertook, in concert with the powerful Duke of Northumberland, to transfer the crown into their own line. With this view a marriage was concluded between Lady Jane Grey and Northumberland's fourth son, Lord Guildford Dudley, in May 1553. Edward VI. was persuaded by his interested advisers to set aside the rights of his sisters Mary and Elizabeth, and, in consideration of her eminent virtues and royal descent, to settle the crown upon Lady Jane Grey and Dudley. The king died July 6th; and it was not until the 10th that this unfortunate lady even knew of the plot in which she was involved. She was very reluctant to accept the crown, but was at last over-persuaded by the importunities of her parents, and the entreaties of her husband, whom she dearly loved. The two dukes had no party among the people, and ten days placed Mary in undisputed possession of the throne; while Queen Jane and her young consort had to bid farewell to all earthly glory. The Tower palace, where they were residing, became almost instantaneously the Tower prison. Northumberland perished at once upon the block; but Lady Jane and her husband would probably have been spared, but for Wyat's ill-managed insurrection, which broke out on the queen's intended marriage with the cruel bigot of Spain, King Philip, and was supported by *Lady Jane Grey's father*, the Duke of Suffolk. The insurrection failed, and not only involved all those in ruin who had directly promoted it, but those in the Tower, who assuredly desired nothing so much as a peaceable and unambitious life. Indeed, Lady Jane's only error was being persuaded to accept a crown to which she had no good title, and for which she did not wish. She took it rather as a burthen than as a favour, and resigned it with as much indifference as she would have laid down a garland, when its beauties had faded and its scent had gone.

Within a week after Wyat's discomfiture, it was determined that Lady Jane and her husband should both die on the same day—Monday, the 12th of February 1554. The last evening of her life was employed by her in religious duties. Having taken up a Greek Testament, and attentively perused it for some time, she discovered a few pages of blank paper at the end of the volume, 'which, as it were, awakening and exciting her zeal to some good and charitable office, she took a pen, and in those waste leaves wrote a most godly and learned exhortation' to her sister Katherine.

In the narrative which follows this letter, it is asserted that Lady Jane, even on the evening of her existence, was harassed by the Catholic divines; for no sooner had she finished the letter, than two bishops, with some other priests, entered her chamber, and employed more than two hours in the effort to convert her. Fecknam, the Catholic dean of St. Paul's, was foremost; but he failed with one who was more than his equal in controversy. What a splendid example of female constancy and firmness, in a girl who had not then attained her seventeenth year!

Lady Jane, that her fortitude might not be shaken, refused a farewell meeting with Lord Guildford, on the morning of the fatal day. It would foment their grief, she said, rather than be a comfort in death, and they would shortly meet in a better place and more happy estate.

The fatal morning at length arrived. It was originally intended that Lady Jane and Lord Guildford should suffer together on Tower Hill; but the Council, dreading the effect of their youth and innocence on the populace, changed their orders, and it was determined that Lord Guildford only should be executed on the Hill, and that Lady Jane's death should take place within the verge of the Tower. Lord Guildford was first led to his fate. From the window of 'Master Partridge's house,' where Lady Jane was lodged, she is said to have beheld Lord Guildford going to execution, and exchanged with him her last parting signal. He passed on to Tower Hill, was brought back in a cart to be buried in the Tower Chapel, and she looked upon his headless trunk. 'O Guildford, Guildford!' exclaimed the unhappy lady, rising even in her agony to the highest sublimity of Christian heroism, 'the antepast is not so bitter that thou hast tasted, and which I shall soon taste, as to make my flesh tremble; it is nothing compared to the feast of which we shall partake this day in heaven.'

The account states that Lady Jane, when sitting in her apartments awaiting the dreadful summons, heard the cart pass under her window, and rose, notwithstanding the efforts of her attendants to restrain her. This statement is not so probable as the other, for she would scarcely have sought so dreadful a spectacle; and as she had carefully avoided an interview with Guildford, lest her firmness might have been destroyed, it cannot be believed that she would willingly view an object still more calculated to disturb her thoughts. Grafton, the chronicler, corroborates the other statement, that Lady Jane's meeting the mutilated body of her husband was entirely accidental; for, he says, Lord Guildford Dudley's 'dead carcas, lying in a carre in strawe, was agine brought into the Tower, at the same instant that the Ladie Iane, his wife, went to her death within the Tower; which miserable sight was to her a double sorrow and grief.' Dudley, we are told, exhibited considerable dignity and fortitude. After some time spent in prayer, he addressed the assembled multitude, merely to request them to pray for him; and placing his head on the block, it was in a few minutes separated from his body.

The Tower, it has been acutely remarked by a German writer of our history, is a remarkable monument of the past, yet not to its advantage; 'for the images of the children of Edward IV., of Anne Boleyn, and Jane Grey, and of the many innocent victims murdered in times of despotism and tyranny, pass like dark phantoms before the mind.'

The place of execution within the Tower, on the green, was reserved for putting to death privately; and the precise spot whereon the scaffold was erected is nearly opposite the door of the chapel of St. Peter, and is marked by a large oval of dark flints. Hereon many of the wisest, the noblest, the best, and the fairest heads of English men and English women, of times long passed away, fell from such a block, and beneath the stroke of such an axe, as may now be seen in the armouries.

So soon as the closing scene of Lord Dudley's life was over, the sheriff announced to Lady Jane that they were ready to attend her to the scaffold; nor did this awful summons shake the fortitude which she had displayed throughout her imprisonment. Howes, in his *Chronicle*, tells us: 'The Lady being nothing at all abashed, neither with fear of her owne death, which then approached, neither with the sight of the dead carcase of her husband when he was brought into the chapell, came foorth, the lieutenant leading her, with countenance nothing abashed, neither her eyes anything moistened with teares (although her gentlewomen, Elizabeth Tylney and Mistress Helen, wonderfully wept), with a book in her hand, wherein she prayed until she came to the said scaffold, whereon, when she was mounted, she was beheaded.'

Another account describes her conduct on the occasion in the following words : 'And being come down, and delivered into the hands of the sheriffs, they might behold in her countenance, so gravely settled with all modest and comely resolution, that not the least hair or mote either of fear or grief could be perceived to proceed either out of her speech or motions; but like a demure body going to be united to her heart's best and longest beloved, so showed she forth all the beams of a well-mixt and temporal alacrity, rather instructing patience how it should suffer, than being by patience any way able to endure the travel of so grievous a journey. With this blessed and modest boldness of spirit, undaunted and unaltered, she went towards the scaffold.' She was entirely occupied in the perusal of a book of prayer, though Fox asserts that her devotions were continually interrupted by Fecknam.

A particular account of her behaviour on the scaffold is to be found in an exceedingly rare tract (neither noticed by Ames nor Herbert), which, though without date, bears internal evidence of having been printed immediately subsequent to her decapitation. That portion of the tract regarding the Lady Jane is as follows :—

'Fyrst, when she was mounted on the scaffolde, she sayd to the people standinge thereabout, " Good people, I com hether to die, and by a lawe I am condemned to the same. The facte, indede, against the Queenes highnes was unlawful, and the consenting thereunto by me, but touching the procurement and desyre thereof by me, or on my halfe, I doo wash my hands thereof in innocencie before God and the face of you, good Christian people, this day;" and therewith she wrung her handes, in which she had her booke. Then she sayd, "I pray you all, good Christian people, to bear me wytnes that I dye a true Christian woman, and that I looke to be saved by none other mene but only by the mercy of God, in the merites of the blood of His onlye Sonne Jesus Christe; and I confesse when I dyd know the word of God, I neglected the same, and loved myselfe and the world, and therefore this plagge or punyshment is happely and worthely happened unto me for my sinnes. And yet I thanke God of His goodnes that He hath thus geven me a tyme and respet to repent. And now, good people, while I am alyve, I pray you to assyst me with your prayers." And then she, knelyng downe, she turned to Fecknam, saying, "Shall I say this psalm?" and he said, "Yea." Then she said the psalm of "Misereri mei Deus," in English, in most devout manner, to thende. Then she stood up, and gave her mayde, Mistres Tylney, her gloves and handkercher, and her booke to Maistre Thomas Brydges, the lyveteuantes brother. Forthwith she untyed her gowne. The hangman went to her to have helped her off therewith; then she desyred him to let her alone, turning towardes the two jentlewomen, who helped her off therewith, and also her Frose paste and neckecher, giving to her a fayre handkercher to knytte about her eyes. Then the hangman kneled downe and asked her forgevenes, whome she forgave most willingly. Then he willed her to stand upon the strawe, which doing, she saw the blocke. Then she sayd, "I pray thee dispatche me quickly." Then she kneeled downe, saying, 'Wil you take it of before I lay me downe?' And the hangman answered her, "No, Madame." She tyed the kercher about her eyes; then feeling for the blocke, saide, "What shal I doo? Where is it?' One of the standers-by guiding her thereunto, she layde her head downe upon the blocke, and stretched forth her body, and sayd, " Lorde, into Thy handes I commende my spirite." And so she ended.'[1]

The lines which this unfortunate lady is said to have scratched with a pin on the walls of her prison in the Tower, viz.—

> '*Non aliena putes homini quæ obtingere possunt,*
> *Sors hodierna mihi cras erit illa tibi,*'

have been thus diversely translated:

> 'To mortal's common fate thy mind resign,
> My lot to-day, to-morrow may be thine.'

> 'Think not, O mortal, vainly gay,
>   That thou from human woes art free;
> The bitter cup I drink to-day,
>   To-morrow may be drunk by thee.'

Of the following lines, ascribed also to Lady Jane, the annexed translations have been given:—

> '*Deo juvante, nil nocet livor malus;*
> *Et non juvante, nil juvat labor gravis:*
>   *Post tenebras, spero lucem.*'

> 'Whilst God assists us, envy bites in vain;
> If God forsake us, fruitless all our pain.
>   I hope for light after the darkness.'

---

[1] Neither Nichols, in his *History of Leicestershire,* nor the *Chronicle of Queen Jane,* nor, it is believed, any other author, mentions the place where the Lady Jane was buried. The general belief is, that her body was interred with that of her husband in the Tower; but the historian of that fortress was not able to find any conclusive evidence of the place where their remains were deposited. There is a tradition that the body was privately brought from London by a servant of the family, and deposited in the chapel at Bradgate.

> 'Harmless all malice if our God be nigh;
> Fruitless all pains if He His help deny.
> Patient I pass these gloomy hours away,
> And wait the morning of eternal day!'
> —See Nicolas's *Life of Lady Jane Grey.*

The apartments in which Lady Jane was imprisoned have been much contested. Beauchamp Tower was certainly the place of Lord Guildford's prison. Many years ago, in converting an apartment in Beauchamp Tower, which had formerly been the place in which state prisoners had been confined, into a mess-room for the officers of the garrison there, several inscriptions were discovered on the walls of the room. They appeared to have been made with nails, or some other pointed instrument, and the greater part of them were undoubtedly the autographs of the unfortunate tenants of the place. Amongst them was, 'IANE. IANE,' which, it has been conjectured, was written by herself, and that some latent meaning was contained in the repetition of her signature, by which she at once styled herself a queen, and intimated that not even the horrors of a prison could force her to relinquish that title.[1] Sir Harris Nicholas, who first recorded the above circumstance, does not consider the suggestion entitled to any consideration; for, independently of its having been proved that Lady Jane was placed in a different apartment from that where this inscription was found, her character and conduct render it extremely un-

---

[1] The document in the British Museum, bearing Lady Jane's signature *as queen*, is supposed to have been the immediate cause of Mary's signing the warrant for her execution.

likely that motives of vanity should have had any place in her wounded mind. Another antiquary has supposed that it was written by Jane's father-in-law, the Duke of Northumberland; but the most rational suggestion is that by Mr. Bayley, who considers it to have been inscribed by Jane's unhappy partner, Lord Guildford Dudley; for nothing is more probable than that, in his separation from his wife, he should have solaced himself by marking the walls of his prison with her name. If it could be proved that it was traced by his hand, so affecting a memorial would speak eloquently of his tenderness, and we might feel convinced that the affection which had been attributed to this interesting pair unquestionably existed.

The Brick Tower is commonly said to have been that in which Lady Jane Grey was lodged. Mr. Hepworth Dixon, who read to the Archæological Institute, in 1866, a very interesting *précis* of the Tower history, may be supposed to refer to the contested inscription in the following passage:—

'In the lower room of the Beauchamp Tower you will find among the crowd of Dudley inscriptions the name of JANE. It is probably the work of her husband, Guildford Dudley, who could not think of her even in the Tower as other than the rightful queen. But Jane herself, after her midsummer game of royalty was over, never used that perilous style.' Mr. Dixon adds of the Latin couplet which, it is said, Jane wrote on her prison-wall, and which Fox has preserved (see *ante*, p. 401): 'If these lines could be found, they would give the room in which Lady Jane was lodged;

but the search has been often made, and always in vain. I am clear that her prison was not the Brick Tower; for in a contemporary journal, kept by a resident in the Tower, and describing her daily life, it is said that she lodged in the house of Master Partridge, and that her window commanded a view of the Tower-green, so that she could see the cart which brought in for interment her husband's headless corse. Partridge's house and Lady Jane's prison I take to have been the house standing between the lieutenant's lodgings and the Bloody Tower.' Still, this conclusion is based upon the identity of the precise spot to which the above anecdote refers, and this point, as we have already seen, is much contested.

The finest portrait of Lady Jane Grey is the beautiful original by Lucas de Heere, now at Althorpe. There are also a very ugly portrait by Vertue, and an original in the possession of Lord Stamford; besides a portrait once in the possession of Mr. Harrington of Breaston, Derbyshire, into whose hands it came from the Misses Grey of Risley.

The substance of this paper relating to Bradgate has been mainly abridged from *The Graphic and Historical Illustrator*, 1839, appended to which are some stanzas, entitled, 'The Ladye's Tower,' thus glancing at the historical associations with which Bradgate is so fraught :—

> 'This lone chapelle, whence prayer to heaven arose,
>   The Ladye's simple Tower that stands beside;
> The nameless limpid rill that gurgling flows,
>   With shadows flitting o'er its foaming tide,
>   Which ever with th' opposing rocks doth chide;

BRADGATE AND LADY JANE GREY.

The greensward hills that bound the gazer's ken,
   And seem the stilly spot from all to hide,
May well detain the pensive pilgrim, when
He quiet lingers here, afar from common men.

There, in departed days, the gentle maid,
   The lovely and the good, with infant glee,
Along the margin of the streamlet played,
    Or gather'd wild-flowers 'neath each mossy tree ;
    And little recked what cares hers were to be,
While listening to the skylark's aerial lay ;
    Or merry grasshopper that caroll'd free,
In verdant haunts, throughout the live-long day,
The beauteous child, as blithe and sorrowless as they.

. . . . . .

Here from her casement, as she cast a look,
   Oft might she mourn the reckless sport to scan ;
And well rejoice to find in classic book,
    Solace,—withdrawn from all that pleasure can
    Impart to rude and riot-loving man :
    Aye, and when at the banquet revels ran
To loud extreme, she here was wont to haste,
   And marvel at creation's mighty plan ;
Or with old bards and sages pleasure taste,
Unknown to Folly's crowd, whose days all run to waste.

. . . .

Beautiful martyr ! widowed by the hand
   That reft thee of thy life ere yet 'twas thine ;
Thy grave to find beneath a guilty land,
    Thou had no need of gilded niche or shrine !
    Fond recollections round thy memory twine—
A sacred halo circles thy brief years;
    'Tis thine, redeemed from sin and death, to shine
Eternally above this world of fears,
Where Christ Himself, thy King, hath wiped away all tears.

Farewell, thou mouldering relic of the past !
  An hour unmeetly was not spent with thee :
Events, as rapid as the autumn's blast,
  Have hurried onward, since 'twas thine to see
  The fairest flower of England pensively
Expand and blossom 'neath thy rugged shade ;
  And here thou stand'st, while circling seasons flee,
A monumental pile of that sweet maid,
Whom men of blood-stain'd hands within the charnel laid.'

ASSASSINATION OF THE HARTGILLS BY LORD STOURTON.

THE scene of this atrocity was Stourton, in North Wiltshire, subsequently celebrated as Stourhead, the seat of Sir Richard Colt Hoare, Bart., the amateur antiquary and topographer.

Stourton was the family seat of Charles Lord Stourton, who was son and heir of William Lord Stourton, who died at Boulogne while in the service of Edward vi. On Lord Charles taking possession of the family mansion, his mother, Lady Elizabeth, who had survived her husband, placed herself under the roof of William Hartgill, and John Hartgill, his son, of Kilmington, a village two or three miles from Stourton. These gentlemen had become entitled to the confidence reposed in them, as well by family connection as by their respectability of character. The Lady Elizabeth had not been long in this family when she received a visit from her son, who proposed that she should enter into a bond to a considerable amount never to remarry without his consent; and who, having pressed this measure with little success by his own persuasion, summoned Mr. Hartgill to enforce it with the influence which he had long gained over his mother as a protector and long-tried friend. But Mr. Hartgill, knowing the overbearing and cruel spirit of Lord Charles, refused to support his demand, unless he would enter into a reciprocal obligation to allow his mother an annuity suitable to her rank; and on that point he firmly insisted.

Soon after this proposal was made, and rejected, on a Whitsunday morning, while Mr. Hartgill and his family were at Kilmington Church, their devotions were interrupted by the appearance of Lord Stourton, who approached the church-door, followed by his defenders in such numbers, and with such weapons (bows, guns, etc.) as afforded little doubt of the hostility of their intentions.

The younger Hartgill, an athletic and courageous young man, who was then at church beside his aged parents, concluding his devotions with an ejaculated petition for the assistance of that 'Lord of Hosts' in whose house and in whose service he was so unjustly assailed, issued forth to encounter the impious Goliath; and drawing his sword at the church-porch, made his way to his father's house, which was only a few yards distant, and which he happily reached unwounded. But his father, whose arm was enervated by age, and his mother, who tottered with infirmity, durst not venture on so perilous a passage, but took refuge with some of their servants in the church tower.

Young Hartgill's motive for this movement was not self-preservation, but a desire to succour his parents; and, accordingly, having taken his long-bow, and given a crossbow and a charged gun to a second person, he proceeded again towards the church, and with admirable bravery repulsed Lord Stourton and some of his men from the churchyard and the outskirts of the house; but as some of them still remained in the church, the descent of the persons in the tower was too hazardous to be attempted. Young Hartgill, however, having devised a method of getting some provisions drawn up into the tower, rode directly for London to procure the interference of the authorities; and on his arrival in town he succeeded so far as to get Sir Thomas Spark, the high-sheriff of Somerset, despatched to take Lord Stourton into custody, and to liberate those persons who were shut up in the churchtower. For, though Mrs. Hartgill was allowed to go into her house on Sunday evening, her husband and his servants were still kept in their close and comfortless confinement by a band of his lordship's retainers, who surrounded the church during young Hartgill's absence.

Meanwhile, the sheriff, as directed by the Lords of the Council, repressed these disorders. Lord Stourton was committed to the Fleet prison, but soon regained his liberty on being bound over to keep the peace. But the desire for revenge continued to rankle in his breast, and he persisted in harassing the Hartgills by destroying their corn and driving away their cattle, till after the accession of Queen Mary, when, on Her Majesty's visit to Basing-end, in Hampshire, they presented a petition for redress. Both parties were now summoned to appear before the Council, when Lord Stourton promised, if the Hartgills would go to his home, and 'deserve his goodwill, they should have not only that, but the value of all the property he had taken from them during the quarrel.' To this proposition they readily acceded; and on a stipulated day they proceeded towards Stourton, accompanied by John Dackombe, Esq., who was to be a witness to their submission to his terms.

But on approaching a house through a lane they were met by half-a-dozen of Lord Stourton's men, who, letting the elder Hartgill and his friend pass, stood before the son with the evident intention of preventing his further progress. He, on observing their number and hostile appearance, turned his horse as if to ride homeward; but immediately perceived a like number of enemies approaching him from that point, and before he could draw his sword, and put himself in a posture of defence, he had received several wounds. He set his back, however, against the hedge, and defended himself for some time against the whole twelve; but exhausted at length by the unequal contest, and by loss of blood from his numerous wounds, he fell into a state of insensibility, and was left by his assailants as dead.

After lying some time in this condition, he so far recovered that, with the assistance of a cook of Lord Stourton's, he got on his horse and rode to the house of Mr. Richard Mumpeston of Maiden Bradley, under whose care he soon recovered his health.

At length the matter was brought before the Star Chamber, and Lord Stourton was sentenced to pay a considerable sum of money to the Hartgills, and undergo a second imprisonment in the Fleet.

Under pretence of having some family business to arrange, which required his presence at Stourton, and after entering into a bond for £2000 penalty to present himself at the Fleet on the first day of term, he obtained a licence to return into Wiltshire; and, soon after his arrival at Stourton, shortly before Christmas, he sent to the Hartgills, stating that he was prepared to pay them the fine imposed upon him by the Star Chamber, and requesting them to appoint a place and time at which they would meet him to receive it, and settle the differences between them. The Hartgills, who had seriously experienced his treachery, informed his lordship they would meet him on the 10th of January, but at no other place than Kilmington Church. On the appointed day, therefore, he went to Kilmington, accompanied by several gentlemen, sixteen of his servants, and several of his tenants, altogether sixty persons; they went not, however, into the church, but into the churchhouse, his lordship observing that the church was 'not a fit place in which to talk of worldly matters.'

Mr. Hartgill, whose suspicions were strengthened by the number of Lord Stourton's retinue, refused to approach him, when he was invited to do so by his lordship, who assured him that he should 'have no bodily hurt.' He received a similar assurance from Sir James Fitzjames Chaffyn, and other gentlemen, and was requested to come into the church-house. But Hartgill, as well as his son, still refused to enter any covered place except the church.

It was at length agreed that a table should be set upon the green. This being done, Lord Stourton put down a cap-case and purse, and calling the Hartgills to him, said, the Council had ordered him to pay them 'a certain sum of money, which they should have; marry (but) he would first know them to be true men.' This was the watchword for Lord Stourton, who, with ten or twelve of his men, seized the Hartgills and dragged them into the church-house, where they took from them their purses, and then bound them with 'two blue bands of inkle' which his lordship had brought with him. One of the purses having been dropped, was picked up by a domestic, Upham; and a torquoise which it contained was presented to Lady Stourton. This Upham received 'two great blows' from his master because he was about to pinion the captives instead of tying their hands behind them; and the younger Hartgill received another blow from the same unmerciful hand because he dared to call the treatment he met with cruel. About this time his lordship, on coming out of the house with his naked sword, and meeting young Mr. Hartgill's wife, 'he kicked at her with his spurs,' says our manuscript, 'also rent a great piece off from one of her hose,' and struck her so violently 'between her neck and head' that she was carried away in a state of insensibility.

The captives were taken to the parsonage house of Kilmington, where they were kept bound, and without victuals, till about one o'clock the next morning, when they were removed to a house of Lord Stourton's, called Bonham, about two miles distant, and within half a mile from Stourton. Here they were placed, bound as before, in separate apartments, and without fires, till the next evening.

About ten o'clock on that evening, his lordship sent to Bonham four of his servants—ready to obey their iniquitous master even to commit murder—to bring the victims of his revenge to his house, with instructions that if they should offer any resistance, or make any noise by the way, they should be despatched on the spot. On arriving at Bonham, the messengers found another of his lordship's men, who had been stationed there to watch the house, and who was engaged to act in conjunction with them.

Then the murderous work began. About ten o'clock at night they took their victims to a close adjoining Lord Stourton's house. There they forced them to kneel down, and knocked them on the head with clubs, his lordship 'standing in the meantime at a gallery door, not a good coyte's cast from the place.' This done, the bodies were wrapped up in their gowns, and carried through a garden into the gallery, where Lord Stourton stood, his lordship bearing a candle to light the murderers! The bearer of old Mr. Hartgill made a false step, and fell into a hole —the intended depository of his burthen. Life being not quite extinct, a groan was heard, when one of the murderers swearing they were not yet dead, his lordship ordered that their throats should be cut, lest they should disturb a French priest who was lying in an adjoining room. This order was executed by a servant with a pocket-knife, while his lordship held the candle; but one of the men relenting, exclaimed, 'Ah, my lord, this is a pitiful sight! Had I thought what I now think, before the thing was done, your whole lands would not have won me to consent to such an act.' To which his lordship answered: 'What, faint-hearted knave! is it any more than ridding of two knaves, that living, were troublesome to God's laws and men's? There is no more account to be made of them than of killing two sheep!' Their bodies were then let down into a 'dungeon' or pit beneath the floor, and two of the men were let down with cords (for there were no steps), to bury them; his lordship all the time watching their progress from above, and urging them to despatch, by observing that the night wore fast away.

The bodies were afterwards disinterred by Sir Anthony Hungerford, then high-sheriff of Wiltshire, whose exertions in discovering them received the thanks of the Council. The bodies were fifteen feet below the surface, covered with earth and two layers of paving, on which were thrown two or three cartloads of timber and shavings.

Lord Stourton was apprehended and committed to the

Tower, charged with the murder, on the 28th of January 1556. He was brought up, with one of his men, for examination at Westminster on the 10th of February, and was remanded to the 26th, when he was arraigned in Westminster Hall, before the Lord Chief-Justice Brooks, the Lord-Steward, and the Lord-Treasurer, appointed by special commission to try him. His four servants were sent to be arraigned in Wiltshire.

In the course of the examination, some of the atrocities of Lord Stourton came to light. It appeared that he had caused, not long before, a barn of one Thomas Chaffin to be set on fire by three of his servants; and then against Chaffin, for saying it was not done without the knowledge of the said Lord Stourton, or some of his servants, he brought an action, and recovering one hundred pounds damages, he took for payment out of his pasture, by force, twelve hundred sheep, with the wool upon their backs, besides all the oxen, kine, and horses that he could find.

Lord Stourton and his four servants were found guilty of the murder. The Hartgills, who had fallen victims to his violent and malicious nature, were Protestants; and as his lordship had always been a staunch supporter of the Roman Catholic religion, and had rendered many services to the Government, it was hoped by his friends that the Queen would have spared his life. But she left him to the laws; and there is no act of Mary's reign that is so creditable to her memory as this exercise of justice, and her horror at the atrocity of his crime.

On the 28th of February, the Council directed the sheriff of Wiltshire to receive the body of Lord Stourton at the hands of Sir Hugh Paulet, and to see him executed. On the 2d of March, he was taken, under a strong guard, from the Tower on horseback, his arms pinioned behind him, and his legs tied under the horse's belly.

His lordship, with Sir Robert Oxenbridge, the lieutenant, four of his servants, and other guards, rode from the Tower for Salisbury, the place of execution; and resting one night at Staines, and a second at Basingstoke, they arrived at Salisbury on the 4th; and on the 6th he was executed in the market-place. It is said he 'made great lamentation at his death for his wilful and impious deed.' It was directed that his servants should be hanged in chains at Meere; and the only mark of distinction shown to Lord Stourton's rank, was his being hanged with, instead of a hempen halter, a silken rope, the privilege of a peer. He was buried in Salisbury Cathedral. 'The visitors,' says the *Athenæum*, 'will not have forgotten the tomb of this most cruel and treacherous of assassins. There formerly dangled above it, from an iron bar, the silken cord in which this savage was hanged. In the manner of his death this treacherous ruffian had regard for his dignity as a peer; and, disgusted at the idea of dying in hemp like a common felon, he was permitted to swing in a noose of stout twisted silk.'

The son of this criminal lord, John, eighth Baron Stourton, was restored in blood, by Act of Parliament, in 1575. This nobleman was one of the peers on the trial of Mary Queen of Scotland. In lineal descent from him is the present Lord Stourton, who is eighteenth Baron. 'This noble family, which derives its name from Stourton, county Wilts, was of considerable rank antecedently to the Conquest; for we find at that period one of its members, Botolph Stourton, the most active in gallantry, disputing every inch of ground with the foreigner; and finally obtaining from the Duke his own terms. Having broken down the sea-walls of the Severn, and guarded the passes by land, Botolph entered Glastonbury when that victorious Norman had made his appearance in the west; and thus protected, compelled William to grant whatsoever he demanded.'—Burke's *Peerage*.

THE RED AND WHITE ROSES.

IN an account of these distinctions we are informed that 'the bages that be beryth by the Castle of Clifford is a white rose;' but, as usual, no reason why. It is quite clear that this, the celebrated cognizance of the House of York, did not originate in the dispute in the Temple Gardens, so dramatically introduced in the play of Henry VI.; nor does it follow that Shakspeare, or whoever wrote it, intended it, as Sir Henry Ellis seems to think, to represent that it did so. There is not a line throughout the scene which can be taken to show an intention on the part of the author to represent that the Lancastrian badges were then for the first time assumed. Richard Plantagenet, as grandson of Edmund of Langley, Duke of York, naturally proposes that those who think with him should signify their opinion by adopting the badge of his house, which is by accident blooming behind him. John of Beaufort, a descendant of John of Gaunt, Duke of Lancaster, as naturally selects the badge of his family—the red rose—as the token of adherence to his side of the question.

The scene, if entirely the invention of Shakspeare (which has been disputed), is full of truth and character, and in any case testifies rather to the pre-existence of those signs of company than to their derivation from this incident. Roses—red, white, and gold—are mentioned as ornaments both of dresses and furniture, possessed by various members of the Plantagenet family from the time of Edward I., who is said to have given for a badge 'a rose *gold*, the stalk *vert*.' There is no positive authority for this assertion, which is to be found in a Harleian MS. (No. 304); but it is very probable that the white and red roses may have been only chosen as differences, as you will find was the case with the ostrich feathers, which are blazoned and depicted gold, silver, and ermine, to distinguish the King's from the Prince's and the Duke of Lancaster's.

Tenure of a manor, by presenting a rose on a certain day, was also a common custom in the middle ages. Brook House, Langsett, in the parish of Penistone, in Yorkshire, is said by Beckwith, in his edition of Blount's *Ancient Tenures*, to have been held even in his day (he died in 1799), by the unseasonable payment of a snowball at Midsummer, and a rose at Christmas; or, as he presumes, a sum of money in default. We have no evidence of the tenure of Clifford Castle by this sort of service; but it may have been held by the annual payment of a white rose, although the fact has not transpired. There is also a romantic story associated with the family of Clifford in connection with a rose, as the popular tradition of Rosamunda, the 'Rose of the World,' the 'filia pulchra,' of Walter de Clifford, the favourite of Henry II., and the victim of Queen Eleanor's vengeance. All we know at present is, that the white rose badge is reputed to have belonged to the Castle of Clifford, and that it came into the possession of the House of York by the marriage of Richard of Coningsburgh, son of Edmund of Langley, with his second wife Maud, daughter of Thomas Lord Clifford.[1]

THE OLDEST ROSE-TREE IN THE WORLD.

Humboldt, in his *Aspects of Nature*, gives the following account of, probably, *the oldest Rose-tree in the world*. In the crypt of the Cathedral of Hildesheim grows a wild rose-tree, said to be a thousand years old; whereas it is the root only, not the stem, which is eight centuries old, according to accurate information derived by Humboldt from ancient and trustworthy original documents. A legend connects the rose-tree with a vow made by the founder of the cathedral, Ludwig the Pious; and a document of the eleventh century states that 'when Bishop Hezilo rebuilt the cathedral, which had been burned down, he inclosed the roots of the rose-tree with a vault which still exists: raised upon this vault the crypt, which was re-constructed in 1061, and spread out the branches of the rose-tree upon the walls.' The stem was, in 1849, 26½ feet high, and the branches covered about 32 feet of the external crypt wall.

[1] Mr. Planché, Somerset Herald; *Journal of the British Archæological Association*, abridged.

APPENDIX.

PEERAGES PER SALTUM.

WHEN Lord John Russell was raised to the earldom, he accomplished a feat which has not been performed anything like a dozen times in nearly a hundred and twenty years. When he ceased to be a commoner, and entered the House of Peers, he passed clean over the heads of all the barons and viscounts, and took his seat next to the Earl of Dudley, at the bottom of the third rank of the hereditary nobility.

The feat is one which doubtless was often performed by court favourites under the arbitrary Tudors, and scarcely less arbitrary and more eccentric Stuarts. But from the days of Sir Robert Walpole, when party government first began, down to this present year, 1861, so far as we are able to learn from the Peerages, Earl Russell has achieved a success which has befallen to the lot of men for the most part of high historic merit.

In 1742, the all-powerful commoner, Sir Robert Walpole, was created Earl of Oxford; but it was on resigning the premiership, after a tenancy of two-and-twenty years' duration. Again, in 1766, we find another great commoner honoured in the same manner—we mean, of course, the elder Pitt, who was then made

Earl of Chatham; but there was a difference in his case, inasmuch as his wife had previously been made a baroness, so that in effect it amounted only to a 'step in the peerage.' Again, in 1797, so greatly was the popular feeling excited by the victory gained by Sir John Jervis over the Spanish fleet off Cape St. Vincent, that the fortunate admiral was at once elevated to the earldom by which his victory still lives in our memories. No other instance that we can find occurs in the annals of the reign of George III., or of the Regency, or of King George IV.; neither Nelson nor Wellington gained an earl's coronet *per saltum;* the former, indeed, never wore one, and the latter went through one, at least, of the inferior grades before he was created Earl of Wellington, though, as a matter of fact, he did not take his seat in the House of Peers until he had climbed up to a dukedom. In 1831, a younger son of the Duke of Devonshire, Lord G. Cavendish, was created Earl of Burlington; but for this act of grace there was the assignable reason that he was ultimately heir to the dukedom, in which his own title must eventually merge. About the same time, King William IV.'s eldest son, by Mrs. Jordan, was raised to the earldom of Munster without passing through the intermediate grades; and her Majesty, on coming to the throne, bestowed the earldom of Leicester on Mr. Coke of Holkham. Since that date, a similar act of graciousness has been extended to no commoners, with the exception of Lord Francis Egerton, on whom her Majesty was advised by Sir Robert Peel to bestow the earldom of Ellesmere in 1846; Sir Maurice Berkeley, the owner of Berkeley Castle, and an ex-Lord of the Admiralty, received at Lord Palmerston's hands the coronet of Fitzhardinge, which his brother obtained from Lord Melbourne, but could not transmit to his successor in the family estates; and lastly, the wife of the present Duke of Sutherland, the daughter and heiress of Mr. Hay Mackenzie of Cromarty, was created Countess of Cromertie, with remainder to her younger children, in remembrance of her maternal ancestor the Earl of Cromertie in the peerage of Scotland, whose title was forfeited in the last century.—*London Review.*

'BELL THE CAT.'

THIS odd name was given to Archibald Douglas, a Scottish nobleman, from an incident that occurred at Lauder, where the great barons of the nation had assembled at the call of the king, James III., to resist a threatened invasion of the country by Edward IV. of England. They were, however, less disposed to advance against the English than to correct the abuses of James's administration, which were chiefly to be ascribed to the influence exerted over him by mean and unworthy favourites, particularly one Cochran, an architect, but termed a mason by the haughty barons.

Sir Walter Scott thus described the strange scene : ' Many of the nobility and barons held a secret council in the church of Lauder, where they enlarged upon the evils which Scotland sustained through the insolence and corruption of Cochran and his associates. While they were thus declaiming, Lord Grey requested their attention to a fable. "The mice," he said, "being much annoyed by the persecution of the cat, resolved that a bell should be hung about puss' neck, to give notice when she was coming. But, though the measure was agreed to in full council, it could not be carried into effect, because no mouse had courage enough to tie the bell to the neck of the formidable enemy." This was as much as to intimate his opinion that, though the discontented nobles might make bold resolutions against the king's ministry; yet it would be difficult to find any one courageous enough to act upon them. Archibald, Earl of Angus, a man of gigantic strength and intrepid courage, and head of that second family of Douglas whom I before mentioned, started up when Grey had done speaking. "I am he," he said, "who will bell the cat;" from which expression he was distinguished by the name of *Bell-the-Cat* to his dying day.'

INDEX.

ABBESS of Amesbury, 4.
Abbess of Lacock, 3.
Addison and the Duke of Shrewsbury, 140.
Ampthill Park, *note*, 33.
Arundel, Earl of, Earl Marshal, 199.
Arundel, Earl of, 'the Renowned Confessor,' 196-199.
Ascham, Roger, at Bradgate, 389.
Ashdown, Battle of, 318.
Assassination of the Duke of Buckingham by Felton, 143.
Assassination of the Hartgills, 407.
Aston Church Window, and the Holts' Arms, 172-174.
Attainder of the Duke of Monmouth, 331.
Aubrey and Britton on the Hungerford Family, 119, 120.

BAKER Family Legend, 176.
Ballad, Anglo-Norman, 379-381.
Barnet, Battle of, and Richard Duke of Gloucester, 309.
Barnes, Juliana, and the *Boke of Seynte Albans*, 351.
Basing House, Sacking of, 86.
Battle Abbey and Cowdray Castle, 71.
Bayntons, the, of Spye Park, 17, 18.
Beaumont, Adam, and Sir John Eland, 205.
Berners Family, 351.
Berners, Lord, translator of Froissart, 352.
Blowing Stone described, 322.
Bodach Glass Legend, 179-182.
Book of Lacock, 7, 8.
Bosworth Field, and Buckingham, 91, 92.
Bradgate and Lady Jane Grey, 382.
Bradgate described, 382, 383; 386, 387.
Brancepeth Castle, Vicissitudes of, 87.

Browne Family and Name, 73, 74.
Browne, Sir Anthony, and his Descendants, 65.
Browne, Mabel, marriage of, 70.
Buckingham and Bosworth Field, 91.
Buckingham, George Villiers Duke of, attempts on his life, 146.
Buckingham, Duke of, his funeral, 151.
Buckingham and Chandos, Dukes of, 97.
Buckingham and Chandos, second Duke of, 99, 100.
Buckingham Family, the, 91.
Buckingham, Villiers, Dukes of, 95, 96.
Burial of Lady Jane Grey, 401.
Burton, Sir Charles, 102.

CALVERLEY Family, the, 49
Calverley, Walter, story of, 49.
Carews of Beddington, 355.
Castle of Brancepeth, 87.
Castle, Donington, and Chaucer, 183.
Castle, Fotheringhay, 23, 26, 28.
Castle of Oakham, 258.
Castle of Pontefract and its Echoes, 214-230.
Castle, Sandal, 304, 305, 306.
Castle of Tutbury, 244.
Catharine of Aragon at Fotheringhay, 33.
Champions, the Queen's, 377.
Chapel on the Bridge, Wakefield, 303.
Charles, Prince, and the Duke of Buckingham, 144.
Charles I. at Southwick Park, 149.
Charles II. and the Duke of Monmouth, 341.
Chartley, Tradition of the Ferrers Family, 133.
Chatillon and Fotheringhay, 24.
Chaucer, Death of, 188.
Chaucer and Donington Castle, 183.

INDEX. 425

Christmas Mummers in the Olden Time, 268-274.
Church of Fotheringhay, 25, 26.
Cicely Duchess of York, 26, 32.
Cicely Duchess of York, her Family, 80.
Clanricarde, Lord, and the Kildare Family, 58.
Clavering, Miss (Lady Cowper), 276, 278.
Cliffords' Mansion, Clerkenwell, 374.
Cliffords and Rose Tenure, 419, 420.
Cliffords of Craven, 368.
Clifford, shepherd Lord, 370.
Constableship of Donington Castle, 190.
Conyers Family, reverses of, 103.
Conyers, Sir John, the Dragon-slayer, 165.
Cornish Miracle Plays, 271.
Coronation of George IV., 377.
Country Gentleman, 17th Century, 251.
Cowper, Lady, her *Diary*, 276-281.
Craven, History of, 368.
Craven, Scenery of, 368.
Crewe Family, the, 242, 243.
Crocodiles and Dragons, 157, 158.
Cumberland, Earl of, 371.

Decorations at Sutton Place, 365, 366.
Deepdene, the Howards at, 200.
Derby, Countess of, at the Siege of Lathom House, 284, 285, 286.
Derby, Earl of, defeated by Lilburne, 288.
Dering, Sir Edward, 88.
Derwentwater's Corpse Lights, 236.
Derwentwater's Farewell, 236.
Derwentwater, James Earl of, 231.
Derwentwater, Notes on, 238.
Despencers and Gaveston, and Edward IV., 217.
De Vexi, Lord of Kildare, 54.
Diary of Lady Cowper, 280.
Dilston or Devilstone Hall, 235.
Donington Castle and Chaucer, 183.
Dragon Hill, 320.
Dragon Legends, 156.
Dragon of Wantley, 159, 160.
Dymoke Family and the Championship, 375-377.

Eagle and Child tradition, 291.
Edmund of Langley at Fotheringhay, 24.
Edward Earl of Kent, execution of, 184.
Ela Countess of Salisbury, 2.
Eland Hall, Yorkshire, 201.
Eland Mill, affray at, 208
Eland, Sir John, tragedy of, 201.
Elizabeth and Mary Queen of Scots, 36, 37, 42.
Elizabeth, Queen, lines by, 195.

Execution of Lord Ferrers, 129-132.
Execution of Lady Alice Lisle, 347.
Execution of the Marquis of Exeter, 354.
Execution of Mary Queen of Scots at Fotheringhay, 38-42.
Execution of the Duke of Monmouth, 333, 334.
Execution of Lord Dudley and Lady Jane Grey, 395-400.
Execution of Lord Stourton, 416.
Exeter, Holland, Duke of, begging, 86.

Fairfax, Sir Thomas, and the Siege of Lathom House, 285, 286.
Farleigh Castle Estate, 104.
Fatalities in Families, 80.
Felton assassinates the Duke of Buckingham, 147.
Felton, John, account of, 140.
Ferrers Family, 384.
Ferrers Family and Oakham Castle, 259.
Ferrers, the House of, 121.
Ferrers, Laurence Earl of, murder by, 124.
Ferrers, Lord, execution of, 129-132.
Fetterlock, Origin of, 25.
Fetterlock plan of Fotheringhay Castle, 25.
Feud, deadly, in Yorkshire, 200-213.
Fitzgerald Earl of Kildare, 54.
Fitzwilliam, Sir William, at Fotheringhay, 37, 38.
Fotheringhay Castle, 23, 28, 44, 45.
Fotheringhay Castle demolished, 45.
Fotheringhay Church, 26, 27.
Fotheringhay and its Memories, 23.
Fotheringhay a prison of State, 34.
Foundling Knight, 254.
Froissart's Chronicles, *note*, 353.
Froude, Mr., his account of Mary Queen of Scots, 46, 47.
Fyndern and the Fyndernes, 242.
Fyndernes' Flowers, the, 245.

Gentleman, Country, 17th Century, 251.
Geology and Dragon Legends, 163, 164.
Gerald the Great, Earl of Kildare, 57.
Gerald eleventh Earl of Kildare, 68.
Geraldine, Fair, 66, 67, 355, *note*.
Golden Horse-shoe, story of, 267.
Goldsmith of Leeds, a tragic tale, 247.
Gooderich Castle described, 136.
Great Stanley, close of his career, 293.
Great Stanley, execution of, 295.
Greenwich Hospital and the Derwentwater Estates, 237.
Grey Family, 384.
Greys of Groby, 391.
Grey, Lady Jane, born, 386.
Grey, Lady Jane, character of, 388.

2 E

INDEX.

Grey, Lady Jane, her scholarship, 390, 391.
Grey, Lady Jane, and Lord Dudley executed, 395-400.
Gundreda, finding of her remains, 298.

HADDON HALL at Christmas, 273-275.
Haddon Hall described, 274.
Hagley, Tradition at, 172.
Hall of Oakham Castle, 259.
Hartgills, the, 408, 409.
Headless Horse Superstition, 52.
Henry v. buried at Fotheringhay, 29.
Heraldic cognizance at Sutton Place, 374.
Hewet, Sir W., the Cloth-worker, 76.
Haytesbury, the Hungerfords at, 116.
Horse-shoes at Oakham Castle, 258, 263-267.
Howard, Catherine, fate of, 193.
Howard, Henry, Earl of Surrey, the poet, 193.
Howard, the Home of, 191.
Howard, John, the eminent Yorkist, 191.
Howard, Thomas, Earl of Surrey, 192.
Howard, Thomas, imprisonment of, 193.
Hungerford badge, knots, etc., 113, 114.
Hungerford Family, the, 105.
Hungerford, Lady, executed at Tybourn, 106, 108.
Hungerfords of Cadenham, 107.
Hungerfords, the, at Charing Cross, 115, 116, 118.
Hunsden House and the Fair Geraldine, 66.
Hungerfordiana, 104.

INVENTORY of the Hungerford Family, 109, 110, 111, 112.

JAMES I. and the Duke of Buckingham, 144.
Joan Plantagenet and her three marriages, 184.
Jeffreys, Judge, end of, 349.
Jeffreys, Judge, portrait of, 345, 348.
Jockey of Norfolk on Bosworth Field, 105, 193.
'Judge Jeffreys' Ground,' 348.

KILDARE, three Earls of, fortunes of, 54.
Kilmington Church, affray in, 408-412.
Kirkby Moorside and Villiers Duke of Buckingham, 96.
Kimbolton Castle, 33.
Knock Taugh, or the Hill of Axes, 58.

LACOCK Abbey, present state of, 14, 15.
Lacock Abbey described, 1, 2.

Lacock Abbey, proprietors of, 13.
Lacock Village, 1.
Laidly Worm, the, 169.
Lambe, Dr., death of, 145.
Lambton Hall Worm, the, 166.
Lancaster, Earl of, beheaded, 219.
Lancaster, Earl of, at Pontefract Castle, 217.
Lathom House, ruins and traditions, 288, 289.
Lathom House, Siege of, 282-296.
Leeds, Dukedom of, 78.
Leeds, Goldsmith of, a tragic tale, 247.
Legend of the Bodach Glass, 179.
Legends of the Red Hand, 171.
Legend of Sir Richard Baker, 176.
Legend at Stoke d'Abernon, 178.
Lesley or Leslie Family, the, 239.
Leven, the brave Earl of, 239.
Leven, Earl of, in the Tower, 240.
Leicester, old, views of, 387.
Lindwurm, or Dragon, in Moravia, 158, 159.
Lines by Lady Jane Grey, 401.
Lines on Bradgate, 405.
Lisle, Lady Alice, 343-349.
Longspé, William, Earl of Salisbury, 2.
Love Passage from the *Diary* of Lady Cowper, 276-280.
Lumley Portraits, the, 19.
Lyttelton, Lord, and the Red Hand, 173.

MABEL BROWNE, romantic career of, 67.
Magna Charta of Henry III., 14.
Marmyons and the Championship, 375, 376.
Marriage of Lord Dudley and Lady Jane Grey, 394, 395.
Mary Queen of Scots at Fotheringhay, 34.
Mary of Valence at Fotheringhay, 24.
Memorials of the Duke of Monmouth, 337.
'Merciful Assize,' Winchester, 344.
Middleham Castle and Richard III., 308-315.
Monmouth, Duke of, capture of, 327-329.
Monmouth, Duke of, his last days, 325-342.
Monmouth Close described, 330.
Monmouth Documents, 342.
Monmouth House, Soho Square, 336.
Montague, the last Viscount, 72.
Montague, Wortley, and the Dragon of Wantley, 161.
Mummers, Christmas, 268-273.
Mummers in Northamptonshire, 272.
Murder of his Steward by Lord Ferrers, 124.
Murder, tragical, 49.
Murder at Stourton, 414, 415.
Mutiny at Portsmouth, 154.

INDEX. 427

NASH'S *Mansions of England*, 273.
Neville of Brancepeth, 87.
Neville, the House of, 80-83.
Nicholas, Sir Edmond, at West Horsley, 359.
Nichols, J. G., his account of Lady Hungerford, 110.
Norfolk, Duke of, at Bosworth, 193.
Norfolk, Thomas fourth Duke of, 194, 195.
Norton St. Philips, Duke of Monmouth at, 326.
Nuns' Boiler at Lacock, 15.
'Nut-Brown Mayde,' ballad, 372.

OAK, celebrated, at Castle Donington, 189.
Oakham Castle described, 262.
Osborne and Leeds Families, 76.
Osborn, the London Bridge Apprentice, 76.
Oxenham Family Legend, 182.
Oxford, John Earl of, 86.

PAPER found in Felton's hat, 148.
Paulets, reverses of the, 84.
Peers' Horse-shoe Custom at Oakham, 260.
Pembroke and Montgomery, Countess of, 373, 374.
Percy, the House of, reverses of, 83.
Perkin Warbeck at Cork, 58.
Photography and Mr. Fox Talbot, 13.
Pindar Fields, Wakefield, 303.
Planché, Mr., his account of the Lumley Portraits, 19.
Plantagenet co-heirs, reverses of, 102.
Pocket-book, the Duke of Monmouth's, 337, 388, 340.
Poems and Songs on the Duke of Buckingham, 153.
Pole, Cardinal, and Gerald Earl of Kildare, 69.
Pontefract Castle described, 230.
Pontefract Castle demolished, 228.
Pontefract Castle and its Echoes, 214-230.
Pomfret and Pontefract, 230.
Pontefract, view from, 228, 229.
Pope on Villiers Duke of Buckingham, 96.
Portraits at West Horsley Place, 361.
Portraits, the Lumley, described, 19-22.
Portraits of Mary Queen of Scots, 43.

RADCLIFFE, CHARLES, Earl of Derwentwater, 232.
Radcliffes of Derwentwater, the, 231.
Raleigh, Carew, birth of, 355.
Raleigh, Sir Walter, burial of, 357, 358.
Raleigh, Sir Walter, head of, 358.

Rebellion of 1745, 223.
Red Hand, baronet's hatchment, 175.
Red Hand Legends, 171.
Red and White Roses, the, 418.
Relics of the Derwentwaters, 238.
Reresbys of Thybergh, reverses of, 101.
Richard II., death of, 223, 224.
Richard II. deposed, 220.
Richard II. in Flint Castle, 221.
Richard II. in the Tower of London, 223.
Richard III., accession of, 311.
Richard III. born at Fotheringhay, 28, 29.
Richard III., character of, 309.
Richard III., his love of music, 313.
Richard III. and Richmond at Bosworth, 314.
Richard III. and Richmond, portraits of, 314, 315.
Rivers, Grey, and Vaughan, executions of, 226.
Robin Hood and Barnsdale Forest, 304.
Rose Tenures, curious ancient, 419.
Rose-tree, the oldest in the world, 420.
Ruins of Bradgate, 394, 395.
Rutland, county, lines on, 258.

SALISBURY CATHEDRAL founded, 5.
Salisbury, Earl and Countess of, 5.
Sandal Castle, Account of, 304-306.
Saxon Standard of the White Horse, 319.
Scouring the White Horse, 317.
Scrivelsby Court described, 379.
Scrivelsby and the Queen's Championship, 375.
Sedgemoor, Battle of, 329, 332.
Serpent or Dragon in St. Leonard's Forest, 162.
Serpent in the Sea, 170.
Sevenoake, Sir William de, 254.
Sherborne and Sir Walter Raleigh, 356.
Shirley Family, the, 121.
Shrewsbury, Duke of, the statesman, 139.
Shrewsbury, the Earl of, 135.
Shrewsbury, the Earl of, and Mary Queen of Scots, 139.
Shrewsbury, Lady, at Lacock, 16.
Siege of Lathom House, 282, 296.
Sieges of Pontefract Castle, 226, 227.
Silken Thomas, tenth Earl of Kildare, 62-64.
Skipton Castle and its Lords, 369.
Snail, gigantic, and the Laidly Worm, 169.
Sockburn Falchion, the, 165.
Spendthrift Sir Edward Hungerford, 117, 119.
Spye Park Legend, 17.
Stafford, Edward, Duke of Buckingham, 93.
Staffords of Penshurst, 89.
Stamford, Countess of, 392, 393.

Stanhope, three Earls, 255.
State Funeral at Fotheringhay, 29-31.
Storm, Great, of 1703, 360.
Staunton Harold and Sir Robert Shirley, 123.
Stourton described, 407.
Stourton Family, 417.
Stourton, Lord Charles, 407.
Stowe, great sale at, 99.
Stowe and the Duke of Buckingham, 97, 98.
Surrey, Earl of, the poet, 66.
Surrey, Lord, at Flodden Field, 106.
Sussex Dragon Legends, 162, 163.
Sutton Place described, 363.

TALBOT, the House of, 135.
Talbot, Sir Gilbert, at Bosworth, 139.
Talbot, the valiant Lord, 137, 138.
Talbot, William, adventures of, 3, 4.
Talbotype, the, 14.
Temple Garden and Red and White Roses, 418.
Thornbury Castle, Gloucestershire, described, 92-94.
Toad in the Hungerford Arms, 117.
Towers of Pontefract Castle, 216.
Tower of London, Lord Dudley and Lady Jane Grey in, 395-403.
Towton, Battle of, 302.
Towton and Waterloo battles compared, 302.
Traditions of Wallington and the Calverleys, 48.
Tragedy of Sir John Eland, 201.
Tresham Family and Rushton Hall, 88.
Trial of Lady Alice Lisle, 344-347.
Trial of Lord Ferrers for Murder, 127.
Trial of Lord Stourton, 419.
Trial of Mary Queen of Scots at Fotheringhay, 35.
Tutbury Castle, 244.

UFFINGTON Castle, White Horse Hill, 316.
Ulster King-at-Arms, Badge of, 173.

VALE of White Horse, the, 316, 324.
Vavasours of Weston, the, 51.
Vere, Lady Harriet, and Lady Cowper, 277–280.
Vicissitudes of Families, by Sir Bernard Burke, 245.
Villiers Duke of Buckingham, 95, 96.
Villiers, George, Duke of Buckingham, assassinated by Felton, 142.
Villiers, John, Earl of Buckingham. 97.

WAKEFIELD, the Battle of, 300, 301.
Wakefield Park, 306.
Wakefield Manor and Sandal Castle, 296.
Wallington Family, 47.
Wallington Border Tower, 48.
Walpole's Notes on the Rebellion of 1745, 233, 234.
Wayland Smith Tradition, 320, 321.
Wentworth, Baroness, of Nettlestead, 339.
West Horsley Manor, 355.
West Horsley Place and the Westons, 350.
Weston Family of West Horsley, 361.
Weston, Prior of St. John's, Clerkenwell, 363.
Westons of Sutton, Family of, 362-367.
White Horse, Vale of, 316-324.
White Lackington, Duke of Monmouth at, 326.
White-breasted Bird Legend, 182.
Will Case, the Great Shrewsbury, 140, 142.
Worm Hill and Worm Well, 168, 169.
Worm of Lambton Hall, 166.
Wyat's Insurrection, 395.

YORK, House of, at Fotheringhay, 28.
Yorkshire Tragedy, the, 51.

www.ingramcontent.com/pod-product-compliance
Lightning Source LLC
Chambersburg PA
CBHW022147300426
44115CB00006B/379